COMPARATIVE AND INTERNATIONAL EDUCATION SERIES

Volume 4

Educational Technology
— Its Creation, Development and
Cross-Cultural Transfer

COMPARATIVE AND INTERNATIONAL EDUCATION

Series Editor: PHILIP G. ALTBACH, State University of New York at Buffalo, New York

NOTICE TO READERS

Dear Reader

An Invitation to Publish in and Recommend the Placing of a Standing Order to Volumes Published in this Valuable Series.

If your library is not already a standing/continuation order customer to this series, may we recommend that you place a standing/continuation order to receive immediately upon publication all new volumes. Should you find that these volumes no longer serve your needs, your order can be cancelled at any time without notice.

The Editors and the Publisher will be glad to receive suggestions or outlines of suitable titles, reviews or symposia for editorial consideration: if found acceptable, rapid publication is guaranteed.

ROBERT MAXWELL
Publisher at Pergamon Press

Educational Technology — Its Creation, Development and Cross-Cultural Transfer

Edited by

R. MURRAY THOMAS
University of California
Santa Barbara USA

and

VICTOR N. KOBAYASHI
University of Hawaii
Honolulu USA

PERGAMON PRESS

OXFORD · NEW YORK · BEIJING · FRANKFURT
SÃO PAULO · SYDNEY · TOKYO · TORONTO

U.K.	Pergamon Press, Headington Hill Hall, Oxford OX3 0BW, England
U.S.A.	Pergamon Press, Maxwell House, Fairview Park, Elmsford, New York 10523, U.S.A.
PEOPLE'S REPUBLIC OF CHINA	Pergamon Press, Room 4037, Qianmen Hotel, Beijing, People's Republic of China
FEDERAL REPUBLIC OF GERMANY	Pergamon Press, Hammerweg 6, D-6242 Kronberg, Federal Republic of Germany
BRAZIL	Pergamon Editora, Rua Eça de Queiros, 346, CEP 04011, Paraiso, São Paulo, Brazil
AUSTRALIA	Pergamon Press Australia, P.O. Box 544, Potts Point, N.S.W. 2011, Australia
JAPAN	Pergamon Press, 8th Floor, Matsuoka Central Building, 1-7-1 Nishishinjuku, Shinjuku-ku, Tokyo 160, Japan
CANADA	Pergamon Press Canada, Suite No. 271, 253 College Street, Toronto, Ontario, Canada M5T 1R5

First edition 1987

Library of Congress Cataloging in Publication Data
Educational technology.
(Comparative and international education series; v.4)
Includes index.
1. Educational technology. 2. Educational technology—
Developing countries. 3. Technology transfer—Developing
countries. I. Thomas, R. Murray (Robert Murray), 1921-
II. Kobayashi, V. N. III. Series.
LB1028.3.E334 1987   371.3'07'8   87-14239

British Library Cataloguing in Publication Data
Educational technology.—(Comparative and international
education series; v.4).
1. Educational technology—Developing countries
I. Thomas, R. Murray   II. Kobayashi, V. N.   III. Series
371.3'07'8   LB1028.3

ISBN 0-08-034994-3 (Hardcover)
ISBN 0-08-034993-5 (Flexicover)

Printed in Great Britain by A. Wheaton & Co. Ltd., Exeter

Introduction to Series

The Comparative and International Education Series is dedicated to inquiry and analysis on educational issues in an interdisciplinary cross-national framework. As education affects larger populations and educational issues are increasingly complex and, at the same time, international in scope, this series presents research and analysis aimed at understanding contemporary educational issues. The series brings the best scholarship to topics which have direct relevance to educators, policymakers and scholars, in a format that stresses the international links among educational issues. Comparative education not only focuses on the development of educational systems and policies around the world, but also stresses the relevance of an international understanding of the particular problems and dilemmas that face educational systems in individual countries.

Interdisciplinarity is a hallmark of comparative education and this series will feature studies based on a variety of disciplinary, methodological and ideological underpinnings. Our concern is for relevance and the best in scholarship.

The series will combine careful monographic studies that will help policymakers and others obtain a needed depth for enlightened analysis with wider-ranging volumes that may be useful to educators and students in a variety of contexts. Books in the series will reflect on policy and practice in a range of educational settings from pre-primary to post-secondary. In addition, we are concerned with non-formal education and with the societal impact of educational policies and practices. In short, the scope of the Comparative and International Education Series is interdisciplinary and contemporary.

I wish to thank the assistance of a distinguished editorial advisory board including:

Professor Suma Chitnis, Tata University of Social Sciences, Bombay, India.

Professor Kazayuki Kitamura, Research Institute of Higher Education, Hiroshima University, Japan.

Professor Gail P. Kelly, State University of New York at Buffalo, USA.

Dean Thomas LaBelle, University of Pittsburgh, USA.

Dr S. Gopinathan, Institute of Education, Singapore.

Professor Guy Neave, Institute of Education, London.

PHILIP G. ALTBACH

Preface

The purpose of educational technology is to promote the efficiency of education by improving the quality of teaching, of educational administration, and of educational research. New types of technology intended to accomplish these purposes appear at an ever-accelerating pace, paralleling the rapid increase of innovations in the general society. As a result, educators face the constant challenge of understanding the nature of technologies, their potential uses, and their strengths and weaknesses.

In keeping with this challenge, organizers of the Western Regional Conference of the Comparative and International Education Society selected as their 1986 conference theme *Educational Technology: Its Creation, Development, and Transfer.* The conference was held on the Manoa Valley campus of the University of Hawaii in Honolulu at the end of December. As a means of charting the course that the conference would take, a series of papers was commissioned ahead of time to highlight selected aspects of the theme. During the conference a host of additional papers relating to the theme were presented by participants.

The chapters of this book are the commissioned papers written by authors chosen for their expertise in the types of educational technology that form the four central parts of the volume—electronic computers, television/radio, print media, and operating systems. The following biographical sketches suggest something of each writer's background.

Dennis O. Harper (Chapter 2, on the development of computers in advanced industrial societies) is a faculty member at the Institute of Education in Singapore, specializing in educational applications of computer technology. His teaching experience over the past two decades includes posts in Australia, West Germany, Liberia, Malaysia, and the United States. He is the author of the widely used textbook *Run: Computers in Education,* a monograph entitled *Computers for Education in Developing Nations,* and the textbook *Mathematics for Photographers.* Dr. Harper is also editor of the *International Logo Exchange,* a periodical focusing on the use of Logo computer language in education systems around the world.

Jiaying Zhuang (Chapter 3, on a decision-making model for the transfer of computer technology into developing societies) is on the faculty of the Shanghai Institute of International Trade. She holds M.A. degrees in both political science and TESL (teaching English as a second language) from the Monterey (California) Institute of International Studies. She is currently completing doctoral studies in international education at the University of California, Santa Barbara, where she specializes in educational-research methodology, including the application of computers in research and instruction.

Claudine Michel (Chapter 5, on the transfer of educational radio/television into developing nations) holds both M.A. and Ph.D. degrees in international education, with strong emphases on child development and instructional psychology. She has produced more than 150 children's television programs over Haitian National Television, many of them in both the French and Creole languages. Dr. Michel's recent publications include "Television and Human Development" (*International Encyclopedia of Education* 1985) and "High-Quality, Low-Cost Television for Children of Developing Nations" (*International Journal of Educational Development* 1985). She currently holds a joint faculty appointment in the Departments of French and of Black Studies at the University of California, Santa Barbara.

John W. Seybold (Introduction to Part III) taught economics at Swarthmore College, functioned as a labor arbitrator, worked in Europe with the American Friends Service Committee on programs to improve the character of east-west relations, and served as the industrial relations director for the commercial printing industry in Philadelphia before starting the world's first computer photocomposition service bureau in 1963. In 1970 he and his son founded Seybold Publications, Inc., publishers of an internationally-respected newsletter, *The Seybold Report on Publishing Systems*. He has been active as a consultant to vendors, publishers, and other users of text-editing and composition systems, and is the author of numerous books and articles in the fields of printing, computer technology, and social organization.

Philip G. Altbach (Chapter 6, on textbooks in comparative context) is professor and chair of the Department of Educational Organization, Administration, and Policy at the State University of New York in Buffalo. In addition, he serves as Director of that institution's Comparative Education Center. He has written widely on publishing and related issues and is author of *Publishing in India, The Knowledge Context, Publishing in the Third World* and other books. Dr. Altbach is also editor of the *Comparative Education Review*.

S. Gopinathan (Chapter 7, on cross-cultural transfer of print media) is editor of the *Singapore Journal of Education* and a professor at the Singapore Institute of Education. He is an author and editor of books and journal articles that range in subject-matter from educational publishing to moral education in developing nations.

Noel McGinn (Chapter 8, on the development of educational operating systems) is a professor of education at Harvard University and presently the director of the BRIDGES Project, a five-year USAID-funded effort to provide planners and policymakers in Third World countries with increased access to research-based information about the effectiveness of alternative policies and programs for education. Dr. McGinn has worked for the past twenty years on issues of educational planning in developing countries, with particular attention to the process of policy formulation. He has coauthored several national studies of education systems (Korea, Mexico, Venezuela) and a series of articles on educational planning and decentralization.

Gail P. Kelly (Chapter 9, on the transfer of educational operating systems into developing societies) is a professor of education at the State University of New York, Buffalo, and president of the Comparative and International Educational Society (1986-7). She has written extensively about French colonialism and the development of education in French West Africa and Indochina in the period between the two world wars. She has authored and coauthored books on comparative education and on women's schooling. Recent volumes include *Comparative Education* (Macmillan, 1982), *Education and the Colonial Experience* (Transaction, 1984), and *New Approaches to Comparative Education* (University of Chicago, 1986).

The two editors, R. Murray Thomas (Chapters 1 and 4) and Victor N. Kobayashi (Chapter 10), brought to their task extensive backgrounds of experience in Pacific-rim nations. Dr. Thomas is an educational psychologist who heads the Program in International Education at the University of California, Santa Barbara. His direct involvement with educational technology spans more than four decades. In 1946-7 he served as radio editor for the University of Hawaii, responsible for producing several educational programs each week over Honolulu radio stations. In the mid-1950s he taught child development over closed-circuit television at the State University of New York (Brockport) and produced educational-television broadcasts in Rochester, New York. Since then, for more than a quarter century, he has worked as a teacher, researcher, and consultant in education systems of Southeast Asia and the Pacific Islands. His writing in the area of educational technology ranges from the college textbook *Integrated Teaching Materials* (1960) to "The Rise and Decline of an Educational Technology: Television in American Samoa" (*Educational Communication and Technology Journal,* 1980) and "Media-Assisted Counseling" (*International Encyclopedia of Education,* 1985).

Dr. Kobayashi is professor of education and dean of the summer session at the University of Hawaii, Honolulu. He has written numerous chapters in books and articles in journals on Japanese education, the philosophy of education, and film productions. He is currently completing a book exploring the implications of Gregory Bateson's ideas for education. These ideas play an important role in Chapter 10 of the present volume.

As a final note, we should explain the style of citing references in the body of the chapters. Wherever a source of information is identified, the numbers immediately following the author's name indicate the year of the publication, and the numbers after the colon refer to the relevant pages in the cited book or article. An example is: (Schramm, 1977: 34-36).

Contents

CHAPTER 1

The Nature of Educational Technology

R. MURRAY THOMAS

There is no universally-agreed-upon definition of *educational technology*. For most people, the term likely brings to mind such electronic gadgetry as film projectors, tape recorders, television sets, and microcomputers used as teaching tools. Other people add such nonelectrical instructional materials as books, photographs, and charts. Still others subscribe to a definition that includes not only items used in teaching but also equipment used in educational administration—keeping student records on microfilm, communicating between schools by radio, correcting entrance examinations with the aid of a computer, and the like.

Even more encompassing are definitions that extend beyond physical materials to include methods of performing tasks that require no special equipment. These can be referred to as *operating systems*. An example of such "non-hardware" technology would be a specific method instructors use for directing a class discussion, such as Socratic method of discourse. Another example would be the particular steps adopted in a country's ministry of education for planning the next five years' development of the nation's school system.

In effect, *educational technology* can mean rather different things to different people. Even those who specialize in this field as a professional pursuit have failed to concur on what exactly should be encompassed by the term (Gerlach, 1984: 24-25; Meierhenry, 1984: 3-4). But in an apparent attempt to satisfy everyone, the Association for Educational Communications and Technology in the United States ended a seven-year struggle with the problem by producing the following "official" definition. It is so all-embracing that it leaves nothing out that could remotely be interpreted as bearing on the conduct of education (Silber, 1981: 21).

Educational Technology is a complex, integrated process involving people, procedures, ideas, devices, and organization, for analyzing problems and devising, implementing, evaluating, and managing solutions to those problems, involved in all aspects of learning. . . .

1

The relationships among [its] elements are shown by the Domain of Educational Technology Model:

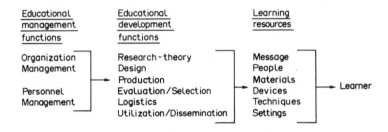

As the subtitle of this volume suggests, our purpose in writing the book has been to analyze (1) conditions that lead to the creation and development of a given educational technology within a society and (2) conditions that influence how such a technology is transferred to other societies and adapted to their needs. It is apparent that attempting to illustrate such conditions for all varieties of modern educational technology would require far more space than a single book could allow. Therefore, we have limited our attention to four varieties of educational technology—computers, broadcast media (television and radio), print media, and selected operating systems. Our choice of these types was guided by four considerations—potential breadth of impact, popular attention, recency of innovation, and technological diversity.

The phrase *potential breadth of impact* refers to the extent of influence that a given technology currently exerts or might exert in the future. Printed materials—especially books and periodicals—are the most obvious example of widespread breadth of impact, both past and present. Throughout the world, the most common instructional tools continue to be printed text materials. For instance, in a recent survey in Latin America of 474 research-and-development projects involving educational technology, over 83 percent concerned printed matter (Chadwick, 1983: 107). And while printed matter will likely continue to play a dominant role in education over the foreseeable future, there are educators today who predict that before long television-and-radio and computers will effect a major transformation in educational practices at both the administrative and instructional levels. Such educators further predict that innovative operating systems—that is, ways of organizing education—will also have wide-ranging influence. So all four types of technology treated in the following chapters are judged to be potentially broad in their impact.

The four types also qualify under the *popular attention* criterion, since each of them is frequently featured in educational literature and in conferences focusing on educational development.

While it is obvious that both television and computers meet the *recency of innovation* requirement, it would appear at first glance that printed materials and operating systems are not of recent origin. However, as the contents of Part III will illustrate, the particular sorts of print technology on which that section focuses are ones which have evolved over the past few decades. As such, they are still in early stages of development and adaptation. Furthermore, certain aspects of the operating systems that are the center of attention in Part IV have experienced changes in relatively recent times and continue to undergo revision.

Computers, television/radio, printed materials, and operating systems also represent a range of diversity in types of technology. The differences among the four have enabled our authors to illustrate how the special nature of a given technology influences the way it is developed and applied in education.

As the chapters illustrate, the four technologies are not mutually exclusive. Rather, they can combine in ways that take advantage of their separate characteristics in order to produce complexes that accomplish educational aims far more effectively than any one type could achieve alone. For example, the publishing industry has moved rapidly toward transmitting words and pictures over distances via television and in controlling typesetting and printing by means of computers. As a further example, computer-controlled, self-instructional lessons can be presented to learners not only in book form but also on television screens that are located either in the school or in the student's home. Therefore, in the following chapters, the authors focus attention both on individual characteristics of each technology and on the educational capabilities that result when such technologies are combined.

In summary, the purpose of this volume is to offer an analysis of conditions affecting the creation, development, and cross-cultural transfer of four varieties of educational technology.

The Organization of the Book

The aim of this introductory chapter is to sketch a background for the subsequent chapters by (1) briefly noting important characteristics of the four technologies, (2) suggesting types of societal conditions that influence their development, and (3) proposing ways the success of a technology can be judged.

The next eight chapters, 2 through 9, are presented in pairs organized under four sections or parts. The parts are arranged in terms of recency. Thus, Part I focuses on computers, the newest of the inventions. Part II treats television/radio, Part III printed materials, and Part IV operating systems. An essay introducing each part reviews highlights in the history

of the technology featured in that section's two chapters. The first
chapter of the pair directs attention to conditions in the advanced
industrial societies in which the particular technology has been created
and developed. Such societies are generally found in nations of Europe
and North America and in Japan. The second chapter focuses on the
transfer of that technology into societies referred to as *developing,
underdeveloped*, or *less-developed*. These are societies generally found in
Asia, Africa, Latin America, and the Pacific Islands. It is apparent,
however, that dividing societies into only two categories—the more
developed and the less developed—distorts reality. The obvious truth is
that societies are arrayed along all degrees of a scale of technological
development. For example, in Asia the educational systems of Singapore and Hong Kong are far more developed technologically than are
the systems of Burma and Nepal. And the modern-technology level of
schools in urban sectors of most countries is more advanced than that of
schools in rural areas. However, for convenience of analysis, our scheme
of using pairs of chapters to inspect technological development and
transfer is still useful. It enables us to compare the conditions and
problems of nations that are typically modern technology's creators with
those which are usually recipients of innovations.

(Throughout the book, the terms *advanced industrial nations* and
developing nations refer solely to levels of technology. The terms are not
intended to suggest that societies which we label *developing* are inferior
to more industrialized nations in social organization, in moral virtue, in
humanitarianism, in cultural sophistication, in artistic endeavour, in public safety, or the like. Indeed, convincing arguments can be adduced to
support the proposal that *technologically developing societies* are, in a
variety of important ways, either equal to or superior to the more
advanced industrial nations.)

Not only does each part of the book center on a particular technology, but each part also shows a different way of analyzing conditions that
influence the development and transfer of educational technology. For
example, Part I (computers) illustrates how a decision-making model
can be used to determine which technologies from advanced industrial
societies can profitably be adopted by developing nations. Part II (radio/
television) views technological development and transfer from a "lessons
learned" perspective. The lessons are generalizations learned about conditions affecting the creation and transfer of an educational technology
over the past few decades. Part III (print media) offers a "contrasting
viewpoints" perspective, showing the way an educator from an advanced
industrialized society can perceive technological transfer as compared to
the way an educator from a formerly colonized, developing society
perceives it. Finally, Part IV (operating systems) illustrates a sociopolitical, historical analysis of the creation, development, and transfer of a
technology.

The dual role of the final chapter of the book is to summarize observations drawn from the preceding chapters and to speculate about the future.

The Four Technologies

The brief overview of key characteristics of the four technologies offered in the following paragraphs serves as a preparation for more detailed analyses that appear in later essays which open each of the four major parts of the book.

Computers in Education

Electronic computers began to offer modest educational applications as early as the 1950s but did not burgeon into their present-day widespread use until after the invention of the microcomputer in the latter 1970s. Since that time, they have assumed both instructional and administrative functions in a rapidly growing number of the world's education systems. As a consequence, educators in advanced and developing nations alike are adding *computer literacy* to *reading and writing literacy* as a skill students will need for succeeding in the technologically sophisticated world of the future.

Today, computers perform a host of functions in the field of education. At the administrative level, they register students in classes, maintain records of pupil performance, keep inventory lists of supplies, do cost accounting, pay bills, print reports, address envelopes, assist in architectural design, and much more. Computers bring great speed and accuracy to each of these tasks, along with the convenience of storing large quantities of information on small disks or tapes.

In their role as *word processors*, microcomputers are rapidly replacing typewriters in both offices and classrooms. Composing a letter or a lesson-plan or an instructional pamphlet on a microcomputer enables the author easily to correct misspellings, move paragraphs from one section of the document to another, insert new material at any place in the manuscript, store the results for later retrieval, and produce multiple copies in a handsomely printed format.

At the instructional level, microcomputers are used by pupils to learn reading, mathematics, science, social studies, music, art, health practices, and games of all sorts. An advantage of the computer as a teacher is that, unlike a lecture or a television program, the typical computer lesson advances at the student's own learning speed. Furthermore, computer programs can be designed to assess how well the student has mastered each step in the learning sequence so that before the student advances to the next step, the computer can provide remedial reteaching of any part of the present segment that the learner has not yet mastered. In effect, computer-assisted instruction can be better adjusted to individual differences in pupils' learning skills than can the typical lecture, textbook, or television lesson.

Accompanying the benefits of computers are a number of drawbacks. Computer "hardware"—meaning the machine itself—is expensive and usually requires repair that depends on the services of a trained technician and the availability of spare parts. Likewise, an item of computer "software"—with "software" meaning a lesson stored on a disk for teaching a particular skill—is typically more expensive than a book or pamphlet on the same topic. Furthermore, how efficiently students will learn from a computerized lesson depends on how skillfully the lesson on the disk has been designed. A key criticism of instructional software produced during the 1980s has been that much of it is not well designed from the viewpoint of instructional efficiency.

In the present book, Chapters 2 and 3 focus on computer technology in education. Chapter 2 describes conditions contributing to the development and educational applications of computers in industrialized societies. Chapter 3 proposes a simple decision-making model that might aid educators in developing societies determine which of those applications would be appropriate for them to adopt.

Educational Radio and Television

Radio and television are both twentieth-century phenomena, with educational radio gaining its distinction after the early 1920s and television after the early 1950s. As instructional media, radio and television display a variety of advantages over the schools' traditional reading materials. Literate and illiterate learners can both profit from radio and television broadcasts, and the blind can follow radio instruction as easily as can the sighted. In addition, information broadcast over radio or television can be more up-to-date than information in textbooks, since a broadcast lesson can be disseminated to the learners shortly after it has been created, whereas months or years pass between the time a book manuscript is completed and the book arrives in the learner's hands. Television has the further advantage of being multisensory. For lessons in which coordinated sights, sounds, and movement are important, television is clearly superior to both radio and printed matter.

However, in addition to their advantages, radio and television also exhibit a number of liabilities. Some of the liabilities derive from the nature of the equipment, which is technically complex. As a consequence, technical skill and spare parts are needed to repair malfunctioning radio and television units. Furthermore, a source of electricity is required to operate such equipment, and under extreme conditions of temperature and humidity the components of both transmitters and receivers can quickly deteriorate. In addition, television receivers are expensive.

Other limitations of broadcast media derive from how well they suit the requirements of effective instruction. Perhaps the most significant shortcoming results from the immutable pace at which broadcast material is presented. Radio and television programs are time-bound; the learner must capture in mind every scene or bit of information at the moment it is presented or else it is lost. In this sense, radio and television lessons are like the traditional classroom lecture in which the teacher refuses to be interrupted with questions from the audience. Thus, unless the broadcast lesson includes a final summary or a review of main points, learners who failed to grasp an idea at its first mention are lost. Although in some forms of educational broadcasting two-way communication is provided, so that learners can ask questions of the instructor via a radio talk-back arrangement, such opportunities are offered in only a few instructional settings. In contrast, reading materials are not time-bound. Students can pore over elusive passages of a book time and again until they master the contents. Therefore, students' individual differences in learning ability are better served by reading materials than by radio and television broadcasts, unless such broadcasts have been tape-recorded and made available to students to use repeatedly.

The two chapters that comprise Part II of this volume focus on educational uses of radio and television. Part II opens with an introductory essay that sketches the historical background of the two media. Then Chapter 4 describes 16 "lessons" that educators have learned about the development of educational radio and television in advanced industrial societies in recent decades. Chapter 5 identifies a further series of "lessons" about conditions affecting the transfer of the two technologies to developing nations.

Educational Print Materials

Despite the recent rapid expansion of electronic media throughout the world's education systems, books and allied printed materials continue to serve today as education's most important technological aids for both instructional and adminstrative activities. In the great majority of the world's classrooms, the most reliable indicator of what is taught is the textbook. In like manner, the most convenient source of information about the way the education system is administered is the collection of printed regulations and reports that govern the system's daily operation.

It is obvious that the printed word has been a powerful force in

furthering technological progress over the centuries. The instructional
significance of written accounts can be illustrated in comparisons between nonliterate societies (such as those of the Pacific Islanders) and
literate societies (such as those of Europe). Before Europeans entered
the Pacific, island peoples lacked a system of writing and thus were
obliged to depend entirely on memory and on direct demonstration for
transmitting technology and historical lore from one generation to the
next. In contrast, the Europeans' tradition of writing, and ultimately of
printing books in large quantities, enabled them to leave detailed
accounts of their discoveries for use by others who lived at later times
and in distant places. Such written records gave Europeans a considerable advantage over the islanders in furthering technological invention,
since literate Europeans had available far larger quantities of detailed
information on a far greater variety of discoveries than did the Pacific
peoples.

The continuing popularity of print materials for educational purposes
is a result of several obvious advantages that books and periodicals have
over other instructional media. Books, unlike television lessons and
computer programs, already exist in great quantities, they cover a nearly
infinite variety of topics, and they require no special equipment for their
use. Books, in contrast to motion pictures and television, can be easily
carried from place to place and studied at the reader's own pace and
convenience. Furthermore, people's long-time familiarity with the process of creating print materials also has played a part in such progress,
in that the technology of publishing has a long tradition throughout most
of the world. As a result, more people in all societies have experience
with educational publishing than with producing educational material for
other types of communication media. And of special importance are
recent innovations in publishing practices that enable people who have
little formal training to issue books and pamphlets of high standard.
Today, an individual equipped with a microcomputer and a photocopying machine can readily publish printed matter of professional quality. Such advantages have enabled educational print materials to stand
up well against the competition offered by a growing array of electronic
media.

Chapters 6 and 7 that comprise Part III of this volume concern
educational print technology. Because textbooks remain the prime determinants of the content of formal education throughout the world, the
two chapters of Part III center attention on the development and use of
modern-day textbooks. As mentioned earlier, Part III illustrates a "contrasting perspectives" way of analyzing conditions affecting technological
transfer. Chapter 6 shows how an educator from an advanced industrial
society, the United States, can perceive the transfer of educational print

technology to Third-World nations. In contrast, Chapter 7 shows how an educator in a formerly colonized Third-World nation, the Republic of Singapore, can view this same type of transfer.

Operating Systems in Education

Among our four technologies, the oldest and still most widespread is that of operating systems, where the term *system* means an established procedure or series of steps for accomplishing an educational goal.

For convenience of discussion, it is useful to divide such systems into two types. The first is that of instructional methodology, which refers to the ways people try to teach information, attitudes, and skills. The second is that of educational administration or management, which refers to ways of organizing the people, facilities, ideas, and agencies that make up the formal and nonformal educational functions of a society. Both of these types have existed since before recorded history, although in far simpler forms than those found today.

Instructional methodology concerns not only procedures designed by educators for use in the classroom, but also child-rearing practices used intuitively by parents in the routine of family living. From earliest times, these practices have included such methods as descriptive lectures, demonstrations, parables, admonitions, threats of reward and punishment, and more.

Educational administrative functions encompass a wide variety of activities that are suggested by such diverse terms as: educational governance, supervision, support services, infrastructure, finance, budgeting, accounting, personnel selection and training, system monitoring and evaluation, facilities procurement and management, equipment maintenance, research, and the like.

To illustrate conditions that can influence those operating systems which are at the top of a nation's educational structure, the two chapters that comprise Part IV of this volume focus on one particularly influential type of institution—the central ministry of education—which resides at the apex of the educational enterprise of most modern-day societies. The Part IV authors' approach is that of sociopolitical, historical analysis. Chapter 8 centers attention on how ministries have been conceived in advanced industrialized settings, with the evolution of France's educational bureaucracy from Napoleon's time serving as the prime example. Chapter 9 then inspects the way ministerial administrative systems may be transformed when they are exported to developing societies. The case analyzed in Chapter 9 shows what occurred when the French version of a ministry of education was transported to French colonies in Southeast Asia during the first half of the twentieth century. The case also includes a discussion of the present-day effects of this transfer after the colonies achieved political independence.

Conditions Influencing the Creation, Development, and Transfer of Educational Technology

Throughout this book, our discussion of educational technology is intended to be both descriptive and explanatory. The descriptive portion tells what has happened in the realms of the selected technologies. The explanatory portion offers an estimate of why things happened that way. Therefore, explanation in this sense means speculation about cause. Each author not only describes the present state of a technology, but also seeks to identify factors which helped produce that state. In preparation for Chapters 2 through 9, the following discussion provides a backdrop against which to view the estimates of causal conditions presented in subsequent chapters. The discussion addresses matters of (1) underlying and immediate causes, (2) similarities and differences between advanced and less-developed societies, (3) general and specific causal conditions, and (4) realms of causal factors.

Underlying and Immediate Causes

For the sake of analysis, it is useful to place causal conditions on two levels, those of underlying and immediate causes. Underlying causes are circumstances in the general society that make possible, but do not directly determine, the educational use of a technology. Underlying causes are like enabling-laws passed by a legislature to permit—but not require—people to take a given action. For instance, in advanced industrial nations in recent years, two of the enabling conditions underlying the advent of computer-assisted instruction in schools have been (1) the invention and low-cost mass production of microchip electronic circuits and (2) sufficiently prosperous economies to afford the purchase of microcomputers for classroom use. In developing societies, two of the underlying conditions affecting the adoption of computer-assisted instruction are (1) characteristics of the society's written language and (2) sufficient foreign-exchange currency or foreign-aid monies to purchase computers from abroad.

Direct causes are conditions that immediately influence the way a technology is applied to solving educational problems. For instance, two direct causes affecting the adoption of computer-assisted instruction are (1) the availability of ready-to-use computer programs for the various subject areas that make up the school's curriculum and (2) the availability of inservice-training courses that will equip teachers to conduct computer-assisted instruction.

Modern Industrialized Societies Compared with Developing Societies

Many of the conditions that account for the creation and development of a new technology in an advanced industrial society are similar to those conditions affecting the transfer of that technology to a developing society. For instance, in both industrially advanced and less-advanced cultures, the economic strength of the society, the enthusiasm of the populace for schooling, and the efficiency of the teacher-training system influence the adoption of new educational technologies. However, in addition to these similarities, there are also significant differences between such societies that make it useful for analytic purposes to separate industrially more-modernized from less-modernized societies. This is the reason for offering a pair of chapters in each of this book's four parts—one of the pair for more-modernized and the other for less-modernized societies.

General and Specific Causal Factors

Causal conditions can also be divided along a general/specific dimension. At the general end of the scale are conditions affecting the adoption of all educational technologies. An example would be a society's financial strength, which influences the degree to which people can provide the funds for equipment and the training of personnel that any technology would require. In contrast, other conditions are specific to a given technology. For instance, the viability of educational television depends on having spare parts and television-repair technicians available to keep transmitters and receivers in working order. Intermediate between the extreme ends of the general/specific scale are factors that influence the adoption of certain groups of educational technology but not others. An example is the availability of electricity in schools, a condition that determines whether computers, television receivers, and film projectors can be used. However, the absence of electricity does not prevent the use of reading materials, maps, charts, models, or chalkboards.

Realms of Cause

The phrase *realms of cause* refers to categories in which causal factors can be divided. There is no single *correct* set of realms, since such categories are merely ways people group or separate-out aspects of cause for convenience of analysis. So the four illustrative categories suggested here form only one set out of many that might be suggested. The four realms have been chosen because they are among those often met in the literature on educational innovation, development, and transfer. The categories are labeled political conditions, economic factors, cultural suitability, and magnitude of change.

Political Conditions

The term *political* in this context refers to the interaction between power and an educational technology, with *power* defined as the ability of a group or of an individual to influence the behavior of other groups or individuals. As the word *interaction* implies, a group's political power can affect the use of a particular technology while, at the same time, a type of technology can affect a group's power. For example, a political group currently in power is often able to control the contents of the nation's textbooks so that the texts picture the group's leaders and their policies in a favorable light. As a consequence, students acquire the government's interpretation of national history and political events, an outcome that serves to legitimate the current government's authority and increase its power.

When political power is used to influence the form of a technology, the form usually does not derive simply from a single source of power. Instead, the content that a technology conveys is typically the result of competing political forces that produce a compromise solution. For example, in numbers of multilingual societies, the demands of various cultural groups require that educational radio and television programs be broadcast in each of the group's languages. Furthermore, the contents of textbooks, pamphlets, and educational television programs are often the result of negotiations among politically active religious and secular organizations that seek to have their beliefs propagated.

When a new technology is introduced on a rather massive scale, the underlying motivation is often, if not always, political. To illustrate, in the early 1960s a series of incidents publicly embarrassed the US government into addressing itself to the educational plight of the US island territory of American Samoa. One incident was the publication in 1961 of a congressional report on the unsatisfactory condition of the islands' school system (*Study Mission to Eastern [American] Samoa*, 1961). Another event was a series of articles in the public press criticizing the US Navy's administration of Eastern Samoa. A third was the up-coming meeting of the South Pacific Commission, scheduled to be held in American Samoa in mid-1962. The Commission is a type of united nations of Oceania, so the United States faced the prospect in 1962 of receiving distinguished political visitors who would observe the administration of the colony first hand. These events stimulated political leaders in Washington to appropriate large sums of money for establishing in the islands a central television facility that would broadcast specially created daily lessons to all of the territory's schools. In short, the threat of further public criticism served as a political force motivating US officials to improve the islands' education system, and educational television was selected as the technology that could most dramatically effect such improvement.

Political power not only influences technology on the macro or national level but also on the micro level, including the individual school. A typical example is a school in which a new teacher introduces an instructional approach that is unfamiliar to the school principal and other teachers. The innovation might be that of sociodrama, of peer tutoring, of an individualized reading program, or the like. The principal and veteran teachers may resent the innovator, since they expect her to follow their lead and adopt their established practices rather than embarrassing the veteran staff members by demonstrating new skills which they lack. Hence, out of resentment or ignorance, the staff may criticize the newcomer so much that her attempt at innovation, as well as her potential future attempts, will be abandoned.

As the classroom example can imply, people who wish to introduce new technologies can profitably recognize ahead of time the important power relationships within the social system they hope to influence. An understanding of these political conditions equips innovators to devise strategies that may maximize the chances that the technology will be adopted. In way of illustration, the process of introducing microcomputers into a school might well begin with a simple demonstration of computer-assisted instruction designed for school administrators and curriculum supervisors. This early acquaintance with the role of microcomputers in the classroom may demystify the technology for those administrators who hold the top political-power positions in the school society. As a consequence, the administrators are less likely to feel threatened by the technology and, instead, may well consider themselves knowledgeable innovators, willing to encourage their teachers to try microcomputers in their classrooms.

In short, political conditions at both the macro and micro levels are crucial factors affecting the adoption of educational technologies.

Economic Conditions

Four of the economic considerations affecting the use of educational technologies are: (1) the financial strength of the society, as reflected in such indicators as the gross national product and the per capita income, (2) the value systems of the people who control the expenditure of funds, (3) decision-makers' estimates of the ultimate expense of a given technology, and (4) cost-benefit comparisons among units of the education system.

In regard to financial strength, it is clear that some societies are economically far better off than others. The annual per capita income in Saudi Arabia in 1984 was $10,224, in Japan $10,200, in the United States $11,338, in mainland China $330, in Burma $180, and in the African state of Chad $88 (*World Fact Book 1986*, 1985). As a result, Saudi Arabia, the United States, and Japan were much better equipped financially to adopt new educational technologies than were China, Burma, or Chad.

It is also clear that decision-makers in different societies allot more funds to those activities they greatly value than to ones they consider less worthy. The high esteem accorded technical skill and efficiency in Germany, Sweden, and Singapore has influenced decision-makers in those nations to invest in quantities of audiovisual equipment for the schools. In contrast, the traditional Muslim schools of Islamic societies, which for centuries have sought to educate youths in the sacred writings of the Qur'ān and the Hadith, have generally avoided adopting such advanced gadgetry. Instead, having pupils memorize passages from the holy books has continued to be their chief pattern of instruction.

It is also apparent that political values are often linked to economic factors. The observation that "money is power" is sometimes reflected in efforts to transfer technology from one society to another, typically in transfers from industrialized nations to developing ones. In recent years, educators in a variety of developing societies have been either enticed or urged by representatives of industrialized nations to import television and radio equipment, computers, and electronic calculators for educational use. Frequently the initial allotments of such items are offered at little or no expense to the recipient societies, or else the purchase is financed by low-interest, long-term loans from the industrialized nations or international banking agencies. In such cases, the motives of the donors appear to be two-fold—a mixture of philanthropy and self-interest. As philanthropists, donors are sincerely convinced that the proferred technology will enhance educational progress in the recipient nation. As promotors of self-interest, donors expect the recipient society to become a continuing market for the donors' electronic wares. As a result, recipients become dependent on donor societies for future purchases of equipment and for expertise. Usually such arrangements include the donor nation's additional intention of strengthening political bonds between the giver and the receiver by having the recipient society become financially and morally obligated to the donor.

A third economic consideration in technological transfer is the decision-makers' estimate of the ultimate cost of a technology. It is not uncommon for educational authorities to focus on the initial expense of installing an innovative technology, yet neglect to calculate accurately the extent of recurring costs for operating the system over the years. In the case of textbooks, the recurring costs are usually minimal, limited chiefly to replacing worn and lost copies. In the case of television, the continuing expense is substantial, since specialized personnel must be retained to operate the program-development and transmission systems, and both transmitting and receiving equipment requires expensive repair and replacement.

Another economic factor is the cost-benefit comparison among elements of the educational enterprise. In some cases, the decision about where best to invest available funds involves a comparison between a technology and some other aspect of the education system. For instance, will the purchase of classroom computers result in better student learning than will raising teachers' salaries? In other cases, the decision involves comparisons between two or more technologies that are intended to serve the same purpose. Will an investment in better-illustrated textbooks yield greater benefits to a larger quantity of learners than will an equal investment in expanding educational radio facilities?

In summary, economic factors can influence in a number of ways the creation and adoption of educational technologies.

Cultural Suitability

The term *culture*, as intended here, refers to both the physical objects (the material culture) and the patterns of thought and social interaction (the psychosocial culture) that typify a group of people. How acceptable a new technology will be in a society depends on how well the proposed innovation fits the existing culture. Sometimes an invention is ahead of its time, meaning that it has appeared before cultural conditions permit its widespread adoption. Such is the case of an early form of the digital computer, whose basic concept was devised in the 1830s by an English inventor named Charles Babbage. His plan included many of the basic elements of modern digital computers, such as punched-card input/output arrangement, the arithmetic unit, memory in which to store numbers, and the sequential control of operations. He called his invention the Analytical Machine, but it was never completed, partly because methods for producing metal parts with sufficiently close tolerances were not yet available (Development . . ., 1985: 564.) Hence, in the nineteenth century the computer concept could not be transformed into a practical instrument that would make it popular. A further century of technological and attitudinal progress was needed to produce the compatible material and psychosocial cultures of present-day industrialized societies.

While the matter of a technology being ahead of its time is of theoretical interest, of far more practical importance is the issue of transferring an educational technology from one culture to another. The problem is demonstrated most dramatically in the attempts to export complex technologies from highly industrialized countries to developing nations. The cultural mismatches that can result during such transfers include a wide range of incompatibilities—problems of physical infrastructures, of climatic conditions, of training facilities, of language use, of religious belief, of work habits, of sex-role traditions, and more.

As an illustration of problems of infrastructures, regions without electrical power find it difficult, if not impossible, to adopt photographic-slide, motion-picture, television, or computer technologies. And societies that lack a stable publishing industry are at a disadvantage in adapting foreign text materials to their own use.

Climatic conditions, though not in themselves cultural, can contribute to important cultural effects. As an example of a direct effect of climate, electronic equipment tends to suffer early deterioration in regions of extreme heat or cold or of high humidity. An example of a cultural outcome of climate is the nature of a society's work-day and work-year. Hot, humid weather reduces the efficiency of staff and students alike during the mid-day hours, thereby affecting the appropriateness of a school-day pattern that was set in a temperature climate when it is imposed on a tropical culture. Furthermore, a school-year schedule evolved in agricultural societies in northern regions—with a long school vacation during the busy farming months of June through August—may not fit patterns of life in either tropical areas or in regions south of the equator.

The cultural element of language is one of the most significant factors in transfers of educational practices. Reading materials, computer programs, and radio and television broadcasts all depend on language. So when the language of the exporting society differs from that of the importing society, either the learners in the recipient society must acquire the language in which the materials were originally cast or else the materials must be translated into the local dialect. The language problem is sufficiently troublesome when books and radio or television broadcasts require only the direct translation of one language into the other. But the problem is doubly difficult in certain cases of computer-technology transfer. Such difficulty occurs when computer programs written in a Western language that uses a romanized alphabet, such as English or French, must be recast for readers of such ideographic or non-romanized languages as Chinese and Arabic. The recasting is not accomplished simply by direct translation of the words at the computer-user's level. Rather, as illustrated later in Chapter 3, a novel arrangement of the computer's basic machine language must be devised in order to effect the transfer.

Religious and philosophical traditions also influence technological exchanges. This matter is perhaps most apparent in the case of operating systems. An example of one important system is "the process of thought by which truth is established." Two alternative approaches to this process are reflected in the question: Is truth to be found in the contents of holy books, or is it discovered by means of empirical science? The question is a serious issue in a variety of present-day societies—Hindu, Buddhist, Muslim, and Christian alike—which are striving for technological modernization and, at the same time, are seeking to retain their religious traditions. The conflict between the two modes of thought are apparent. Religious doctrine typically depends for its acceptance on unquestioning faith in the correctness of the answers offered in sacred writings. In contrast, empirical science encourages people to doubt past answers, to devise alternative proposals, and to test the validity of these alternatives by means of data collection and logical analysis. But then, as philosophers have proposed, the most suitable source of "truth" may vary from one aspect of life to another, with the truth about morality, art, love, the purpose of life, and the like not discoverable by means of empirical science.

In any event, many traditional operating systems within a society's educational structure are in conflict with systems introduced from other cultures so that the educational practices finally adopted often represent some sort of compromise between the old and new.

The typical work habits in a society also affect the transfer of technologies. Educational radio and television schedules in societies of devout Muslims require adjustments for daily prayers and holy days, and the efficiency of broadcast personnel during the annual Islamic month of fasting is often reduced. In cultures of the South Pacific such family responsibilities as visits to relatives in distant villages have traditionally taken precedence over job commitments. As a result, both the staff members and the students may absent themselves from school with little or no prior notice. Traditional attitudes toward the ownership and use of property can cause problems in maintaining control of the equipment needed in teaching. For instance, in cultures with a tradition of communal ownership of property, pupils and teachers alike may feel free to permanently "borrow" the books, audiotape recorders, transistor radios, maps, charts, and drawing equipment that the school's instructional methods require.

Therefore, a variety of cultural factors help determine how successfully a given educational innovation will be assimilated by a society.

Magnitude of Change

A further dimension of causality is the extent of change required for the use of an educational technology. Observations of the adoption of technologies suggest the rule of thumb that: Other things being equal, the greater the extent of change required, the less likely a technology will be adopted widely in a society, and vice versa. Thus, some technologies are not accepted, or else win only limited acceptance, because they require too many readjustments of traditional methods of instruction or administration. Frequently teachers avoid attempting a new instructional technique because it requires too much from them in energy, time, patience, or skill to become adept in its use. Altering old teaching habits in order to master new ones entails not only the expenditure of energy but also the risk of a teacher's looking foolish by committing embarrassing errors when attempting new techniques in the classroom. In addition, teachers who have traditionally perceived themselves as the classroom's chief performer—lecturing, conducting recitations, leading class discussion—can feel demoted to a less prestigious educational role when they are asked to have reading materials, radio, television, or computers deliver the content of lessons.

Thus, the amount of change required in existing habits and the fear of failure or of decreased prestige can affect people's willingness to accept a new technology.

Summary

The foregoing sampling of factors that govern the creation and use of educational technologies has been only illustrative, not definitive. Far more causal elements than those described above interact in complex ways to determine which technologies are adopted under various conditions, as will be shown in Chapters 2 through 9. The matter of how such factors converge to effect technological change is still far from completely understood. As Chadwick (1983: 114) observed when describing the state of educational technology in Latin America: "There is a growing realization of the need for new procedures to analyze and evaluate the probable impacts of technological innovation . . . and thus reduce difficulties and resistance to innovation generally."

Judging the Success of an Educational Technology

An important kind of information people seek about a technology is "how good" or "how effective" or "how successful" it is. And because not everyone applies the same criteria in judging success, it is useful to recognize some common methods of assessing technological efficiency. The following description of methods is intended to orient readers to typical indicators of success used in appraisals of the four technologies described in Chapters 2 through 9. The two categories of criteria reviewed below are those of: (1) popularity and (2) effectiveness and efficiency.

Popularity

The logic underlying the popularity criterion is that a technology is successful to the degree that it is widely accepted in the educational community. Popularity is usually judged in terms of either availability or use. *Availability* refers to how many regions or schools or classrooms have the technology at hand. How many books and journals are in school libraries? How many textbooks are there per pupil? How many classrooms have television receivers? And what is the average number of microcomputers per school? *Use* refers to how frequently or intensively the technology is employed for either administrative or instructional purposes.

The distinction between availability and use is important, since some technologies that are widely available stand idle much of the time, whereas others are in constant use. As a result, statistics about the number of motion-picture projectors or photocopying machines in schools do not accurately represent the magnitude of the role these sorts of equipment play in the education process.

The matter of availability-versus-use is related to the typical pattern that modern-day technological innovations often display in their stages of development and implementation. The first stage is that of initial possibilities. When such media as programmed books, television, or microcomputers are introduced, prognosticators speculate about how these devices are likely to contribute to the improvement of education.

At the second stage—that of research and development—educational applications of the medium are tried out, refined, and assessed, with the tryouts often accompanied by glowing accounts of the technology's effectiveness.

The third stage consists of widespread adoption of the innovation, as educators hope it will solve their vexing administrative and instructional problems. This widespread acceptance is frequently stimulated by (1) the advertising efforts of companies which produce the equipment that the technology involves, (2) politicians and administrators who wish to be seen as part of the educational vanguard, and (3) educators—such as university professors and instructional supervisors in school systems—who seek to enhance their professional standing by displaying expertise in this new field.

The fourth stage is one of partial disillusionment, or at least of increased caution, when evidence about the limitations of the technology is revealed in educators' daily experience and in the results of research studies. This fourth stage is marked by a reduction both in the rate of schools acquiring the technology and in the frequency with which already-acquired equipment is used. At this fourth stage, the innovation settles into the somewhat permanent role it will fill until some new event either diminishes or enhances its function.

Effectiveness and Efficiency

Educational administrators sometimes distinguish between the words *effectiveness* and *efficiency*. They use *effectiveness* to mean how well a technology does its assigned job. In other words, does the technology reach the goal it is expected to achieve? If videotapes are used for teaching world history to high-school students, do the students subsequently do well when tested over the subject-matter? If college entrance examinations are scored by a computer, are the results of the scoring accurate? If elementary-school pupils use self-instructional booklets in learning to add and subtract fractions, can the pupils then accurately solve daily-life problems involving fractions?

Efficiency, on the other hand, refers not only to whether the desired goal has been achieved but also at what cost in terms of money, time, energy, and personnel displacement. If children learn as well from Textbook A as from Textbook B, then Textbook B is the more efficient technology because it costs less. If students learn nearly as much from a set of photographic slides as they do from a motion-picture film, and the film costs 10 times more than the slides, the slight gain in learning from the film may not be worth the extra expense. If student records that are kept in file cabinets are as accurate in their content as records entered into a computer, which of these systems—file cabinets or the computer—will be more economical when costs in terms of time, space, energy, money, and convenience are considered? Thus, the term efficiency refers to the cost-benefit or cost-effectiveness of a technology.

Several different approaches have been used for estimating the effectiveness of educational technologies. One method is the opinion-survey in which people who use such media are asked to describe a technology's strengths and weaknesses. The advantage of the survey is that it provides information from a diversity of people who use the technology in the classroom or office. A shortcoming of this approach is that it often lacks precision in depicting the factors that have influenced the opinions of the respondents.

Another approach has been referred to as action-research. In action-research, no attempt is made to control experimentally the variables involved in the real-life operation of the technology, although efforts are made to identify and assess such variables as accurately as the ongoing daily conduct of education permits. However, a problem with action-research is that it typically involves so many uncontrolled or unmeasured variables that it is difficult, if not impossible, to estimate how much each of the variables has contributed to the final results of the study.

A third approach is that of controlled experimentation in which researchers seek to limit the number of variables affecting the outcome of an administrative or instructional use of technology. When all but one or a few variables are controlled, the researcher can conclude with greater confidence which of the non-controlled variables have apparently contributed to the outcome of the learning experiment. However, the laboratory conditions that are so often needed for controlling all factors except one or two can render the experimental conditions so different from the real-life conditions of the typical classroom that it is impossible to know what the experiment's results properly imply for daily educational practice.

In short, each of these popular approaches to assessing the worth of educational technologies has its own strengths and weaknesses. Thus, using a combination of the three can help balance out the weaknesses, but doing so requires far more time and effort than would be involved in using one of the approaches alone.

Analyses of the great quantity of educational-technology research of recent decades have led to several informative conclusions. One relates to trends in the kinds of educational technology that attract the greatest research attention. Meierhenry (1983: 101-2), after surveying thirty US higher-education institutions and research centers which offer doctorates in library science and communications, observed that "most research activities relate to the ebb and flow of current technologies." He explained that:

> At one time emphasis was on programmed instruction; at another, it was on instructional systems; at still another it was on instructional television . . ., [whereas] the majority of studies now under way involve mainframe and microcomputers and some type of interacting learning systems that usually involve either television or videodisc . . . . Such trendiness belies the idea that researchers on technology have really moved away from doing research on the impact of a medium of technology and toward a total set of factors that influence human learning.

A second conclusion concerns the question: Are various newer technologies as effective for instruction as traditional face-to-face teaching? Schramm (1977: 34-35) reviewed hundreds of experiments with instructional television and radio, motion-picture films, computer-assisted and programmed instruction, photographic slides, filmstrips, audiotapes, models, and the like. He concluded that "students can learn a great deal from any of the media. Under most of the conditions tested, they could learn as much as from face-to-face teaching, about many subjects." Thus, as a general rule, one medium is not necessarily more effective than another. Decisions about which medium to adopt can depend on (1) the conditions in the particular instructional of administrative setting and (2) the media's comparative costs in terms of such variables as time, money, the expense of personnel training, and administrative complexity.

As the reviews of the assessment literature attest, most comparative studies of instructional technology have centered on such general questions as: "Is a lesson via television more effective than a lesson taught via photographic slides?" Or more specifically: "Is a computer better than a workbook for teaching mathematics?" When the results of such studies are compiled so that generalizations can be derived about the relative effectiveness of different instructional technologies, it appears that no widely applicable conclusions can be drawn. In effect, comparisons of television per se with computers per se, or of books in general with audiotapes in general, provide no help for deciding what instructional devices will be most efficient in helping particular kinds of students master particular objectives under particular learning circumstances. As Schramm (1977: 27) has noted, "There is no shortage of research on instructional media, only a shortage of the kind of research that would be most helpful to us."

What kind of research, then, is needed? Authorities in the field suggest that research should focus not simply on a type of technology or a type of subject matter but, rather, it should comprehend the entire complex of important variables that interact to determine learning effectiveness. These variables include the characteristics of the technology, characteristics of the learners, the specific skills or subject-matter being taught, the attitudes and skills of instructional personnel, and the physical conditions of the learning setting. But even the results of such complex studies are not sufficient to guide decision-makers in determining which technology will be most suitable for a given instructional or administrative task. Information about effectiveness needs to be combined with other data before a judgement can be reached. The other needed data relate to feasibility and to efficiency in the sense of cost-benefit ratios. Conditions that influence feasibility and efficiency include such variables as political conditions, cultural suitability, and the extent of change required by a technology.

Conclusion

The aim of this chapter has been to sketch a setting within which subsequent chapters can be viewed. More precisely, the purpose has been to introduce the four representative technologies, to identify types of causal factors that influence their development and adoption, and to describe methods commonly used for assessing the technologies' success.

With these matters in mind, we turn to the introductory essay for Part I, where the evolution of computers is reviewed, followed in Chapter 2 by a description of the recent state of educational computer technology in industrialized societies. Chapter 3 then offers a decision-making model that could be applied by educators in developing societies to determine which, if any, of the computer applications in advanced nations they might wish to adopt.

References

Chadwick, C. (1983) Educational media in Latin America: A brief overview. In J. W. Brown & S. N. Brown, *Educational Media Yearbook 1983*. Littleton, Colorado: Libraries Unlimited.

Development of digital computing (1985) In *The New Encyclopedia Britannica*, Vol. 21. Chicago: Encyclopedia Britannica.

Gerlach, V. S. (1984) Trends in instructional technology research. In J. W. Brown & S. N. Brown, *Educational Media Yearbook 1984*. Littleton, Colorado: Libraries Unlimited.

Meierhenry, W. C. (1983) Current research in educational media and technology: A survey. In J. W. Brown & S. N. Brown, *Educational Media Yearbook 1983*. Littleton, Colorado: Libraries Unlimited.

Meierhenry, W. C. (1984) A brief history of educational technology. In J. W. Brown & S. N. Brown, *Educational Media Yearbook 1984*. Littleton, Colorado: Libraries Unlimited.

Schramm, W. (1977) *Big Media, Little Media*. Beverly Hills, California: Sage.

Silber, K. H. (1981) Some implications of the history of educational technology: we're all in this together. In J. W. Brown & S. N. Brown, *Educational Media Yearbook 1981*. Littleton, Colorado: Libraries Unlimited.

Study Mission to Eastern (American) Samoa (1961) Washington, D.C.: US Government Printing Office.

World Fact Book 1986 (1985) Washington, D.C.: US Central Intelligence Agency.

PART I: COMPUTER TECHNOLOGY

An Example of Decision-Making in Technology Transfer

The purpose of this introductory essay is to offer (1) a brief history of the development of computer technology and (2) a description of the essential operating components of digital computers. Chapter 2 then reviews the current place of computers in the education systems of advanced industrial societies, with attention centred primarily in the United States. Chapter 3 follows with a suggested decision-making model that may be applied by educators in developing societies as they determine the ways that computer technology can best be adapted to solve educational problems they face. The case used for illustrating decision-making in technology transfer is that of teaching the reading and writing of English in the People's Republic of China.

The Growth of Computer Technology

The history of electronic computers is like the progress of a railroad locomotive that barely creeps along for a great distance, then suddenly speeds ahead at an astonishing, ever-accelerating pace. The creeping progress extended from ancient times until after World War II, when the dash towards the future began.

Apparently the earliest notion of a computing machine appeared several thousand years ago in the form of the abacus—a series of counting beads on a wooden frame—still used by shopkeepers in the Orient to calculate their sales. But not until the mid-seventeenth century did the French scientist and philosopher Blaise Pascal invent the first mechanical calculating device consisting of dial-wheels and gears that permitted him to add and subtract up to eight columns of digits. A short time later the German mathematician G. W. Leibniz improved Pascal's mechanism so it could multiply, divide, and extract square roots. And in 1820 de Colmar offered a commercial version of a similar device called an arithmometer. But despite the soundness of the theory on which these devices were based, they failed to become popular because their mechanical limitations rendered them untrustworthy.

As mentioned in Chapter 1, in the 1830s an English inventor named Charles Babbage envisioned a machine he called The Analytical Engine. It would embody the principal elements found in present-day digital computers—a punched-card system for putting data into the machine and taking the results out, a unit to carry out arithmetic computations, a memory unit for storing numbers, and a system for controlling the sequence of operations that needed to be performed. However, the machine-tool industry of the early nineteenth century was not equal to the task of fashioning the highly precise metal parts that Babbage's invention required, so a proper operating version of his engine was never produced. As a result, his plan lay neglected for over 100 years.

It would be almost the middle of the twentieth century before a working electronic computer was devised. But between the time of Babbage's proposal and the close of World War II, there had been many separate advances in mathematics, science, and engineering which eventually would converge to make the first successful computers possible. As one contributing discovery, in the mid-nineteenth century the British mathematician George Boole devised Boolean algebra, a mode of decision-making that would provide the switching logic for present-day digital computers. In the 1880s Hermann Hollerith, a statistician in the US census bureau, invented a punched-card system for automatically tabulating census returns, thereby unwittingly creating a technique later used for entering data into computers. During this same period, discoveries about the properties and use of electricity were being announced at a growing rate. Thomas Alva Edison improved dynamos and produced a reliable electric light (1879). The comparative advantages of alternating current and direct current were demonstrated. Then Heinrich Hertz in Germany showed that certain metals give off electric current when exposed to light, and thereby he established the basis for the photoelectric cell or "electric eye" (1887). Lee Deforest in the United States in 1907 invented the audion, a forerunner of the vacuum tubes that would become essential elements of the first electronic computers which appeared nearly a half-century later.

So it was that the creation of electronic computers in the mid-twentieth century was not the result of a sudden insight on the part of one or two scientists. Instead, it was the consequence of many separate theories and inventions that had been stimulated by the ferment of scientific activity in Europe and North America from the latter 1800s into the twentieth century. This activity provided the preparatory conditions for present-day computer technology.

Today's remarkable pace of computer development can be illustrated with figures describing improvements in the machines' speed, capacity, size, versatility, and cost over the past forty years, but particularly since the 1960s. The first electromechanical machines, such as the Harvard Mark I completed in 1944, used electrical switching elements to process data that had been entered into the computer on punched cards. To accommodate all the switching equipment, the machine was huge—50 feet long and eight feet high. Such early versions were the pioneers, followed during the period of 1946-58 by what are known as the first-generation of computers.

The first-generation devices used vacuum tubes instead of electric relays to perform logical functions, making them 1,000 times faster than their pioneering predecessors. Techniques for magnetically storing operating instructions in the machine and enlarging the memory functions also evolved during this period.

At the time of the second generation, from 1959 into the mid-1960s, the vacuum tube was replaced by the transistor, a 1947 Bell-Laboratory invention that was far smaller, more energy-efficient, and more dependable than the vacuum tube. As a result, second-generation computers were both faster and more compact than their forebears, capable of performing as many as 100,000 functions a second.

Third-generation computers evolved during the late 1960s and well into the 1970s, with their chief distinguishing characteristic being the miniaturization of computer components. Advanced microtechnology now enabled engineers to form integrated solid-state electrical circuits by embedding thousands of transistors and other electrical elements into a silicon chip no larger that a young child's fingernail. In the United States, an important condition stimulating efforts to reduce the size of computers while increasing their efficiency was the government's interest in rocketry and space exploration, particularly in competition with the Soviet Union. Large sums were invested in research on miniaturizing hardware needed in the space-travel program. A further stimulus was commercial competition for the rapidly evolving markets for computers in business and manufacturing operations, in education, and in recreation (computer games). Not only did one computer manufacturer compete with others within a given nation, but fervid competition developed between countries, particularly between Japan and the United States, with a variety of other nations entering the lists as time passed.

During this period and up to the present day, computers have been categorized into three sizes—main-frame, mini, and micro. Main-frames are the largest type, sometimes filling one or more rooms. They are fast and powerful, solving highly complex problems of air travel, manufacturing, government operations, and the like, while permitting a variety of users to process data simultaneously.

Minicomputers are middle-sized, small enough to be placed on a table or desk, but still sufficiently fast and sophisticated enough to solve the problems of a fairly large school system or business organization.

Microcomputers are chiefly a product of the early and mid-1980s.

They are often referred to as *personal computers* or *home computers*, because so many people in advanced nations now own such devices. In schools, microcomputers serve not only instructional purposes but also as aids in conducting research and performing administrative functions. The larger microcomputers are about the size of a standard electric typewriter. The smaller ones are the size of a typical textbook, weighing only a few pounds and easily transported. Despite its diminutive size, a modern-day microcomputer is a powerful instrument, displaying far greater speed and memory capacity than the second-generation main-frame devices had.

Miniaturization of computer hardware after the mid-1980s advanced at an astonishing pace. By the mid-1960s, up to one million electronic elements could be built into a square silicon chip no broader than two-tenths of an inch square. As a result, computers could be reduced in size, power consumption, and weight by a factor of nearly 100,000. Their dependability increased at the same rate, their speed of operation improved 100 times, and the amount of storage memory grew between 10 and 1,000-fold (Kubitz, 1985: 947).

In the early and middle 1980s, advances in technology produced fourth-generation computers. Although the distinctions between the third and fourth generations are not at all precise, one difference be-tween the two stages has been in the number of integrated-circuit components implanted in each silicon chip. Whereas a single third-generation chip contained thousands of components, a fourth-generation chip of similar size holds one-hundred times more elements. These developments have so reduced size and cost that manufacturers have been able to produce sophisticated, easy-to-use microcomputers well within the buying power of the typical school and home.

The fourth generation has also introduced diverse new uses. Not only can a microcomputer correct spelling errors in a manuscript, but it can read the manuscript aloud. And microcomputers play all manner of games—chess, checkers, dice, slot-machines, and roulette along with simulated war encounters, business ventures, and historical events. They can translate material from one written language into another, such as from English to Spanish. They can cast simple oral dictation into printed form. They can publish books, magazines, and newsletters, complete with illustrations. And the list goes on and on.

Another feature of the fourth generation has been the increase in computer networking, a system of connecting widely separated compu-ters by means of telephone lines and microwave relays so that informa-tion can be shared by a great number of users. Airline reservations, banking functions, stock-market orders, library-information services, in-teruniversity operations, cooperative research ventures, law-enforcement identification of criminals, government communications, and business inventories have all profited from networking.

An additional fourth-generation characteristic has been the growth of research into *artificial intelligence* (simulating human thought by means of computers) and the allied field of *robotics* (computer-directed machines that perform human-like tasks) (Shute, 1985). Theorists working on artificial intelligence assume that if they can program a computer to produce the same sorts of solutions to problems that a human would produce, science will have taken a significant step toward understanding human thought processes. This understanding should aid educators in devising more efficient teaching techniques. Furthermore, as engineers combine simulated human thought with limb and muscle movements, they are able to create robots that carry out increasing numbers of the tasks humans have traditionally performed. Computers can already calculate figures much faster and more accurately than humans, and robots can manipulate both large and small objects with greater strength and precision than humans—all of this without suffering fatigue, boredom, distraction, or depression. Over the past decade, robots have taken over a host of jobs in the fields of manufacturing, construction, research, and medical treatment, with new developments in robotics appearing at a rapidly increasing rate.

Because of such technological advances, industrial societies by the latter 1980s have become so dependent on computers that if all computers suddenly stopped, life in those societies would be immeasurably disrupted. The supply of electricity, gas, and water to schools, homes, and factories would cease. No airplanes, trains, automobiles, or military weapons of recent vintage could function. The supply of food to most markets would stop. Records of inventories in business and industry would be lost. Space travel would cease, and the government's ability to collect and record taxes would end. The stock market would collapse. And these are only a few of the consequences. In effect, within a period of hardly more than two decades, computers have become indispensable components of the world's advanced-technology cultures.

The Structure of Digital Computers

So far we have identified high points in the history of electronic computers but have yet to describe the components essential to a computer's operation. This is a task to which we now turn.

Computers are of three classes—analogue, digital, and hybrid. Analogue computers operate on the basis of continuous variables, just as a thermostat operates along an unbroken array of temperatures, ranging gradually from very cold to very hot. In contrast, digital computers operate on the basis of discrete variables, just as a typical electric-light switch can assume only two positions—completely on and completely off. Hybrid computers combine certain features of both analogue and digital devices. But because analogue computers are rarely used in the field of education, the following description is limited to digital varieties (even though digital machines may include some analogue elements).

In computer parlance, each binary on/off switch in a digital circuit is called a *bit*. Since a bit has only two possible positions (1 for on, 0 for off), it cannot hold or convey much information. However, when eight bits are clustered to form a unit called a *byte*, the large quantity of on/off permutations that this 8-bit sequence is able to assume can represent a great variety of different symbols. For example, a single meaningful character—such as a letter of the alphabet, a number, or a punctuation mark—can be assigned a set code of eight on/off (1/0) combinations. The byte pattern representing letter A is 01000001, the pattern for letter B is 01000010, and so on. However, since great quantities of bytes are needed for the complex operations of the computer, bytes are usually not referred to as single units but, rather, as *kilobytes*, a term often abbreviated as K or KB. The prefix *kilo* normally means 1000. However, a digital computer's counting system is based on the number 2 rather than 10, so one kilobyte contains 1024 individual bytes (since 2 multiplied by itself ten times equals 1024). The operating capacity of computers is often referred to in terms of kilobytes or in the next larger unit, *megabytes*. (A megabyte is commonly defined as equal to 1024 kilobytes, though some writers have defined it as equaling only 1000 kilobytes.) Teachers who use microcomputers in the classroom or educational researchers who use them in the office are familiar with such phrases a "128K" or "512K" in reference to the byte capacity of the central memory unit of a particular machine. The larger the K, the greater the quantity of information the machine can accommodate at one time.

With the meaning of bytes now in hand, we turn to the basic components typically found in computers, with our illustration focusing on the microcomputer, since it is the type used most widely in educational settings.

Computers are constructed to perform four basic functions. They must be built to receive information from a user (input), to manipulate the information (processing), to provide the results of the manipulation to the user (output), and to save the results (storage).

The Input Phase

The most common mechanism for inputing information is a keyboard modeled after that of a typewriter. However, information already stored magnetically on a disk or tape can also be used to input information as directed by the user at the keyboard. Or, as a third option, a device called a *modem* can be connected to a computer and used to cradle a telephone receiver, thereby permitting information from a distant source to be entered into the computer via a telephone line.

In order to operate, the computer needs two kinds of input—instructions and data. A set of instructions—commonly referred to as a *program* or an *application*—tells the computer how to process data that will be recieved. For example, one set of instructions (a word-processing program) will direct the computer to behave like a typewriter—producing lines of words and numbers that form a business letter, journal article, or book manuscript. A different set directs the computer to serve as a drawing board (a graphics program), allowing the user to draw figures, maps, charts, and the like. Another set enables a user to place musical notes on a staff, thereby creating a musical score that the computer not only prints but also plays aloud in four or more harmonized parts (music-composition program). Still other instructions equip the computer to organize business inventories or income-tax forms and calculate the totals for the various quantities in the form (spread-sheet program). And these are but a few of the thousands of available programs telling computers how to manipulate data.

The second kind of information to be input is called *data*. In the case of word-processing, the data are the contents of the business letter or the book manuscript that the user wants to produce. Data for a graphics application are the lines, shapes, words, and numbers the user plans for his chart or diagram. Data for a music-composition program are the tunes, harmonies, and lyrics the user creates to form the song she has envisioned.

It is possible for a user to input her own program, that is, to create her own set of instructions about how to process data. When a user assumes such a role, she is functioning as a *programmer*. However, the task of creating a program that contains instructions of any great complexity is extremely difficult, sometimes requiring several years' effort. Therefore, most people use programs that experts have already developed and tested to ensure they operate as intended.

The difficulty that programming entails is related to levels of computer languages. Each computer language is a set of rules—vocabulary, grammar, syntax—that permits a user to tell the machine how to move data about, what sort of logic to follow, what conclusions to draw, and how to store and report the results. Nearly every computer program depends on several different levels of language, ranging from low to high. The lowest level is called machine language, since the rules are all in terms of basic machine bytes, requiring the user to cast all instructions in binary zeros and ones. But hardly anyone understands the layout of, say, a 512K circuit well enough to make any sense at all at the machine level. And in any event, working at that level to carry out such jobs as word processing or graph designing is so slow and tedious that requiring people to operate at the machine level would be entirely unreasonable. Therefore, experts have devised intermediate-level languages (interpreters and compilers) that translate such a high-level language as English into low-level machine instructions and vice versa. The hierarchy of languages that participate in a typical program is usually complex. It takes more than one linking language to bridge the gap between everyday speech or thought and the machine's millions of byte patterns. The process is similar to that used by a French-speaking visitor in the Orient who wishes to communicate with a Mongolian political leader. His wish is fulfilled through a chain of intermediaries—one translator who speaks French and English, another who speaks English and Mandarin Chinese, and a third who speaks both Mandarin Chinese and the Mongolian leader's dialect.

In summary, two sorts of information are entered into the computer. One is a program of instructions. The other is a set of data. Programs usually have been stored on magnetic disks or tapes, so they are entered from a disk drive (turntable) or tape drive, under the user's direction at the keyboard. Data are usually entered from a keyboard or else by a small box (called a *mouse*) that the user slides by hand across the table to direct an arrow across the computer's videoscreen, showing the user what information is being entered.

The Stage of Processing and Storing Data

The internal operations of a microcomputer are performed by a cluster of interacting elements that are embedded in silicon chips. At the center of this cluster is the *central processing unit* (CPU), the computer's "brain" that performs all manipulations of data as dictated by machine-language instructions fetched from the machines's memory. There is also a set of electrical conductors called a *bus* that carries electronic signals to various elements of the computer. Another unit of the processing system is the *read-only memory* (ROM), which contains a variety of programs that control essential operations of the computer.

A fourth component is the *random access memory* (RAM), capable of storing and retrieving characters within a millionth of a second. The one major limitation of this memory unit is that when the computer's power is turned off, everything stored in RAM is lost. Therefore, if data are to be retained beyond the time the user is operating the computer, they must be transferred for permanent storage onto a thin, flexible electromagnetic plastic circle called a *diskette* or *floppy disk*. This transfer is accomplished by the user inserting a diskette into a device called a *disk drive*, which is rather like a phonograph turntable. The disk drive is extremely fast, able to read and write continuous information at the rate of 60,000 characters a second. Microcomputer diskettes measure either $5\frac{1}{4}$ inches or $3\frac{1}{2}$ inches in diameter, with the smaller size holding larger amounts of information (819,200 characters on a double-sided disk) than the older $5\frac{1}{4}$ size. An alternative to the plastic floppy disk is the *hard disk*, a rigid metal platter coated with magnetic material, capable of storing far more information than a floppy disk the same size. A hard disk can hold as much as 10 or 20 megabytes (over 10 million or 20 million characters) or, in slightly larger versions, more than 300 megabytes (Lu, 1985: 144, 180).

The foregoing elements, then, are principal components of the processing and storage functions of the typical microcomputer.

The Output Phase

There are several ways computers can report the results of their work. One is a visual representation on a video screen. As the user works at the keyboard or moves the mouse across the table, the screen immediately displays the results of that work. If the computer is being used as a word processor, the screen shows the exact text that the user is presently writing. If the computer is serving as a drawing device, the screen shows the lines and spaces as they are created. These images can be either monochrome or in a range of colors.

A second type of computer output is that of printed pages. There are three main kinds of printing devices in common use. One is the letter printer, rather like an electric typewriter which prints out text material from the raised letters on a plastic ball (or "daisy wheel" or plastic thimble). Another variety is the dot-matrix printer, which forms letters, numbers, and graphic designs by means of tiny, closely clustered dots. A third variety is the laser printer, which employs a laser beam to trace the computer's message across a page in the form of electrical charges which attract a special "dust" that is sealed onto the paper at a high temperature.

Another way to output information is to transmit the computer's signals to distant computers by means of a modem that connects the computer to a telephone line.

Microcomputer output can also take the form of sound. Music composed on a computer by means of such a program as *ConcertWare* is played aloud by the computer, simulating whatever musical instruments the composer has chosen to include. Likewise, text material written on such a program as *Smooth Talker* will be output as spoken words. Both of these programs are designed for the Apple Company's Macintosh microcomputer.

Thus, just as there are various ways that information can be entered into a microcomputer for processing, so also there are diverse ways the results of the processing can be reported to the operator.

Such, then, is the way computers do their work. They accept programs and data (input), manipulate the data in ways the programs direct (processing), and subsequently report the results of their work (output).

Conclusion

The dual intention of this essay has been (1) to describe highlights in the historical development of computers in order to suggest conditions that influence the evolution of such a technology and (2) to identify principal computer components and common terms used in discussions of computers. The essay thus serves as a foundation for the next two chapters which focus on computers in the service of education.

As mentioned in Chapter 1, each of the four parts of this volume illustrates a different viewpoint toward analyzing conditions which influence the development and cross-cultural transfer of educational technology. The perspective adopted for Part I is a *state-of-the-art* and *decision-making* approach. The state-of-the-art portion appears in Chapter 2 as a review and assessment of the current condition of computer applications in the education systems of advanced industrial societies. The decision-making portion appears in Chapter 3 as a suggested pattern of thought that educational leaders in developing nations could follow when choosing which computer applications from advanced societies will likely suit their society's educational needs.

References

Kubitz, W. J. (1985) Computer technology and telecommunications. In Torsten Husen & T. Neville Postlethwaite, *International Encyclopedia of Education*. Oxford: Pergamon, Vol. 22, pp. 747-955.
Lu, Cary (1985) *The Apple Macintosh Book*. Bellevue, Washington: Microsoft (2nd Ed.)
Shute, Valerie (1985) Artificial intelligence. In Torsten Husen & T. Neville Postlethwaite. *International Encyclopedia of Education*. Oxford: Pergamon, Vol. 1, pp. 333-340.

CHAPTER 2

The Creation and Development of Educational Computer Technology

DENNIS O. HARPER

In advanced industrialized nations, the amount of research and publication related to computers in education during the past five years has been staggering. The aim of Chapter 2 is to summarize this body of knowledge under the following major sections:

1. Extent of the educational use of computers
2. Types of educational functions that computers perform
3. Conditions that influence the extent of computer use in education
4. Problems related to computer education and early predictions that have not been fulfilled
5. Ways of assessing the success of computers in education
6. New developments in the offing
7. Prognosis for the future of computer education in advanced nations

To cover these matters in detail would require a book for each. Therefore, only the principal findings related to the topics are offered in the following pages, with an extensive reference section at the end of the chapter provided for readers interested in delving deeper into each topic.

How Widely are Computers used in Education?

In earlier decades, books and instructors in the education system were about the only means available outside the family and immediate community for transporting information from generation to generation. But over the past four decades, this changed dramatically since nearly everyone in advanced industrialized societies gained access to television, to radio, and, at a rapidly growing rate, to computers (Haefner, 1985: 176).

The purchase of computers for school use in such nations as the United States has been increasing at such a pace that it is difficult to

35

keep track of how many machines are now in American classrooms. The most comprehensive survey of the instructional uses of school computers has been undertaken by the Center for Social Organization of Schools at Johns Hopkins University under the supervision of Henry Jay Becker (1986). Becker's summary of a 1985 survey based on a probability sample of 2,300 US public and non-public schools suggests that: One million computers were in American elementary and secondary schools.

- More than fifteen million students used them during 1985.
- Computers were used by half-a-million teachers (one-fourth of the nation's teaching force).
- Half of US secondary schools–meaning 16,500 schools–owned 15 or more computers.
- More than 7500 elementary schools owned 15 or more computers.
- In the typical school, about 150 students used computers during the year, and four to five teachers used computers regularly in their teaching practice.
- Of secondary-school teachers using computers, about 40 percent were in the fields of mathematics and computer-technology.
- The major category of student use of computers was computer-assisted-instruction followed by computer-programming, discovery-learning and problem-solving, and word processing.

Although Becker's survey demonstrates the growing availability of this rather expensive technology, questions remain about the cost-benefit of microcomputers in schools. In Becker's words: "How much better off are the schools for their investments? How much more effective have teachers been with their new instructional tools? How significantly has the curriculum changed to become more appropriate to the needs of children? And how much better off are the students for their experiences?" (Becker, 1984, 1986: 30).

In response to Becker's queries, other surveys have made it clear that the advantages computers offer to teachers are now perceived as more limited than was suggested in earlier optimistic visions of computer enthusiasts (Brophy & Hannon, 1985: 49). Such sobering observations about the educational potential of computers have been reported not only for North America but for England as well (Lesgold, 1983; Fletcher, 1983).

While recognizing the support for computers that Becker's figures suggest, Roblyer (1985: 40) points out that such support "is not sufficient foundation upon which to build a future for computer-based methods. In the first place, it seems likely that breakthrough discoveries of the kind technology has realized in science and medicine may simply not be possible in education."

Although such cautions are being sounded about the educational potential of computers, activity in the field is progressing apace, as reflected in the growing quantity of research and printed material on the subject.

Research and Development. Bergheim & Chin (1984: 30) report that "although no part of the 1984 US Department of Education budget was specifically earmarked for computer education, school administrators are creative in how they channel federal funds." For example, in 1983 US $529 million was available to schools from the Chapter II Education Consolidation and Improvement Act, which carries no federal stipulations on how the funds must be used. Some 60 to 70 percent of this money was spent on computer education (Bergheim & Chin (1984: 30).

Printed Matter. Thousands of new computer-related publications have appeared in the last five years, and it is estimated that computer books are now being published at a faster rate than works of fiction (Bartimo, cited in Sunners, 1985: 5). In addition, at least three on-line data bases can now be tapped which index the contents of microcomputer magazines: Computer Database (Dialog Information Services); Microsearch (The Source); Microcomputer Index Services (Dialog Information Services) (Sunners, 1985: 5).

Sunners (1985: 11) also analyzed *ERIC's Current Index to Journals in Education (CJIE)* and discovered that the frequency of computer-education articles increased exponentially from 2 in 1976 to 714 in 1983. Sunners also learned that 1,563 computer-education descriptors had been used a total of 13,720 times in indexing the 1,795 computer-education articles in ERIC from 1976 to late 1984. Table 1 summarizes these 13,720 citations under major categories.

TABLE 1. *ERIC Computer-Education Citations*

Category	Number of citings
Educational and Technological Change	395
Educational/Age Level	1509
Publication Types	248
Research/Measurement/Testing	365
Administration	379
Curriculum and Program Development	388
Learning/Instruction	1864
Special Needs Students	151
Microcomputers and Subject Areas	1473
Computer Education	2097
Media and Technology	401
Library and Resource Centers	261
Information Retrieval	299
Teacher Education	202

The above figures seem to indicate widespread use of computers in American education. Melmed (1984: 79) extrapolates Becker's data to estimate that 1,250,000 computers were in place by September 1986.

"Assuming an average school day of five and a half hours, or 330 minutes, and a school population of 40 million students, 1,250,000 computer units provides for an average of about 10 minutes of computer time per day for each student." Considering that the average American child watches six hours of television daily, it is hard to conceive that the estimated 10 minutes has nearly as much influence on the child's learning as does home television. However, Melmed also points out that "by considering the possibility of yet another doubling to an acquisition rate of 500,000 computer units annually, this leads under the same assumptions, by around 1989, to an average of 20 minutes of computer time per day per student." Some older students may even receive 30 or 35 minutes of experience which accounts for about 10 percent of their school day. Perhaps, in their case, computers already make a difference in student achievement. Of course, having machines available does not indicate how frequently and for what purposes they are used in the school's instructional plan.

What, then, are some of reasons schools are buying computers in the numbers outlined above? The major explanations would include: (1) advertising efforts by computer hardware and software manufacturers, (2) politicians and administrators wishing to be seen as modern, (3) professors and teachers wanting to display expertise in a new field, and (4) pressure from parents.

These factors help account for many schools buying microcomputers before knowing what to do with the machines. "I'm very skeptical about the decision making at the schools," writes Henry Becker. "Schools are buying micros like overhead projectors or movie projectors. You may have two or three. That's like ordering two or three books for the whole school" (cited in Bergheim & Chin, 1984: 29). Such buying habits, which fail to fit purchases into a reasoned instructional plan, may well impede effective classroom use.

Thus it is clear that microcomputers are being purchased at a rapid pace by schools in advanced industrial societies. It is also clear that prophesies of a few years ago about the major role computers would play in learning programs have not been fulfilled. Today, the number of supporters of widespread use of such electronic media is somewhat limited, apparently for several reasons. One reason is that both administrators and teachers are confused about the roles computers can most effectively play in education programs. "Many teachers who have tried microcomputers in their classrooms, usually with initial enthusiasm, have been discouraged by practical problems of implementation and by low quality of software. Consequently, unless they are teaching computer programming courses, they usually stop using them altogether or begin to use them only in ancillary roles" (Brophy & Hannon, 1985: 51).

Some school districts are finally appointing computer coordinators to direct hardware and software purchases (Bergheim & Chin, 1984: 29). However, one overburdened individual is often in charge of training the entire teaching staff, developing a curriculum, and establishing computer laboratories in every school in the district, thus producing an excessive workload that leads to inefficiency and low staff morale.

In summary, although the increase in computer hardware (both at school and home), in computer-education research, and in computer publications has been impressive, the impact of computers on existing curricula is still quite limited. Much of what is happening can be categorized as small-scale experiments and basic computer awareness and literacy.

In a pessimistic vein, Seymour Papert (cited in Ebisch, 1984: 38) has written that: "Computers are not having any effect now. There's been a lot of ballyhoo about computers revolutionizing the schools, but in fact the relative number of computers in schools is so small that it's negligible. They aren't really having any effect. They can't have any effect." Perhaps Papert's 1984 opinion is unduly negative but may still be close to summarizing the present extent of the educational use of computers in advanced industrial societies.

What Variety of Functions do Computers Perform?

When considering the functions that microcomputers can usefully perform, it is important to realize that different styles of learning are typically promoted by print, by TV, and by computers. Norton compares the three technologies in this fashion:

> When one learns to read and write, one learns to organize experience sequentially and linearly to create universes of discourse that propose and test hypotheses about the world beyond direct experience. When one learns to encode and decode experience using the electronic image [television and videotape], one learns the mechanism for interpreting experience that taps the non-rational, emotive domains of understanding. When one learns to program and use the computer, one learns to create universes of imagination and to seek patterns of interaction among experiences (Norton, 1985: 18).

As Norton's observations imply, it is an error to assume that learning from computer software, videotapes, and printing involves identical processes. However, consistently good educational computer software may not be available until schools sort out which medium is best for which learning goals and which students' learning styles. Using a computer simply to display written text, as a book does, is not an efficient use of the medium.

Papert sees computers as having a more fundamental effect than do other technologies, including television and print media:

> Even the best of educational television is limited to offering quantitative improvements in the kinds of learning that existed without it. Sesame Street might offer better and more engaging explanations than a child can get from some parents or nursery school teachers, but the child is still in the business of listening to explanations. By contrast, when a child learns to program [a computer], the process of learning is transformed. It becomes more active and self-directed. The knowledge is acquired for a recognizable personal purpose. The child does something with it. The new knowledge is a source of power and is experienced as such from the moment it begins to form in the child's mind (Papert, 1980: 2).

In other words, unlike television, computers interact with the user so that it is impossible for the student to address a computer passively. "The computer takes your attention because there's so much that's being called for that YOU have to put in" (Rhodes, 1986: 15).

So what can students learn or teachers teach via computers that they could not easily accomplish otherwise? Walker (1983: 103) has suggested that computers' contribution to instruction includes: more active learning, more varied sensory and conceptual modes, less mental drudgery, learning at a rate nearer the speed of thought, instruction that is better tailored to individuals' learning rates, and more independent learning. In addition, Tetenbaum and Mulkeen (1986: 102) argue that at the present time the major contribution computers can make to education is that of serving as a catalyst during a period of societal change by providing:

> . . . an occasion to explore educational issues, to release new energies, to rethink what we do, to reconceptualize schools, and to create a basis for change. Schools remain largely unchanged since the turn of the century. They are not only out of step with the present, they are not anticipating the future. . . . Computers have triggered educators' awareness. Now thoughtful, well-developed proactive strategies are necessary so education can productively and meaningfully enter the twenty-first century.

The question of what is appropriate and what is not appropriate when using computers in education is fundamental to the eventual success or failure of this technology. US representative Albert Gore, Jr., the author of the National Educational Software Act of 1984, stated that, "the potential for computers to improve education is enormous—more dramatic than any invention since writing. Yet the potential is not being met. Simply put, our schools are being swept up in a tidal wave of technology without any idea of how to make wise use of it" (cited in Bonner, 1984: 64).

To summarize, there is at present a measure of confusion in advanced industrial societies about the most effective roles computers can play in education. At the same time, there continues to be a great deal of experimentation with their potential educational roles. And though a complete cataloging of such roles is well beyond the scope of this chapter, the following list of major areas can suggest the range of applications that have been tried.

The Writing Process: Some feel that writing should be seen as a series of tasks rather than as the manufacture of a product. Computers may be used to make some of those tasks less forbidding to students. A major advantage of pupils' composing written material on a computer rather than with pen on paper is that the computer screen allows learners to alter phrases and correct errors without fearing that the words they are putting down are set in final form and inviolate.

Science: Computer simulations of science phenomena and the computer's ability to store and analyze data are major advantages of computers for science instruction.

Social Studies: The computer allows students to do "real research" by using actual data from available data bases. It can also be used for simulating situations in history or present-day social conflicts that require resolution. And computers can serve as agents of social interaction when students must communicate effectively with each other in completing cooperative projects.

Mathematics: Drill and practice of mathematical concepts via computers is very common. However, problem solving may well be the key to teaching mathematics, and any proper use of computers in the classroom can properly focus on thinking skills.

Special Education: Computers are opening additional doors to learning for the disabled, deaf, blind, and orthopedically handicapped.

Logical Thought: As microcomputers have become more powerful and more teachers display interest in their potential, schools have begun slowly to change the emphasis of their computer-education programs from (1) drill and practice (still the primary mode of use in the late 1980s) and teaching students to write programs to (2) simulations and problem-solving software.

Instructional Management: Schools are using computers for managing school and class records, organizing school-wide objectives, maintaining individual pupils' daily progress assessments, managing materials, reporting student progress, and administering and scoring tests. Because computers conceivably can take over certain of the teacher's laborious tasks, more time can be available for direct attention to the learners. Business and industry have long used computers to handle much of the drudgery, and perhaps education will begin to exploit some of this potential, as illustrated in an example offered by former US Secretary of Education Terrel H. Bell:

> Take today's English teacher. If you're meeting 30 students in a class and teaching five periods a day in a typical high school, you have 150 papers to mark. We know from the word processing software we have now—spelling, punctuation, grammar—that what teachers have to spend hours going over can be done with a computer. Test scoring, analysis of tests, and printouts that show each student's learning needs will relieve hours and hours of teacher toil. This is the kind of detail work where computers have fantastic potential (Bell, cited in Ebisch, 1984: 36).

Educational Administration: Participants in a recent delphi survey conducted in the US (Waggoner & Goldberg, 1986: 8-12), identified the following administrative areas in which computers are seen to have potential application (percentages reflect number of times an item was mentioned): Decision tools (56 percent), budget (44 percent), record-keeping (33 percent), tracking students (33 percent), communications (22 percent), policy-setting (22 percent), access to information (11 percent), reduction of paper-work (11 percent), and teaming (11 percent) (Waggoner & Goldberg, 1986: 12).

Educational Research: Computers have effected major improvements in research techniques. To locate studies that have been conducted in the past on a topic, a researcher need no longer hunt by hand through the library's card catalog or periodical indexes and abstracts. Rather, by typing into a computer-terminal a few key words related to the topic, the investigator immediately receives an extended list of pertinent books and articles that would have taken days to locate by means of a traditional library search.

At the stage of outlining the structure of the research design, the computer, serving as a word processor, facilitates the preparation of an outline which can be easily expanded and altered as new ideas occur. Whatever questionnaires or diagrams are needed in the study are readily created and printed by the computer. And if letters are to be sent to a sample of respondents, the letters can be prepared in a single form in the computer, yet the salutation of each letter individually addressed to the person who will receive it.

When quantitative data have been collected, the computer will facilitate its compilation, perform statistical analyses, and print out the results in tables and charts. Not only are complex statistical functions performed almost instantaneously, but they are performed more accurately than would be possible by hand. The final report of the research is also prepared on the computer, then printed in multiple copies of a quality rivaling that of a professional print shop.

In summary, computers have served a wide variety of instructional, administrative, and research functions in education.

A Lesson from the Past

As educators ponder the place computers will assume in educational programs, they can identify similarities between what the schools are doing and thinking about microcomputers these days and what they did and thought about television three decades ago. Wagschal (1984: 252) argues that in North America the typical school day proceeds as if television did not exist.

> There are at least three explanations for the failure of television to capture the interest and imagination of public school educators, and these explanations will prove instructive for educators who are now coming to grips with the computer revolution. First, the schools that purchased television sets rarely had the foresight to set aside money for equipment repairs and maintenance. Second, these schools never found an effective way to train teachers to integrate television into their ongoing instructional programs. Third, and perhaps most important, a majority of teachers had (and still have) an extremely snobbish attitude regarding the quality of commercial television and its consequent usefulness in the classroom.

Wagschal (1984: 252) then compares this to what he perceives is currently happening with computers in the school.

> As the case with television, most schools have stretched their budgets to the limit to purchase computer hardware and software. Therefore, they have little money set aside to repair and maintain the machines they have purchased. Moreover, as was true in the case of television, few schools have been able to afford the large-scale teacher retraining efforts that will enable teachers to make computers an integral part of classroom instruction. Most discouraging, however, is the fact that teachers' attitudes toward computers in the schools have some striking parallels with their previous and present attitudes toward television.

It is not difficult to see why most educators see little need for instructional television. No essential change has taken place in classroom practice, so that television is considered to be just an "add-on" to the curriculum—a supplementary medium not essential for instruction. The computer is also in danger of being treated as an "add-on", the victim of "benign neglect" (Berman & McLaughlin, cited in Winner & Holloway, 1983: 32). It is undeniable that television in the home plays a major role in the lives of children. And computers are likely to play an even more important role. Should not educators, then, become actively involved so as to ensure that computers are used effectively? This question identifies a key challenge faced today by advocates of educational technology. And meeting the challenge requires an understanding of conditions influencing the educational utilization of computers.

What Conditions Contribute to the Current Development of Computers in Education?

First, we shall consider societal conditions that make educational applications of computers possible. These conditions include both direct and indirect political, economic, and cultural influences as well as traditions in educational organization and innovation.

Political Factors

Political conditions in both developed and developing countries are possibly the most critical factors contributing to the current state of computers in education. Some indirect political conditions include a competitive need for technology, the threat of public criticism if technology is not advocated (no one wants to labeled a neo-Luddite), increasing populations, and the growing use of telecommunications.

Direct effects of politics on computer education include:

(1) The power of political groups to influence the adoption of computers in schools. The two largest professional organizations that exert such influence are the International Council for Computers in Education (ICCE) and the International Federation for Information Processing (IFIP).

(2) A growing political concern that the back-to-basics movement will not prepare students adequately for the future. Just what are *The Basics*? Judah Schwartz of Harvard suggests that if schools view their mission merely as the transmission of mechanical knowledge of basic skills (reading, writing, calculating), then schools will not be needed since, in five or ten years, these skills can be taught to children on computers in their homes (Richards, 1982 cited in Tetenbaum & Mulkeen, 1986: 96). Intertwined in this controversy is the issue of whether, in the immediate technological future, *literacy* in modern societies should include *computer literacy*. In other words, how should computer

literacy contribute to, or coexist with, reading and writing literacy. Tetenbaum & Mulkeen (1986: 96) summarize the issue in the following manner:

> Basic literacy is a necessary but not sufficient mission for the nation's schools. The problems of overpopulation, hunger, environmental rape and pollution, inadequate energy supplies, and urban decay cannot be solved by people who are merely literate. Nor can society, which is entering a rapidly changing technological era, function effectively with a citizenry prepared only in the basic skills. Schools must go further in their mission, setting as their goal the development of individuals capable of independent learning in a world where continuous change will demand their continuous education; capable of problem solving in a world where the challenges are increasing in number and complexity; capable of critical thinking in a world growing so complex that evaluation of myriad information and resources will be a daily fact of life; and, capable of flexibility in a world where few things will remain constant.

(3) National, state and district teacher-education, and credentialing policies that have become highly political issues. Some state legislators are making computer literacy mandatory for obtaining a teaching credential. (However, the question of exactly what the term *computer literacy* means is often left up to the director of the individual teacher-training program.) One example of an intensive inservice program is New York University's cooperation with political boards to provide "the first ancillary certificate program," a multilevel training program in educational computing available to the city's 62,000 teachers (Bergheim & Chin, 1984: 36).

Economic Conditions

It is apparent that economic factors are often connected to political factors. Indirect effects of the economy on computer education include a prosperous economy able to commit sufficient resources for supporting computers in education, the invention of increasingly lower cost equipment and software, and competition among manufacturers to bring out more efficient products.

Computer education is very expensive. Besides the basic computers themselves, there are costs associated with peripherals (printers, monitors, ribbons, paper, modems, extra disk drives), software, facilities development, maintenance, auxiliary materials (books, kits), curriculum development, teacher training, and the preparation of teacher trainers. Achieving a balance between what can be most efficiently learned with a computer and what can be efficiently learned via other methods is a key question to be answered by researchers in the years ahead.

Funding for the introduction of computers into education and for financing the upkeep of such an expensive technology is a serious problem, both for the education system and for the producers of the software programs that need to be carefully designed to accomplish the schools' learning goals. It is apparent that publishers of software and books are still reluctant to spend large amounts of time and money for research and development for computer education. On this issue, Alfred Bork has written:

> We ... were asked by a new software company for personal computers which was considering education as a market, what would it cost to do a complete first-through-sixth-grade mathematics series. The series would completely replace textbooks and would have to be highly interactive. We estimated the costs to somewhere between $3 and $5 million. We wanted to find out if these figures were realistic. We discovered that there were about half a dozen recently published mathematics textbooks in the U.S.A. We asked these publishers what the costs were to produce these series. Three of them were willing to figure it out. By the first it cost $2 million; the second was $5 million, and the third was $8 million. These were textbooks and no computers were involved. Therefore a large amount of money is spent already on curriculum development, and I find it hard to believe that we are somehow going to do it cheaper by computer. We will get poor material if we don't use the same care in developing computer-based learning material as we do on our best curriculum material for any other learning medium (cited in Waggoner & Goldberg, 1986: 8).

According to the delphi survey mentioned earlier, the main component of cost in producing educational software is labor. Such labor includes teams of experts representing the content, process, and technical skills required to produce pedagogically sound material that takes advantage of the available technology. These expenses can balloon because, unlike the textbook market, machine-based materials—particularly for computer—are too often machine specific, meaning that software designed for one manufacturer's machine—such as an Apple—will not operate on another's (an IBM or Commodore). Hence, the producers of software must create multiple sets of the same curriculum materials.

Most participants in the delphi survey concurred that "the continued introduction of technology into the workplace will INCREASE net costs for educators" (Waggoner & Goldberg, 1986: 12), chiefly because (1) teachers and administrators were not prepared to make sound purchasing decisions in the area of new technologies, (2) software development has become increasingly expensive, and (3) progress in the realm of computer technology is so rapid that software quickly becomes outmoded and requires replacement to keep up with the times.

Cultural Influences

Cultural factors also play an important role in determining the use of computers in education. One direct cultural cause is people's apprehension that life is becoming too mechanized, so they resist contributing to a "computer culture." Another cause is the concern that there are other societal problems that need to be solved before computer-education is addressed (teenage crime, illicit drugs, the threat of war, environmental pollution).

An important direct cultural cause is teachers' hesitance to change. To many teachers, a computer is intimidating and difficult to master, so they avoid the computer for fear of committing embarrassing mistakes. Furthermore, teachers are often quite satisfied with their present instructional methods and thus see no reason to adopt a new technology. Some educational technologists feel that this resistance can be overcome by having classroom teachers themselves develop computer-education curricula in conjunction with instructional technologists and curriculum designers, enabling teachers to recognize that a computer is a tool whose overall benefits are potentially large and are far from being exhausted. Winner & Holloway (1983: 31) have concluded that:

> The potential change stemming from computer-based education is more than a good idea or a technical novelty, it is a culture change, different enough to be described as a revolution . . . . Earlier technical innovations, such as slide projectors or audio tape recorders, are only different in format, not in content or, most importantly, process. Phrases such as "curricular change" (Wheatley, 1980) and "computer cultures" (Papert, 1981) suggest the difference in the magnitude of the change involved. It is "a qualitatively new kind of relationship" not a culture itself, of course, but a process which will "advance different cultural and philosophical outlooks" (Papert, 1981: 88).

Although these benefits exist, it may well take years to alter preservice and inservice education to implement the necessary changes. There still are relatively few locations where training is available to practicing teachers or to those students studying to obtain teaching credentials.

Deck has cited a variety of reasons teacher-training programs are slow to respond to the technological revolution, reasons that include "declining enrollments, budget cuts, an inability to identify qualified computer instructors, and the realization that it takes a tremendous effort and

commitment of time to learn the technology well enough to teach on a
college level" (Deck, cited in Tetenbaum & Mulkeen, 1986: 100). Bork
(1984: 33) reasons that the needed innovations in teacher-education
programs are not likely to occur quickly from internal pressures, since
schools are generally conservative and slow to change. "Even educational institutions most in favour of changes promote relatively trivial
changes that do not fundamentally affect the institutions."

Traditions in Educational Organization

Despite efforts of computer enthusiasts to increase the educational applications of microcomputers, the extent to which computers are used in
the classroom has begun to slow. Respondents to a survey in the
mid-1980s identified four barriers to full use of computers in the schools
(Waggoner & Goldberg, 1986: 11): (1) organizational workload and
incentive system, (2) lack of teacher preparation to use computers, (3)
poor quality of educational software, and (4) the way teachers spend
their time. Point four was seen as the major barrier. The authors
concluded that "until significantly different organizational arrangements
are made—from released time and differentiated workloads to better
staff development opportunities and better access—then we may expect
to see only a relatively few successful developments occur, because
extraordinary time commitments and exceptional motivation will be
necessary to produce them."

Patterns of Educational Innovation

Oakes and Schneider (1984: 76) claim that the creeping pace of change
comes not from a lack of good ideas nor from an absence of enthusiasm
but, rather, from a poor understanding of how change happens in
schools and a paucity of specific implementation strategies that might
promote change:

> For the last 20 years school innovations have been introduced
> almost exclusively by the research, development, and diffusion
> mode, which usually begins with the development of a sound edu-
> cational innovation that meets the needs of the school. However, it
> is the policymakers who study it, determine its effectiveness, and
> mandate its implementation. What of the people, primarily
> teachers and students, who are the objects of the proposed change?
> The innovation loses its power because it gets disseminated by
> experts, who want teachers to understand or at least adopt the
> changes with little if any input. When it is solicited, input is usually
> gathered after the genuinely important issues have been settled.

To a considerable degree computers in education have been a grass-roots phenomenon, brought about by individual teachers forging ahead in using computers even without being told to do so by researchers or policymakers. Therefore, Oakes and Schneider's warning of dangers in the mode of implementing change may not be as necessary as such warnings were two decades ago with the introduction of "new math" and of television, both of which had less grass-root interest than do computers. It is true that in many industrialized countries, commercial interests and government agencies were the first to call educators' attention to the idea that computer literacy was important. Yet it was generally not the administrators but, rather, the students and computer-using teachers who heeded the call. Youth were among the first to embrace the new technology and see its possible applications. Motivated teachers then became "movers" in utilizing microcomputers for instruction and recommending computers to colleagues. This bottoms-up movement can be seen in such American organizations as Computer Using Educators (CUE), a California group of over 8,000 teachers involved with using computers in education. Similar grass-roots organizations have formed in Canada (ECOO), Australia, Japan, Argentina, and the United Kingdom.

How Accurate were the Prophets' Predictions?

The professional literature is now filled with criticism of computer education. This was not always the case. From 1977 to 1983 there was no end of articles claiming the tremendous benefits of computers in education. However, the use of this technology has now reached a new next level in its development, following the earlier stage of heady optimism. This new phase is one of critical examination of prior prophesies. The following examples illustrate the nature of such disenchantment by comparing past computer enthusiasts' expectations with present reality.

One of the benefits of computer education that is now being examined is the earlier claim that working with computers is exciting and inherently enjoyable. Brophy and Hannon (1985: 52) claim that "in fact, once the novelty wears off, learning by computer becomes just another method, akin to learning with the aid of television, film-strips, listening centers with headsets, etc. A few students can be expected to retain high enthusiasm indefinitely, but most will not."

Technology advocates may also have overestimated teachers' excitement about computers. Enthusiasts assumed that training teachers to produce their own software through programming would be both interesting and beneficial. Yet, in reality, most teachers lack the time and energy that such tasks demand.

Another prophesy was that the costs of computers would decrease dramatically as a result of mass production and competition among manufacturers. And while prices have indeed dropped markedly, by now the costs may be about as low as they will become. This means that computers are still expensive, when compared to books and other print media.

The excitement during the latter 1970s and early 1980s over computer games was often interpreted to mean that instruction via computers would move quickly and be fun. However, as Rockman (1985: 55) suggests, this is not necessarily so.

> Computers can also be frustratingly slow moving, especially when students can supply the answers to questions instantaneously and with certainty of their correctness, and yet must take the time to type them in [to the computer] and get verification from the computer before being able to move on to the next step.

The prophets also failed to predict a variety of the limitations of microcomputers in the classroom. For example, the following 7 shortcomings cited by Walker (1983: 105-107) were seldom if ever mentioned in optimists' predictions.

1. Microcomputers can supplement conventional education, but they cannot substitute for it.
2. Today's microcomputers are hard to use, and teachers prepared to use them are in short supply.
3. New products and systems are being created and marketed in such profusion, with such speed, and with so little standardization that systematic, long-term planning is nearly impossible.
4. Good programs are scarce because creating them for today's microcomputers is difficult, time-consuming, and expensive.
5. We are only beginning to understand how to use microcomputers in education; therefore, it is easy for a school or teacher to err, look foolish, or do harm.
6. Programs for teaching explicit, formal models can be created readily with known techniques, but it is much more difficult to use computers to teach subject matter that involves judgement, intuition, improvisation and creativity.
7. Microcomputers will not solve (and may aggravate) several of the most serious current problems confronting education—notably equity, school finance, and divergent public expectations.

Our attention will now focus on the question as to whether or not computers promote the efficiency of education by improving teaching and the administration of educational systems. This, as outlined in Chapter 1, is the purpose of educational technology.

"Perhaps the most disappointing feature of the move toward having computers in the classroom has been the lack of understanding on the part of many professional educators as to what this technology could mean to the improvement of the learning process" (Norris, 1985: 65). The vast majority of teachers simply do not know how to use computers to promote educational efficiency and are not being adequately trained to use technology. There appear to be two major reasons for this: (1) training teachers to use computers is very complicated and (2) many people have a distorted view of what computers can do for education.

Norris (1985: 66) reports that experiences in nearly a dozen Model Education Centers has shown us that "the training of teachers to understand and manage technology to its fullest capability is indeed a complex and time-consuming task . . . . However, adequate time and support must be given for training, preparation for classes using computer technology and for reflection upon the changes that are being made. Time for these activities must be built into the schedule and strongly supported by teachers and administrators."

Another reason computers are not meeting their predicted potential is that many of the early pioneering instructors who used computer education "became disenchanted with the drill and practice software available at the time and have not ventured back to examine more recent software products which schools who more recently became microcomputer owners have been able to use at least somewhat successfully" (Bonner, 1984: 71).

Even today the majority of commercially available software can only be characterized as either poorly constructed or trivial. Much of the public-domain and pirated software that so many teachers use fails to fully exploit the computer's vast potential for bettering the efficiency of education. Part of this difficulty arises from *atomization*.

> Much of today's software tends to atomize or fragment the learning process, thus resulting in what Sartre (1977) calls "serialization." Because persons must adjust themselves to a mechanical learning device, closely monitor its instructions, follow its commands, and supply appropriate responses at the right time, a state of isomorphism is reached whereby a student's intentions are subsumed by the directives that are issued. This means that the learning process is ahistorical, since an inanimate object establishes the framework for all learning (Murphy & Pardeck, 1985: 101).

A further barrier to computers being used to their potential is that some educators overestimate that potential. They see computers as a technological "quick fix."

Considering that the schools are in fairly desperate trouble, there's great danger of putting in a technological "fix" that will make it appear that something is being done, while nothing is being done to address the actual problems that give rise to this "rising tide" of mediocrity and illiteracy. In other words, computers just may be a powerful distraction that will leave the original problems—money, teachers, time, and energy—untouched (Weizenbaum, cited in Ebisch, 1984: 36).

We seem safe in concluding that the measure of disillusionment about computers observed among educators in recent times has resulted from overly optimistic predictions by early advocates, a shortage of high-quality educational software, and a lack of adequate instruction for teachers and administrators in the realistic potential of computers.

How Should the Success of Computers in Education be Judged?

The task of assessing the success of computers in the education system of advanced industrial societies is most complicated, for the worth of computers can be judged from a variety of perspectives. Furthermore, data about computers in schools change rapidly and are often difficult to obtain. In the following paragraphs consider some of the factors affecting such judgements.

The figures at the opening of this chapter about quantities of computers in American schools suggest that the number of computers has grown rapidly, yet there are still not enough available for pupils to spend much time using them. Thus, how useful are those figures for appraising the success of computers in American education? In response, Rockman, (1985: 46) has drawn an analogy with educational television. While many educators now say that educational television has failed, Rockman notes that one-third of American teachers currently use television on a regular basis. Does this mean that educational TV is a failure because all teachers are not using television? If in twenty years only one-third of the students and teachers are using computers, will computers also be labeled as a failure?

How useful are data on sales of computer equipment to schools as keys to the role of computers in education? Or are such figures only indicators of the success of the sellers of computers and computer programs; promoters of retraining courses for workers and teachers; and writers and publishers of the industry's books and magazines? In 1983, for example, US schools spent nearly $500 million on personal computers and programs (Menosky, 1984: 40).

And do figures on the amount of use of computers in schools accurately reflect the medium's educational value? Fraser (1985: 89) raises this issue in observing that there is "sometimes a tendency to search for problems that can be solved by a machine already purchased, rather than analyzing problems and determining what means (possibly including a microcomputer) can be used to solve the problem." Or do teachers who have computers available simply use them because they feel obligated to put this expensive equipment to work and thus justify its purchase?

A further question in assessing the influence of computers involves the relationship educators see between pupil learning and deliberate instruction. Papert has proposed that:

> In some cases I think the skeptics might conceive of education and the effect of computers on it too narrowly. Instead of considering general cultural effects, they focus attention on the use of the computer as a device for programmed instruction. Skeptics then conclude that while the computer might produce some improvements in school learning, it is not likely to lead to fundamental change. In a sense, too, I think the skeptical view derives from a failure to appreciate just how much Piagetian learning takes place as a child grows up. If a person conceives of children's intellectual development (or for that matter, moral or social development) as deriving chiefly from deliberate teaching, then such a person would be likely to underestimate the potential effect that a massive presence of computers and other interactive objects might have on children (Papert, cited in Harper, 1986: 2).

Such, then, are some of the complex issues that bear on the evaluation of computers in education. But what conclusions can be drawn from assessments of computers in terms of traditional instructional goals and traditional evaluation methods? The following brief review addresses this question for the areas of (1) drill and practice, (2) tutorials, (3) simulations, (4) programming, and (5) attitudes and motivation. But at the outset, we should recognize that computer-education research is notable for its abundance, its frequent poor quality, and its inconclusiveness. There are numerous unquantifiable variables that might affect the outcome of most evaluation studies, with some of the variables still unrecognized. Since it is virtually impossible to control all variables, it is difficult to identify causal relationships between the use of computers and the learning results that students exhibit. With these qualifications in mind, let us consider the nature of research results.

In the past twenty-five years, most educational software has been designed for mathematics drill and practice as a supplement to the regular curriculum. It follows that the vast majority of computer education research studies have investigated this type of software. Slesnick (1984: 15), in summarizing drill and practice studies, concluded that:

We have an abundance of evidence that drill and practice in arithmetic, when used as a supplement to traditional instruction, will result in significant gains in computational skill. This is true in regular as well as compensatory classes [Burrows (1982), Dence (1980), Ehrlich, et al. (1982), Jamison, et al. (1974), Pitschka & Wagner (1979), Vinsonhaler & Bass, (1972)]. There is some evidence that computerized drill reduces the time required for mastery of the target skills although it results in the same end performance as traditional methods of drill [Tsai (1977)]. There is no corresponding difference in understanding of math concepts or in attitude toward mathematics [Overton (1981)]. When drill programs are used as a replacement for traditional instruction in arithmetic or other subjects, like algebra, music, or spelling, there is generally no significant difference in student achievement [Diem (1982), Jamison, et al. (1974)]. Drill and practice as well as tutorials works when used as a supplement to traditional instruction.

In general, the effectiveness of tutorials (using the computer teaching the learner) closely parallels those for drill and practice programs (Slesnick, 1984: 2).

Research on the effectiveness of simulations is sparce, probably because the high cost of designing these complex programs that can simulate life situations has rendered them little used in the classrooms, although their use is increasing rapidly.

The teaching of programming (that is, teaching students how to create a plan that directs the computer to carry out particular functions) can be viewed as necessary to provide the student with a skill useful in a future vocation. Some people also believe that the sort of logical analysis required in programming will transfer to higher-level skills or skills in related content areas. In other words, advocates of discovery-based programming languages such as Logo often claim that mastery of programming will improve students' general skills of problem solving, analyzing, and planning. Thousands of researchers throughout the world have been investigating this matter (Harper, 1986). The results are as yet inconclusive, with the effect of each computer program dependent on a variety of circumstances. Studies analyzed by Slesnick (1984: 3) showed that computers do seem to have a positive effect on student attitude, but this improved attitude is toward computers, not toward the subject matter of the program (Burrows, 1982; Cavin, et al., 1981; Chrisholm & Krishnakumar, 1981; Gustafson, 1982; Overton, 1981; Reynolds & Simpson, 1980; Shannon, 1982; Splittgerber, 1979).

Three pessimistic observations—though somewhat in jest—about the computer's effectiveness in education relate to (1) solving life's problems, (2) young children, and (3) human memory. Computer scientist Joseph Weizenbaum of the Massachusetts Institute of Technology writes:

> Take the great many people who have dealt with computers now for a long time—for example, MIT seniors or MIT professors of computer science—and ask whether they're in any better position to solve life's problems. And I think the answer is clearly no. They're just as confused and mixed up about the world and their personal relations and so on as anyone else (Weizenbaum, cited in Cufarro, 1984: 46).

Sloan (1984: 545) has questioned the value of using computers with young children:

> Are we in danger of now further subjecting the child to a technology that would seem to eliminate entire sources of sensory experience and living imagery—while accentuating out of all proportion images of a very limited type, all the while inserting the latter directly into the child's mind during its most plastic and formative years? What is the effect of the flat, two-dimensional, visual, and externally supplied image, on the development of the young child's own inner capacity to bring to birth living, mobile, creative images of his own? Indeed, what effect does viewing the computer screen have on the healthy development of the growing but unformed mind, brain, and body of the child?

And Podemski (1984. p. 574) hypothesizes that computers can weaken memory:

> Just as we have replaced the child's active imagination (that is, the exercise of assimilation) through television imagery and certain toys, so the computer has the potential to replace nearly all the mental functions of the child. . . . Reliance on an external device, the computer—can easily weaken that faculty. . . . If the capacity to imagine has been undercut by television, interactive computer graphics threatens to complete the assault.

However, these observations about what might happen to children and to memory are still at the speculative stage, as yet unsupported by substantial research evidence.

The following issues concerning effectiveness have been identified as deserving research attention. Questions that Peterson (1984: 12-15) believes should be studied are:

- Do some students "need" computers more than others?
- Are computers better placed in a laboratory or in the classroom?
- Should the curriculum be standardized or innovative?
- Should equipment be standardized or is variety preferable?

According to Roblyer (1985: 40), researchers should:

- determine if certain methods or kinds of materials narrow the gap in achievement among content areas.
- know whether certain levels of skill training profit more from computer use than others. Roblyer states that "some have suggested that computers can enhance learning at basic levels, but that computer influence diminishes when students become more skilled" (Kulik, Bangert & Williams, 1983). In their review of research findings, Jamison, Suppes & Wells, (1974) found that more gains were observed with computer-based instruction for remedial students than with regular students of those at higher levels.
- investigate the rate of retention as well as achievement gains.
- study the impact of various instructional approaches—many more studies need to address the controversial issue of directed versus discovery learning methods as implemented with computers.

Researching the effectiveness of computers in education can profitably be followed by investigating whether computers are efficient as well. Supporters of CAL (computer-assisted learning) claim that computers will eventually reduce the cost of education because computers will increase the learning rate, decrease "wait time" for individualized instruction, and time will be saved on the part of the teacher (planning, preparation, record keeping) (Stowitschek and Stowitschek, 1983: 25). However, not all of the research supports the efficiency of computer use in computer-assisted and computer-managed instruction. "In fact, the only commonality among the many studies is the failure to produce clear, consistent results on efficiency factors" (Stowitschek and Stowitschek, 1983: 27).

In estimating the efficiency of computer-aided instruction, (Schwandt & Wiederanders, 1985: 32) have questioned the price paid for the instructional improvement that computers may foster:

> We have exhausted ourselves with differentiated assignments, multimedia presentations, and a creative array of classroom dynamics models. Each effort has paid dividends, but seldom have those dividends been proportional to the drain placed on the teacher's professional energies.

Evaluations of computer-assisted instruction as summarized by both

Stowitschek and Bork suggest that research has not clearly demonstrated the general superiority of computers regarding either effectiveness or efficiency in instruction.

> Although most agree on the potential of CAI, studies rarely have reported a significant difference in students' achievements over other forms of instruction, and only a few studies report a savings in time. Part of the problem is that effectiveness and efficiency factors apparently have not been isolated or empirically studied (Stowitschek and Stowitschek, 1983: 27).

> Although it seems clear, for reasons not fully discussed, that the computer will become more important in education, it is not yet clear whether the computer will improve education, helping to overcome some of our current problems, or whether it will lead to further deterioration in the educational systems of many countries. The effectiveness of the use of the computer in education may be an important factor in determining which countries will succeed in the future. There is nothing magical about computers. Like all technological developments, the computer itself is not good or evil. Rather it is the way it is used by humans which is the critical factor, in education or elsewhere (Bork, 1984: 33).

What New Developments Appear in the Offing?

The cutting edge of technology offers the promise of computer-related innovations that could have sweeping effects on education. Since education does not have the resources to develop new technologies such as videodiscs or new chips, it has had to make use of technologies developed for other purposes. These innovations include:

- The morpheme generator—"An electronic device that with instruction will sound out any message within its programmed capabilities. The implications for the handicapped, for the foreign language speaker, and for the semi-literate are enormous" (Coates, 1983: 45).
- The speech processor—Spoken messages up to the rate of 300-400 words per minute are fully understandable. This new capability opens rapid learning to the visually limited. To everyone it could be a new avenue of learning while traveling, or jogging, or engaged in other activities which preclude reading. The device is particularly useful for dyslectic students.
- Satellites—"Closely coupled with cable television is the technology

of space communication that will permit the ready exchange of
information from one local cable TV network to another. But more
important than improved domestic TV, communications satellites
will permit all the information of any country in the world to be
available throughout the rest of the world. The full knowledge of
all mankind upon request to any part of the world will first be
useful to scientists, scholars, and entertainers. Then educators,
businessmen, and recreationists will move in" (Coates, 1983: 49).

- Interactive video—"Interactive video will be a lot more important.
  We already have a microwave network in our schools and we'll
  soon have a two-way interactive capability which will allow us to
  transmit information by video. Couple that with the microcomputer
  and we'll not only have a powerful communications tool for teacher
  training but we'll be able to use it as a medium for instruction"
  (Sturdivant, cited in Ebisch: 43).

- Artificial Intelligence (AI)—John Seely Brown, head of the Cognitive and Instructional Sciences group at Xerox Palo Alto Research
  Center in California and specialist in artificial-intelligence research
  in education, writes that "AI offers the possibility of making the
  computer the ultimate in congenial tools, one that is sensitive and
  responsive to its user. Its unique quality is that it can serve as a
  cognitive tool—an active participant, an assistant consultant or
  coach" (Brown, cited in Green, 1984: 29).

- Intercomputer networks, facsimile printers, integrated information
  and video terminals, brain-sized computers, and intelligent robots
  are all only a few years away (Butler, 1983: 14-17).

What is the Prognosis for Computers in Education in the Future?

Three scenarios for the future appear possible: (1) computers will radically change the present education system for the better, (2) computers
will radically change the present education system for the worse, or (3)
computers will have little or no affect on education. This section will
examine these three alternatives.

Careful observers appear to agree that it will take a tremendous
amount of work for the education community to adapt present-day and
future information technology so that it makes the optimal contribution
to learning and educational administration. Seymour Papert, co-founder
of the popular computer language of Logo, in his classic book *Mind-
storms* (Papert, 1980), describes how the necessary radical changes in
education might be achieved:

We are at a point in the history of education when radical change is possible, and the possibility for that change is directly tied to the impact of the computer. Today what is offered in the educational "market" is largely determined by what is acceptable to a sluggish and conservative system. . . . Thus, not only do good educational ideas sit on the shelves, but the process of invention is itself stymied. . ... Conservatism in the world of education has become a self-perpetuating social phenomenon. Fortunately, there is a weak link in the vicious circle. Increasingly, the computers of the near future will be the private property of individuals, and this will gradually return to individuals the power to determine patterns of education. Education will become more of a private act, and people with good ideas, different ideas, exciting ideas, will no longer be faced with a dilemma where they either have to "sell" their ideas to a conservative bureaucracy or shelve them. They will be able to offer them in an open marketplace directly to consumers. There will be new opportunities for imagination and originality. There might be a renaissance of thinking about education (Papert, cited in Harper, 1986: 7).

It is the idea of an educational renaissance that has excited so many teachers about the computer. They see today's schools as either having too many problems or as being institutions not in tune with the "information age." Not only can computers reduce much of the drudgery of test-correcting and record keeping, but the computer has the potential to alter and create curricula. Haefner (1986: 175) argues that present day subjects will disappear.

If we look ten years ahead, I think we will see even more cognitive task substitution. If we anticipate, e.g., the "speech writer" (spoken word to text), do we really believe that young people will bother any longer to learn to spell? What will happen in a world in which simultaneous translation can be done by hand-held machines at least for simple sentences? Can we really anticipate that people are going to worry about learning foreign languages at school?

Curriculum developers will thus need to revise their notions about how curriculum-planning is best accomplished in light of technologies that demand different skills of the citizens of the future.

But McMeen (1986: 45) does not envision widespread utilization of advanced technologies in the conservative public schools until they "find themselves in a more critically defensive position in terms of the challenge of libraries, museums, homes, and private schools—all of which may embrace technology more completely than the public schools." The future of the school as we know it today may rest on whether school

personnel will be in the forefront of change or whether commercial and
other organizations will take the lead in using technology for educational
purposes. Haefner (1986: 177-178) warns that educators must be careful
that this task is not taken over completely by commerce. But he believes
that computer education should be done within the educational system
itself as this would allow educators to "control the way we deal with
information, with knowledge, with wisdom within the system of information technology, as we have tried to do before with human brains."
As yet, relatively few educators appear to have taken this challenge
seriously.

Although many have visions of a radical change in education caused
by computer-related technology, others feel that computers will have
little if any true effect on schooling practices. If computers are used as
no more that electronic workbooks and drill-and-practice machines, and
are administered by a rigid, authoritarian, mechanical rules, then they
may simply reinforce rote-learning practices of the past. Teachers could
constantly send children to machines so that what little individual con-
tact between teacher and learner exists now would diminish. Haefner
(1986, p. 178) argues that such an unfortunate result can be avoided if
teachers stop saying to school boards and finance ministers that "with a
computer in my school I can drill everyone to become a first-class
mathematician." He proposes instead that:

> We don't need that many mathematicians as mathematical expert
> systems are around everywhere . . . we need a new approach in
> education: we need new philosophical insights, new objectives, new
> goals for education within a humanistically computerized society.

There is also a compromise position regarding computers. What is
perhaps a rather widespread opinion among educators who have considered these matters is that books and teachers will not lose their importance in the instructional process, but teachers will consider the computer
a dynamic contributor to the learning process if it is properly utilized.

Finally, Wagschal (1984, p. 254) has offered both pessimistic and
optimistic predictions for the year 2004:

> [The Pessimistic View] The hardware and software with which we
> will interact in our daily lives will have been developed primarily
> by large corporations intent on profits. The structure of the electro-
> nic society of the year 2004 will be extremely hierarchical, with
> monolithic control exerted from the top. Our children will have few
> opportunities to practice critical thinking skills and independence.
> The gap in educational opportunities between the wealthy and the
> poor will have increased manyfold. And the schools, still relying

primarily on paper-and-pencil exercises, will have little choice but to serve as holding tanks for youngsters who are receiving the profoundest aspects of their education in other quarters.

(The Optimistic View) Computers will be as common in the classroom as they are in the outside world, and the gap between the educational opportunities afforded the rich and those afforded the poor will have narrowed. Teachers will be helping their students learn to evaluate critically the information and values that the students' home computers purvey. And the schools, relying primarily on computers and teachers for instruction, will play a central role in the moral and intellectual development of youngsters.

References

Baltz, B. L. (1978) Computer graphics as an aid to teaching mathematics (Doctoral dissertation, The Ohio State University, 1977). *Dissertation Abstracts International* **38** 697A.

Bartimo, J. Q. & Bunnell, A. David. (1984), *InfoWorld*, November 26, p. 54.

Becker, H. (1984) Schools uses of microcomputers: Report #2. *Journal of Computer, Math, and Science Teaching*, January.

Becker, H. (1986) Computers in the schools: A recent update. *Classroom Computer Learning*, January.

Bergheim, K. & Chin, K. (1984) Computers in the classroom. *InfoWorld* September 10, pp. 28-37.

Boas, E. E., Jr. (1979) An analysis of instructional delivery systems in vocational education comparing computer-managed instruction, teacher-delivered module (paper), and lecture-demonstration for the same instructional model (Doctoral dissertation, Temple University, 1979). *Dissertation Abstracts International*, **39** 2624A.

Bonner, P. (1984) Computers in education: Promise and reality. *Personal Computing*, September.

Bork, A. (1984) Computer futures for education. *Creative Computing*, November.

Bracey, G. (1982) What the research shows. *Electronic Learning*, **2** (3), pp. 51-54.

Bradley, B. (1984) Let's do more with computers than study computers. *Learning*, October.

Brady, H. & Levine, M. (1985) Is computer education off track?: An interview with Judah Schwartz, *Classroom Computer Learning*, February.

Brophy, J. & Hannon, P. (1985) On the future of microcomputers in the classroom. *The Journal of Mathematical Behaviour*, **4**, pp. 47-67.

Burrows, S. (1982) Learning signed number arithmetic: A comparative study. *The Computing Teacher*, **10** (4), pp. 55-56.

Butler, T. (1983) Technological horizons. *Instructional Innovator*, March.

Cavin, C. S., Cavin, E. D. & Lagowski, J. J. (1981) The effect of CAI on the attitudes of college students towards computers and chemistry. *Journal of Research in Science Teaching*, **18** (4), pp. 329-333.

Chrisholm, T. A. & Krishnakumar, P. (1981) Are computer simulations sexist? *Simulation and Games*, **12**, pp. 379-392.

Coates, J. F. (1984) What principals should know about telematics, their impact on education. *NASSP Bulletin*, April.

Cufarro, B. (1984) Microcomputers in education: Why is earlier better? *Teachers College Record*, June.

Deck, L. (1984) American schools and the adaptation of computer technology (Part II). *Educational Computer*, January, p. 24.

Dence, M. (1980) Toward defining the role of CAI: A review. *Educational Technology*, **20** (11), pp. 50-54.

Diem, D. (1982) The effectiveness of CAI in college algebra (Doctoral dissertation, Florida Atlantic University, 1982), *Dissertation Abstracts International*, **43**, 1456A.

Ebisch, B. (1984) Trying to predict the future. *Popular Computing*, October.

Ehrlich, K., Soloway, E. & Abbott, V. (1982) *Transfer Effects from Programming to Algebra Word Problems* (Research Report 257). New Haven, Connecticut: Yale University, Department of Computer Science, December.

Fletcher, T. (1983) *Microcomputers and Mathematics in Schools*. London: Department of Education and Science, Government of Great Britain.

Fraser, H. W. (1985) Microcomputers in schools: Questions to be asked. *The Educational Forum*, Fall, pp. 87-96.

Green, J. O. (1984) Artificial intelligence and the future classroom. *Classroom Computer Learning*, January.

Gustafson, B. (1982) An individual teacher-directed spelling program compared with a computer-based spelling program (Doctoral dissertation, Iowa State University, 1982). *Dissertation Abstracts International*, **43**, 991A.

Haefner, K. (1985) The challenge of information technology to education. *Education and Computing*, August.

Harper, D. O. (1986) *RUN: Computer Education*. Monterey. CA: Brooks/Cole.

Harper, D. O. (1986) Logo bibliography, *Logo '86*, June.

Jamison, D., Suppes, P. & Wells, S. (1974) The effectiveness of alternative media: A survey. *Review of Educational Research*, **44** (1), pp. 1-67.

Lesgold, A. (1983) When can computers make a difference? *Theory into Practice*, **22**, pp. 247-252.

McMeen, G. (1986) The impact of technological change on education. *Educational Technology*, February, pp. 42-45.

Melmed, A. (1984) Educational productivity, the teacher and technology. *T.H.E. Journal*, March.

Menosky, J. A. (1984) Computer worship. *Science 84*, May.

Murphy, J. W. & Pardeck, J. T. (1985) The technological world-view and the responsible use of computers in the classroom. *Journal of Education*, **167** (2).

Norris, W. C. (1985) Improving education through technological innovation. *T.H.E. Journal*, June, pp. 65-68.

Norton, P. (1985) An agenda for technology and education: Eight imperatives. *Educational Technology*, January.

Oakes, J. & Schneider, M. (1984) Computers and schools: Another case of ". . .The more they stay the same"? *Educational Leadership*, November.

Overton, V. (1981) Research in instructional computing and mathematics education. *Viewpoints in Teaching and Learning*, **57** (2), pp. 23-36.

Peterson, D. (1984) Nine issues: Will education be different (better) in the year 2000? *Popular Computing*, Mid-October.

Pitschka, R. & Wagner, W. (1979) *Improving Fourth Grade Math Scores with Computer Assistance*. Santa Clara, CA: Santa Clara County Office of Education.

Podemski, R. (1984) Implications of electronic learning technology: The future is now! *T.H.E. Journal*, May.

Ragosta, M. (1983) Computer-assisted instruction and compensatory education: A longitudinal analysis machine. *Mediated Learning*, **1** (1), pp. 97-126.

Reynolds, D. & Simpson, R. (1980) Pilot study using computer-based simulation on human transactions and classroom management. *Science Education*, **64** (1), pp, 35-41.

Rhodes, L. (1986) On computers, personal styles, and being human: A conversation with Sherry Turkle. *Educational Leadership*, March.

Richards, J. (1982) Profile: Who's in charge? *Classroom Computer News*, March/April.

Roblyer, M. D. (1985) The greening of educational computing: A proposal for a more research-based approach to computers in education. *Educational Technology*, January, **25** (1), pp. 40-44.

Rockman, S. (1985) Success or failure for computers in schools? Some lessons from instructional television. *Educational Technology*, January.

Sartre, J. P. (1977) *Life Situations*. New York: Pantheon Books.

Schrader, V. E. (1984) The computer in education—Are we over our heads? *NASSP Bulletin*, May.

Schwandt, L. C. & Wiederanders, D. (1985) Microcomputers and the ulitmate goal of education. *Educational Technology*. **25** (8), pp. 32–33

Shannon, D. (1982) Aural-visual interval recognition in music instruction: A comparison of a computer-assisted approach and a traditional in-class approach (Doctoral dissertation, University of Southern California, 1982), *Dissertation Abstracts International*, **43**, 718A.

Slesnick, T. (1984) Mandates aren't good enough: Here's an alternative. *Classroom Computer Learning*, April.

Sloan, D. (1984) On raising critical questions about the computer in education. *Teachers College Record*, Summer, 539-547.

Splittgerber, F. (1979) Computer-based instruction: A revolution in the making? *Educational Technology*, 19 (11), pp. 20-25.

Stowitschek, J. J. & Stowitschek, C. E. (1983) Once more with feeling: The absence of research in teacher education. *Exceptional Children Quarterly*, December.

Sunners, E. G. (1985) Microcomputers as a new technological innovation in education: Growth of the related literature. *Educational Technology*, August.

Tetenbaum, T. J. & Mulkeen, T. A. (1985/86) Computers as an agent for educational change, *Computers in the Schools*, Winter.

Tsai, S. & Pohl, N. (1977) Student achievement in computer programming: Lecture vs. computer-aided instruction. *The Journal of Experimental Education*, **46** (2), pp. 66-70.

VanDusseldorp, R. (1984) Evaluation of the implementation and management of microcomputers for instruction. *AEDS Monitor*, July/August.

Vinsonhaler, J. & Bass, R. (1972) A summary of ten major studies on CAI drill and practice. *Educational Technology*, **12** (7), pp. 29-32.

Waggoner, M. D. & Goldberg, A. L. (1986) A forecast for technology and education: The report of a computer conferencing delphi. *Educational Technology*, June, pp. 7-14.

Wagschal, P. H. (1984) A last chance for computers in the schools? *Phi Delta Kappan*, December.

Walker, D. F. (1983) Reflections on the educational potential and limitation of microcomputers, *Phi Delta Kappan*, October.

Wheatley, G. H. (1980) Calculators in the classroom: A proposal for curricular change. *Arithmetic Teacher*, **7** (6), pp. 26-27.

Winner, A. A. & Holloway, R. E. (1983) Technology integration for a new curriculum. *The Journal of Computers in Mathematics and Science Teaching*, Summer.

CHAPTER 3

Computer Technology Transfer to Developing Societies: A Chinese-Language Case

JIAYING ZHUANG AND R. MURRAY THOMAS

This chapter is designed to accomplish three purposes. The first is to introduce a decision-making scheme for analyzing the conditions that affect the transfer of an educational technology from an advanced industrialized nation into a developing society. The second is to illustrate the application of this scheme in the transfer of educational computer technology from Western nations into the People's Republic of China. In our example, we use the case of employing microcomputers for teaching people in mainland China to read and write English, which is the most frequently studied foreign language in China. The third purpose is to demonstrate the particular influence of one cultural condition—the nature of a society's written language—on the transfer of computer technology, with the Chinese language serving as the illustration.

A Decision-Making Model of Technological Transfer

As noted in Chapter 1, the transfer of educational technology into developing societies is being reviewed in Part I from a decision-making perspective. As a result, the question that defines our assignment in the present chapter is:

What systematic process can be followed for helping ensure that wise judgements are made when the importation of an educational technology is being contemplated?

One way of answering this question is illustrated below as a plan for arriving at decisions. The scheme is labeled *a decision-making model* because it is intended to serve as a relatively simple, practical guide for people whose task it is to judge (1) what decisions are called for in the transfer of an educational technology into a developing society, (2) what conditions most likely affect each of the decisions, (3) the range of options available at each decision point, and (4) considerations that can significantly influence the choice among the options. The model is described as "simple" because it seeks to identify only some of the more significant elements that are involved in the decision-making process. We have called it a "practical guide" because we believe it can aid decision-makers as they attmept to sort out the complex conditions they face when deciding what to do about the adoption of a technology. After sketching the main features of the model, we illustrate its application by analyzing the case of importing computer technology into the People's Republic of China.

The model consists of two major phases, with each phase comprised of a series of suggested steps. In Phase I, the aim is to select a way of applying the technology that seems both valuable and feasible for the developing society. In Phase II, the dual aim is to (a) judge more precisely the conditions affecting the importation of the application identified in Phase I and (b) estimate the most practical form that the adoption of the technology might take.

Phase I: Selecting a Technology Application to Analyze

STEP 1: SURVEYING THE TECHNOLOGY'S USE ELSEWHERE. How has this type of technology (computers) been used for educational purposes in other societies, particularly in advanced industrial societies?

STEP 2: ASSESSING THE APPLICATIONS ELSEWHERE. What has been the success of each application identified at Step 1? That is, what have been the advantages and disadvantages of each application in terms of (a) increased efficiency in performing educational tasks (cost benefits in funding, time, personnel, accuracy, and complexity of operation), (b) feasibility, meaning how readily it might be put into practice, and (c) political, economic, and cultural side-effects that can occur?

STEP 3: ESTIMATING WHICH APPLICATIONS MIGHT BE MOST SUITABLE. In view of the needs of the developing society's education system, which of the applications analyzed at Step 2 appear most suitable in terms of (a) political/educational importance, (b) cultural suitability, (c) educational efficiency, and (d) feasibility.

Phase II: Analyzing in Detail the Transfer of a Technological Application Selected in Phase I

STEP 1: IDENTIFYING NEEDED DECISIONS. What are the specific decisions that should be made during the process of judging the appropriateness of the selected application?

STEP 2: PLACING DECISIONS IN ORDER. Which decision needs to be made first, which needs to be made second, and so on?

STEP 3: DEFINING THE FIRST DECISION-STEP IN GREATER DETAIL. What subquestions or subproblems does the first step in the decision-making progress involve?

STEP 4: SUGGESTING OPTIONS. What are reasonable alternative answers to the first subquestion under the first major decision?

STEP 5: ESTABLISHING CRITERIA. What criteria or standards should be used for comparing the alternative answers with each other in order to identify the most suitable answer or solution?

STEP 6: APPLYING THE CRITERIA TO THE OPTIONS. Which of the alternative answers or solutions best meets the criteria?

STEP 7: IDENTIFYING CONDITIONS FOR IMPLEMENTATION. What conditions are needed for carrying out the solution identified at Step 6?

STEP 8: PROVIDING THE CONDITIONS. What should be done to bring about these conditions?

STEP 9: REPEATING STEPS 4 THROUGH 8. What is the second subquestion in the sequence? (Steps 4 through 8 are then carried out for the second subquestion. Then the cycle of 4 through 8 is repeated for each subsequent major decision and its subdecisions in the sequence.)

Applying the Decision-Making Model to China—Adopting Microcomputers for Teaching Reading and Writing in English

In the following application of the model, we briefly illustrate each step as directed by that step's guide question. When we attempt this task, we quickly recognize that the process of definitively working through the model completely for computer technology would require far more space that this chapter allows. Therefore, in Phase II of the process we work through only one cycle of Steps 4-8. We then analyze in some detail the way background knowledge about both the developing society's culture and the characteristics of the technology can influence the decision-making process.

Phase I: Selecting a Technology Application to Analyze

This phase includes two steps in surveying other nations' uses of computers. Then, from among those uses, we select at Step 3 an application that seems appropriate for China to adopt.

Step 1: Surveying the Technology's Use Elsewhere

We are assuming that when a nation's educational leaders learn of a technological innovation in another society, an initial question they are likely to ask is: What have been the educational applications of this technology elsewhere?

These steps can take the form of a survey of the use of computers in education in the United States, Japan, and Western Europe. The survey methods can include: (1) educators in China inspecting educational books and journals imported from such societies, (2) Chinese educators spending time in the advanced industrialized countries, searching library holdings and seeing first-hand the uses of computers in educational settings, and (3) inviting foreign consultants to China to describe computer applications in the consultants' societies.

In preparing the present chapter, we used the second of these approaches. We began by inspecting the overview survey prepared by Dr. Harper as Chapter 2 of this book. Then we conducted a computer search of library holdings—of books and periodicals—to identify more detailed descriptions of computer applications in education. The phrase *computer search* in this context refers to the capability of modern libraries to produce immediately, by means of a computer network, a list of recent publications on any topic, along with a summary of the contents of each article or book. (For a way that developing nations can take advantage of advanced nations' computer-search capabilities, see Thomas, 1980.)

Thus, from our computer search in an American university library, we generated an extensive list of educational applications which we organized under three headings: (1) administrative, (2) instructional, (3) evaluation, and (4) research and development. Samples of uses under each category are as follows:

1. ADMINISTRATIVE APPLICATIONS. Keeping records, planning budgets, accounting for expenditures, writing letters and reports, assigning students to classes, testing students, reporting students' progress, assigning teachers to schools.

2. INSTRUCTIONAL APPLICATIONS. Giving instruction in all subject-matter fields at all educational levels, pre-school through university,

with the instructional setting being either in-school, on-the-job, or at-home.

For convenience of analysis, the specific applications can be listed under such subject-matter categories as: language arts (reading and writing one's native language or a second language), mathematics, social sciences, humanities, natural sciences, health education, visual arts, music (composition and appreciation), business practice, industrial skills, and such professions as those of medicine, law, architecture, education, and the like.

3. EVALUATION APPLICATIONS. Creating test items, storing items in a test-item bank, scoring tests, computing statistical results, reporting evaluation outcomes, compiling case studies, and preparing assessment profiles for individual students.

4. RESEARCH AND DEVELOPMENT APPLICATIONS. Conducting a search of the professional literature related to a research or development project, writing up the research plan, preparing research instruments (tests, questionnaires, interview schedules), gathering data, compiling and organizing the data, analyzing the data and computing statistical results, preparing and publishing reports of the project.

Step 2. Assessing the Applications Elsewhere

In the survey of computer uses in the advanced industrial societies, information should be sought about advantages and disadvantages of each application in regard to (a) cost-benefit efficiency in performing educational tasks, (b) feasibility, and (c) political, economic, and cultural side-effects. This information enables educators in the developing society to profit from the experience of people in other nations who have already tried out the applications. For example, we learned some general characteristics of this experience in Chapter 2—in Dr. Harper's review of the present state of computers in education in industrialized societies. But even more helpful are the more specific advantages and disadvantages of particular applications described in journal articles which assess those applications in detail.

Step 3: Estimating which Applications Might be Most Suitable

With the results of Steps 1 and 2 in hand, educators are prepared to select those applications that might prove well suited to the conditions of the developing society. To increase the efficiency of this selection process, we suggest that the potential applications be judged according to four categories of criteria: (a) political/educational importance, (b) cultural suitability, (c) educational efficiency, and (d) feasibility. To illustrate in the case of China how this task can be performed, we shall compare three of the possible computer uses taken from our listing under Step 1 above. The three are: assigning teachers to schools, teaching reading and writing a foreign language (in this case, English), conducting a search of professional literature bearing on a research topic. For each of these potential uses, we first describe the main characteristics of the computer application, then estimate how well that application would likely fulfill the four criteria.

ASSIGNING TEACHERS. The purpose of this application is to improve the efficiency of assigning teachers to schools by using a computer to match schools' instructional needs with teachers' background preparation, skills, and interests. How well, then, does this option appear to meet our four selection criteria?

(a) Political/Educational Importance: We decide that the political/ educational importance is moderately high. There have been complaints in the education system about teachers being underqualified for, and dissatisfied with, the positions to which they have been assigned. Improving the assignment process could contribute to achieving the country's national-development and educational goals.

(b) Cultural Suitability: We judge such a system to be moderately suitable for Chinese culture, in that people are used to being directed by the government to accept particular roles in the society. However, some teachers might passively resist the system, since at present they are able to engage in some measure of personal negotiation outside official channels in determining the school in which they will teach.

(c) Educational Efficiency: Some increase in educational efficiency could be achieved if teachers were willing to accept the positions to which the computer directs them.

(d) Feasibility: This would appear to be a serious problem, since the plan would require a nationwide computer network, or at least a system for each province or region. Furthermore, major difficulties could be expected in gathering information about schools' current needs and teachers' characteristics—information that would be entered into the computer.

Having now estimated the suitability of the first option, we turn to the second.

TEACHING READING AND WRITING ENGLISH. This plan would entail the use of microcomputers to teach individuals to read and write the foreign language that is most often studied in China. When we apply the selection criteria, we arrive at the following conclusions:

(a) Political/Educational Importance: We judge the importance to be quite high. The government urges citizens to learn English as a contribution to the nation's current emphasis on modernization, because help with the modernization plan is being sought from English-speaking sources rather than from the Soviet Union, as was the case in the 1940s and 1950s.

(b) Cultural Suitability: English is a very different language from Chinese. Thus, the lack of similarity between the languages makes English difficult to learn.

(c) Educational Efficiency: The efficiency in teaching English might well be improved, since many present-day teachers of English in China are themselves weak in English. Carefully prepared computer programs could ensure that students were instructed more accurately and systematically. Furthermore, under the present method of one teacher instructing a large class of pupils, the learners fail to receive much individual assistance. But the use of microcomputers could enable each student to progress at his or her own pace and receive continual evaluation feedback and correctives for errors.

(d) Feasibility: Such a plan would appear to be practical, particularly if it began as a small-scale project in which software and methods of implementation were developed and refined before the procedure was disseminated to a broader population.

Searching the Research Literature. This project would require that titles and summaries of published research studies be stored in a computer so that students and researchers could retrieve a list of summaries simply by entering key words (descripters) into the computer.

(a) Political/Educational Importance: The importance appears to be only moderate. The project would be in keeping with the government's modernization goals, but it would affect only a very small segment of the population.

(b) Cultural Suitability: The project would not conflict significantly with the culture, because it would touch only people engaged in research and development planning. However, it would represent an unfamiliar approach to scholarship.

(c) Educational Efficiency: Such an innovation could increase research and development efficiency by saving time and improving the comprehensiveness of literature reviews.

(d) Feasibility: At present, practicality would prove to be a significant problem. If the system were to be of widespread aid, it would require a standardization of computer language for Chinese applications, a system of abstracting and storing research results in computers, and a way of providing scholars access to the computer network.

What we have attempted in the above paragraphs is to perform a rough screening of three potential applications suggested in the earlier survey of computer uses in industrialized societies. These rough-screening judgements can be used for preparing a simple chart displaying the comparative advantages and disadvantages of the three uses in terms of the four criteria. In the chart below we have ranked the three uses on each of the criteria. The most desirable application, in terms of a criterion, is given the rank of 1. The next most desirable is ranked 2, and the least desirable is ranked 3. These rankings are not intended to be "scientific" or precise. Rather, the chart serves only as a visual aid as we consider the question: Which of the applications might be the most profitable to analyze in greater detail?

APPLICATION POSSIBILITIES	CRITERIA				
	Political/ Educational Importance	*Cultural Suitability*	*Educational Efficiency*	*Feasibility*	*Average*
Assign Teachers	2	2.5	3	3	2.6
Teach English	1	2.5	1	1	1.4
Search Literature	3	1	2	2	2.0

If we consider all four of the criteria to be of equal importance, then we can simply total the four rankings for each application and divide by 4, thereby deriving an average ranking for each application. But if we consider one criterion to be more important than another, this simple averaging will not suffice. Somehow, we need to weigh the more important criteria to reflect their greater significance. One way to do this is merely to keep in mind that a particular criterion, such as feasibility, may be so crucial to the success of an application that it should exert overriding influence if it is ranked very low. In other words, if an application were ranked number 1 on political/educational importance, cultural suitability, and educational efficiency but was very low in feasibility, then we might wish to give feasibility more weight than the rest in our choice of an application to adopt.

However, in our present circumstance, this problem has not occurred, for "teaching English language" has been awarded high rankings on three of the criteria. Hence, we select this option as the application we will analyze in greater detail in Phase II of our decision-making scheme.

Phase II: Analyzing Conditions Affecting the Teaching of Reading and Writing English

Our task in Phase II is to work through the 9 steps of our scheme for identifying the conditions that will likely influence the adoption of our selected technological application. As noted earlier, each step is defined by a guide question.

Step 1: Identifying Needed Decisions

The guide question is: What are the specific decisions that should be made during the process of judging the appropriateness of the selected application?

Perhaps the simplest way to perform this act is to engage in "brainstorming." That is, we generate—in a spontaneous, random order—a list of questions about using microcomputers to teach English language, disregarding for the moment how these questions might be efficiently organized. To illustrate, here is the list we produced by brainstorming:

What kinds of microcomputers (the machines themselves) would be best, where can they be obtained, and at what cost?

Where would we find suitable software (computerized lessons) for teaching English to speakers of Chinese?

Is such software already available?

What software would be needed?

What should be the objectives of the series of lessons?

Who would the learners be, and how would they be selected?

If there is no appropriate software already available, who should prepare it, and what sorts of training would they need in order to do the job properly?

What would be the learning setting? In other words, where would the lessons be taught?

How large should the project be at the outset? That is, how many computers would be needed, and how many learners would participate?

How would the project be evaluated?

Who would conduct or supervise the learning program? What skills and what kind of training would they need?

If the program is judged to be successful, how should it be disseminated to serve more learners?

What can we learn from other societies about the use of microcomputers for teaching reading and writing?

Step 2. Placing Decision-Questions in Order

The guide question is: In what order can the decision-questions be efficiently answered? We organized the original questions in the following pattern.

1. What should be the objectives of the lessons?

1.1 Who would the learners be?
2. What kinds of microcomputers (the machines themselves) would be best?
    2.1 Where can they be obtained?
    2.2 What would they cost?
3. What software (computerized lessons) would be needed for teaching English to speakers of Chinese?
    3.1 Where would we find suitable software?
    3.2 If there is no appropriate software already available, who should prepare it?
    3.3 What sort of training would people need in order to create software?
4. How large should the project be at the outset?
    4.1 How many computers would be needed?
    4.2 How many learners would participate?
5. What would be the learning setting? In other words, where would the lessons be taught?
6. Who would conduct or supervise the learning program?
    6.1 What skills would such people need?
    6.2 What training would be needed to prepare them for their assignments?
7. How will the program be evaluated?
8. If the program is judged to be successful, how should it be disseminated to serve more learners?

During the process of reorganizing the questions, we made two discoveries. First, our original question about "learning from other societies" did not fit at any particular point in our outline, since this question could profitably be asked at each step of our decision-making process. We decided that it should parallel all the other questions—we should ask it at every step in the sequence. Second, we recognized that in our original set of queries we had neglected to ask about how the lessons would be conducted? Therefore, between question 5 and 6 in our list we could properly ask: What instructional steps would comprise the teaching method? So we now insert this question as number 6 and renumber the subsequent questions accordingly.

Step 3: Defining the First Decision-Step in Greater Detail

The guide question is: What subquestions or subproblems does the first step involve?

The first decision-question is: "1. What should be the objectives of the lessons?" Also, "1.1 Who would the learners be?" Additional subquestions that we now create and integrate into the outline are:

1. What should be the objectives of the lessons?

1.1 Who would the learners be?
1.2 What is the most suitable source of the specific objectives?
1.3 What prerequisite skills or characteristics would learners need?
1.4 To what level of expertise in reading and writing should the lessons carry the learners?
1.5 How can the objectives best be stated for instructional purposes?

Step 4: Suggesting Options

The guide question is: What are reasonable alternative answers to the first subquestion under the first major decision? Therefore, we generate options for answering subquestion 1.1: Who would the learners be? In another brainstorming effort, we produce the following types of people as likely candidates for computer-assisted English-language lessons.

(A) Government employees who might encounter English-language reading materials in their work.
(B) Secondary-school students enrolled in English-language classes.
(C) University students enrolled in English-language classes.
(D) People planning to travel abroad.

Step 5: Establishing Criteria

The guide question is: What criteria or standards should be used for comparing the alternative answers with each other in order to identify the most suitable answer or solution?

Before setting criteria, we need to decide at what level of difficulty the lessons should start. Should they start at a beginning level, requiring no previous knowledge of English, or should they start at some more advanced stage? We decided to start at a beginning level so that (a) the lessons can serve the largest number of learners and (b) the lessons will build the learners' knowledge as a consistent progression of instruction from the most basic concepts to more advanced levels. In light of the foregoing decision, we set three criteria for accepting students into the course. The students should (1) have a good reading knowledge of Chinese, because in the computer programs the explanations of the English lessons will need to be written in Chinese, (2) have little or no previous knowledge of written English, (3) be contributing significantly to the government's modernization efforts.

Step 6. Applying the Criteria to the Options

The guide question is: Which of the answers or solutions best meets the criteria? To provide a quick view of how well our four types of potential candidates meet these criteria, we can rank the four on a simple chart.

TYPES OF STUDENTS	CRITERIA			
	Read Chinese	*Read No English*	*Contribute to Modernization*	*Average*
Government Employees	1.5	1.5	1	1.3
Secondary Students	2.5	1.5	3	1.8
University Students	1.5	4	2	1.9
Travel Abroad	2.5	3	4	2.4

In ranking the types of learners, we have assumed that (a) the government employees we have in mind are those who are likely to face English-language reading matter in their job but who do not as yet know any English and (b) the people traveling abroad are not government employees. We are also assuming that most students, upon graduation, will engage in work that contributes to the government's modernization effort.

The ranking process leads us to plan the instructional program initially for government employees, later expanding it to secondary school students if its success warrants wider dissemination.

Step 7: Identifying Conditions for Implementation

The guide question is: What conditions are needed for carrying out the solution identified at Step 6?

As a first condition, we need a method of finding government employees who read Chinese fluently, who cannot read English, and whose job would be performed more efficiently if they read English. As a second condition, we need employees who will have the time available to pursue the English-language program.

Step 8: Providing the Conditions

The guide question is: What should be done to bring about these conditions? In the city in which the program is to begin, representatives of the program can interview administrators of government departments and government-operated business and manufacturing firms to learn which employees fit the requirements stipulated under Step 7.

Summary

We have now completed the cycle of steps that provide the answer to the first subquestion: Who would the learners be? We are thus prepared to return to Step 3 to find the next subquestion: What is the most suitable source of the specific objectives? Focusing on this issue, we again work through Steps 4-8 to arrive at a considered answer to the second subquestion. And thus the process continues until all of the questions in the outline at Step 2 are answered. The final result is a complete plan for teaching the reading and writing of English by means of microcomputers.

Because our purpose has been to illustrate the decision-making model rather than to work completely through the English-instruction example, we depart at this point from carrying out the cycle of Steps 3-8 with additional subquestions. We turn, instead, to the kind of detailed knowledge decision-makers need regarding both the importers' culture and the foreign technology.

Cultural and Technical Conditions Affecting Technology Transfer: Characteristics of the Chinese Language, English and Computers

An important reason for the frequent disappointing results in transferring a technology from one culture to another is that the decision-makers who engage in the transfer lack sufficient knowledge of either the importers' cultural conditions or the nature of the technology or both. For example, enthusiastic educational consultants from an industrialized nation often encourage educators in developing societies to adopt a technology without the consultants understanding enough about the potential recipients' culture. Or enthusiastic educators in developing societies seek to import a technology without understanding enough about its characteristics. The outcome can be a mismatch of culture and technology.

Consequently, making wise choices at each step of our decision-making model requires a considerable background knowledge of factors that can influence the choices. It is our aim in this final portion of the chapter to illustrate this point with an analysis of (1) written Chinese as compared to English, (2) the transitional state of written Chinese, and (3) the problem of adapting imported computer technology for use with written Chinese and, in particular, for teaching the reading and writing of English. The background knowledge covered in this section is necessary if decision-makers are to arrive at an informed answer to questions 2 and 3 in our earlier list: (2) What kinds of microcomputers (the machines themselves) would be best? (3) What software (computerized lessons) would be needed for teaching English to speakers of Chinese?

Significant Characteristics of Written Chinese and Written English

English is essentially a phonetic language which uses 26 letters as the basic writing units. Each letter has only one—or at most, only a few—

ways to be sounded. Therefore, the 26 letters can be organized into combinations that represent all of the thousands of words that make up the spoken English language. Written Chinese, in constrast, consists of ideographs, which originally were simplified pictures of objects—wood, mountain, sun, moon.

WOOD   MOUNTAIN   SUN   MOON

With the passing of time, ancient scholars added new strokes to their existing picture symbols in order to express more complex ideas. For example, the following characters evolved from simpler ideographs.

樹   峰   暗   服

TREE   PEAK   DARK   CLOTH

Today the total number of ideographs in traditional Chinese is estimated at fifty or sixty thousand. No single person would know all of them. Only around five or six thousand characters are in common use. This ideographic system has been both a blessing and a curse for Chinese society. Its greatest advantage has perhaps been its lack of dependence on spoken language. Over the centuries, scholars who learned the ideographs could read materials written by other scholars who spoke entirely different dialects. Native speakers of Korean or Japanese or of any of the dozens of Chinese dialects could all understand documents written in the picture language. Likewise, throughout the centuries, as local dialects changed in pronunciation and vocabulary or syntax, scholars could still read the ancient documents. This nonphonetic characteristic of Chinese ideographs helps account for China's ability to maintain the longest unbroken written history of any of the world's cultures—from around 1740 BC to the present.

Attempts to Modernize Written Chinese

When reading and writing were to be skills required only of learned scholars, the complex ideographic system was adequate for the society's requirements. However, such a complicated writing system has disadvantages which render it unsuitable for efficiently meeting the needs of a modern society in which a large quantity of manpower is required for the tasks of reading, writing, recording, typing, and printing. As the Chinese government has sought to raise the educational level of the populace, the traditional writing system has been a barrier to achieving universal literacy. In present-day China, a great portion of school time in primary and secondary education is spent on memorizing, reading, and writing characters. Yet graduates of middle schools or colleges still often commit errors of pronunciation, writing, and lexicon. They frequently encounter characters which they can pronounce but cannot write, or vice versa. Therefore, to foster widespread literacy, both Chinese and foreign scholars have sought to simplify written Chinese. These attempts, which began centuries ago, became most intense in the twentieth century, and today they continue to be a serious concern of the Chinese government. The two main alternatives have been (1) to write Chinese in a phonetic form, using roman-alphabet symbols to represent the sounds of syllables and (2) to retain the ideograph system but with simplified characters so that there are fewer forms to memorize. Each of these alternatives carries particular advantages and disadvantages, as the following discussion suggests.

Romanization—Adopting a Phonetic Alphabet

Efforts by Chinese and foreign scholars to romanize written Chinese began as early as 1605 (Chen, 1939), but the greatest number of alphabetizing systems have been proposed over the past century. Yet none has been universally acclaimed or adopted.

In 1912, soon after the establishment of the Republic of China, the Ministry of Education decided to standardize the sound system. It adopted 3 steps to reach this end: (1) identified all the sounds in the Chinese language; (2) identified the phonemes in the sounds; and (3) designed signs for those phonemes, with each phoneme represented by a unique sign. After almost six years of debate over diverse methods proposed by scholars, the Ministry adopted a system based on 38 simple characters that had not existed in written Chinese but were invented to represent the phonemes (Chen, 1939). This system, sometimes called the Mandarin sound system, is still used in schools in Taiwan.

Several other romanization systems have also been tried. One is the Yale version, based on the 26 letters of the English alphabet and utilizing a sound system similar to that of English, thereby making the approach popular with speakers of English.

Scholars in the People's Republic during the 1950s developed still another approach, known as *pinyin*, to standardize the pronunciation of Chinese. Pinyin uses 21 initials (including 18 consonants and 3 consonant combinations) and 35 finals (including 6 vowels and 29 combinations of vowels or vowels-and-consonants). The system also includes four signs to indicate the tones of the language, since the meaning of a word in spoken Chinese is influenced by the tone with which it is uttered. Because this system has been logically organized and is relatively easy to learn, all schools in mainland China and many schools overseas now teach pinyin to learners of Chinese.

Today, many Chinese scholars see such a romanization of their written language as an inevitable development. However, they admit that such a change will take time. Because of both cultural and technical conditions, it may not occur in the near future.

Consider first the cultural problems. Because language is so closely woven into a culture, changing the writing system used by one's forebears for thousands of years is like asking people to give up an intimate component of their identity. Therefore, many Chinese resist romanization of their language. Furthermore, if the younger generation are not taught to read the traditional characters, how will the history and literature of the past become available to them? Will they not lose touch with their heritage?

In addition to cultural resistance to romanization, there are serious technical problems to solve. Western civilizations's languages, written in phonetic alphabets, typically are structurally-inflected. They depend on structural changes in words (suffixes, prefixes, altered vowels and consonants) and auxiliary words to produce diverse meanings and grammatical functions deriving from a root word. In English, the word *invest* implies different meanings when it becomes *invested, investing, investor, investment, may invest, should invest* and the like. But, as noted above, Chinese is a tonally-inflected language in which the same basic sound, when uttered with a rising rather than a falling tone, will have a different meaning. This poses problems for devising a phonetic form of writing. Not only does a symbol, such as a letter of the alphabet, need to represent a sound, but there also needs to be a way of indicating the intended tone pattern. The various systems mentioned above have introduced ways of meeting this tonal requirement.

A further problem in romanization is both cultural and technical. Even though all people in China use the same writing system, spoken language differs from one region to another. There are at least eight major dialects used within the majority ethnic group, the Han people, who make up about 94 percent of the population. Each of the eight dialects is spoken by millions (Hu, 1979). For instance, Mandarin is used by approximately 70 percent of the population or 700 million people. In contrast, Fujian, which has the smallest number of speakers among the eight major dialects, is used by around 11 million. Furthermore, the 60 million non-Han peoples speak dozens of other languages and dialects. Hence, if the written language is changed into a phonetic form, documents written phonetically in one dialect cannot be read by people who speak a different dialect. Therefore, if romanizing

Chinese is to be most successful, all Chinese need to speak a single language in common. And indeed, for purposes of both national unity and inter-regional communication, the government has for years vigorously promoted the teaching of a form of Mandarin (pu tong hua) as the national tongue, while still permitting the maintenance of regional and local dialects.

Such has been the romanization or phonetization movement. Consider now the competing system for modernizing written Chinese, that of simplifying the ideographs.

Simplifying the Characters

In an effort to solve the written-language problem, the government in 1952 set up a research committee charged with reforming written Chinese (Wu, 1955). The committee not only tried to standardize spoken Chinese by designing the phonetic pinyin system and promoting the use of spoken Mandarin (pu tong hua), but also endeavoured to simplify the written language. The simplification process followed four procedures: (1) If simpler forms originally existed in the historical past, then these simplified versions were to be substituted for the more recent complex forms. (2) If the meanings and pronunciation of certain complex characters were similar to those of simpler characters, then the simpler characters would replace the complex ones. (3) Commonly-used radicals were to be written in a simpler form. (4) New characters were to be invented to replace very complex ones (Wu, 1955).

In January 1956, the State Council published the "List of Simplified Characters," consisting of 515 simplified ideographs and 54 simplified radicals. To ease the transition from the traditional system, these simplified forms were introduced at a gradual rate into all publications, including newspapers, journals, trade books, and textbooks. Not until July 1959 did most of the simplified characters appear in all publications (Zhou, 1978).

Before the simplified forms were introduced, the average number of strokes required to write a character had been 16.08. Simplification reduced the average to 8.16. Studies of the proportion of simplified characters in daily writing showed that they constituted approximately 30 percent of all characters used, so that the total number of strokes needed to write a typical manuscript could be 15 or 20 percent fewer than the number needed in traditional writing (Zhou, 1978). Although the government tried to simplify characters even further, the effort was abandoned because of the confusion encountered with attempting to express thoughts clearly in too few ideographs. Thus, the system used in mainland China today is still based on the list published in 1956. Chinese people in other parts of the world, such as in Taiwan and Hong

Kong, continue to use the nonsimplified forms.

With this sketch of language reform in mind, we turn next to the problem of adapting computers from the West for use with written Chinese.

The Language of Computers—Solving the Problem in China

Many educational technologies have characteristics in common. For example, motion-picture projectors, slide projectors, radios, television receivers, and computers all require a source of electricity. However, each technology also has characteristics which make it unique, and this uniqueness can pose problems that require solutions peculiar to that form of technology. In the case of computers, there are unique problems of language that are not faced with other technologies. This point is illustrated in the transfer of computer technology from Western-language cultures into Chinese culture.

As a developing society, China is currently pursuing the task of importing computer technology from advanced industrialized societies, particularly from the United States. We have already contrasted important characteristics of the English and Chinese languages that can affect this transfer. To further complicate the problem, consider next the nature of computer languages. As noted in the essay introducing Part I, a computer operates at different levels of language. At the most basic level is the machine language, where a person has to work with highly complex combinations of on-off switches in order to get the computer to do desired work, such as solving an algebraic equation or writing a letter to a friend. Relatively few people understand computers well enough to do this, nor do many people have the time and patience to work out the switch patterns that will accomplish the job. Therefore, computer experts have devised programs (patterns of on-off combinations) that translate machine language into the sorts of language people commonly use in daily life. In other words, there are multiple levels of language-translation within computer programs, extending from machine language at the bottom through assembly language in the middle and through one or more strata of higher language levels to "normal everyday language" at the top. In effect, such programs, referred to as *software*, are necessary for converting computers into "user-friendly" instruments that a wide range of the general public can efficiently employ for solving problems, including educational problems.

The interaction between a nation's form of written language and the levels of computer language holds important implications for the transfer of computer technology into the education systems of developing societies. For example, if we wish to transfer an English-language program into a language that requires no more than the 26 letters of the

English alphabet (or even fewer of those letters, as is true with such languages as Indonesian and Samoan), then this translation can be accomplished simply at the top level—the user level—of computer languages. We need not reconstitute the entire programming language at the machine and assembly levels. However, with languages that differ markedly from English, as is true with Chinese or Arabic or Thai, the entire hierarchy of computer languages may need to be reconstructed, beginning at the machine or the assembly level. Furthermore, the task of creating a system of writing a language like Chinese becomes additionally complicated when the language contains a great many written characters and involves tonal inflection.

Keeping in mind these complexities of interaction between written languages and levels of computer language, we turn next to four alternative solutions the Chinese currently face in transferring computer technology into their society. They can (1) popularize the learning of English, (2) adopt a romanized, phonetic version of Chinese for use with the computer, (3) develop a system of writing in ideographs, or (4) program computers so they translate foreign-language documents (as in English) into Chinese romanization or characters. At present all four of these systems are being used, with each approach yielding its own advantages and disadvantages. In the following paragraphs, we first describe each option, then propose how suitable it might be for the project we have in mind—the teaching of written English to people who are already fluent readers of Chinese characters.

Solution 1: Computers for Chinese People Who Already Read English

For Chinese computer-users who already know English, the problem of transferring computer technology into their society is easily solved. Computers—both hardware and software—simply need to be imported from the West. There is no reason for Chinese scientists to devise equipment or programs to accommodate the complexities of written Chinese. However, this approach is impractical for encouraging the widespread use of computers, and it is obviously not suitable for the project we have in mind. While it is true that English is the most popular foreign language taught in Chinese schools today, the level of proficiency of the great majority of graduates is inadequate for the demands of most user programs that would be imported from abroad. Hence, this solution is practical for only a small number of high-level intellectuals, such as computer experts who need to know English in order to learn about the most recent technological progress in the field of computer science. As a consequence, for our present purpose, this first option is unsuitable.

*Solution 2: Using a Latinized (Romanized) Phonetic Version
of Chinese*

A number of computer programs have been designed to use latinized
(romanized) phonetic systems for writing Chinese by means of a computer. To illustrate how such an approach works, we can inspect a Chinese
word-processing program designed by Intech Systems. The program is
based on pinyin. Instead of using a keyboard, the system requires that
the operator touch the viewing screen to select choices of displayed
items. The input process—that is, the act of writing each Chinese
character–involves the following three steps.

STEP 1: CHOOSING THE INITIALS (CONSONANTS OR CONSONANT COM-
BINATIONS). The computer screen first shows the 26 English letters.
Assume that we wish to write the character 万 , which has the sound
wan. Since *wan* starts with the initial *W*, we press touch W on the screen.

STEP 2: CHOOSING THE FINALS (VOWELS). The screen next displays all
of the *W* sounds in romanized form, accompanied by a commonly
recognized Chinese character.

wa 瓦	wang 王	weng 翁
wai 外	wei 危	wo 我
wan 完	wen 文	wu 五

We touch the screen where *wan* is displayed, and we move on to
Step 3.

STEP 3: CHOOSING THE CHARACTER. The screen displays all of the
traditional characters whose pinyin romanizations are written *wan*. The
characters appear in four rows according to their four different tones,
with the tone symbol at the far left of each row.

```
一   弯剜湾挽豌
／   丸完玩顽
∨   宛莞挽惋晚婉绾皖碗
＼   万腕
```

We touch the desired character 万 , which is thus entered into the computer.

At present, this Intech system is probably the easiest one to use. However, it requires a special, rather expensive computer terminal.

Other computer programs based on the pinyin system, such as Asiangraphic, use a similar approach, except that they can be run on standard computer terminals. With such systems, after the romanized form and the tone of a character are selected and entered into the computer, the screen typically displays all the characters that have such a sound combination. And because the Chinese language has many characters which have the same pronunciation, these programs usually have to adopt other aspects of the character to distinguish it from other ideographs that sound the same. For instance, the Asiangraphic program provides a list of 26 English letters, each of them representing a commonly-used radical. Thus, to input the character 佐 , the operator enters *zuòr* which is composed of three parts: (1) the sound *zuo*, (2) the tone`, and (3) the radical (represented by the letter *r*).

In China a program has been designed which takes the foregoing approach one step further. Instead of inputting one character at a time, the operator inputs words and phrases. The program divided the language into three levels—characters, words, and phrases. In the modern Chinese language, many words are comprised of more than one character. With this type of program, the computer operator can directly input the sound of a character or a word or a brief phrase, thereby shortening the inputting time (*People's Daily*, January 4, 1986).

All of the foregoing programs appear logical and relatively simple to use. However, they demand that users have a good knowledge of both the characters and the sound system. Therefore, users who have not mastered the pinyin system find it difficult to select the correct words. As a consequence, people outside of mainland China (such as in Taiwan) or even older people in China may need to learn the pinyin system before they can use such programs.

Solution 3: Constructing the Chinese Characters

The third solution involves using radicals of the Chinese characters as the basic "input" or writing units. Although every Chinese character is composed of its unique pattern of strokes, there are only six basic strokes used in forming all the patterns. Certain combinations of these six strokes are called *radicals*, which appear in characters that have a similar meaning. For instance, one radical means water. See how it appears in the following characters:

湖 (lake)   洗 (wash)   江 (river)

酒 (wine)   海 (ocean)   汤 (soup)

Thus, a number of computer writing programs designed in China have employed the basic strokes and commonly-used radicals. One method of changing machine language so as to construct Chinese characters is called ZN 26-key Stroke Code, an approach created by Zhen Yili. From Zhen's examination of the structure of the Chinese characters, he identified 26 major radicals as the main roots of the Chinese writing system. The 26 roots appear as keys on the computer keyboard. Apart from the 26 root radicals, Zhen invented another 69 extended stroke combinations. Altogether there are fewer than 100 strokes or stroke-combinations for the computer to process, thus solving the problem at the machine-language level of assigning binary codes to the multitude of Chinese characters (*People's Daily*, December 18, 1985).

A similar program designed by the Computer Research Center under the Economic Planning Commission of Sichuan Province also uses 26 basic radicals. According to reports, once a user memorizes where the radical keys are located on the keyboard, he can write as easily as with a pen or in typing English. On average, it takes 3.42 stikes on the keyboard to write one character. Experiments suggest that after three days of training, a user's speed in typing Chinese characters approaches that of typing English words on a computer. Because this system is easy for writers of Chinese to learn, by 1986 it had been adopted by more than 100 enterprises in China (*People's Daily*, December 11, 1985).

While reports suggest that these systems for constructing characters are easily mastered, they all require that users already have a good command of the Chinese written language. For people still in the process of learning to write, or ones who are at a relatively low literacy level, such programs may be inappropriate. Thus, companies outside of China that design computer software for processing Chinese written language often create programs that contain two parallel systems. Two sets of characters, simplified and nonsimplified, are stored in the machine's memory so the computer operator can choose either simple or complex characters.

Solution 4: Using an English-Chinese Translating System

China's Communications Research Institute reported in late 1986 that its staff had invented a computer system which translates four English sentences into Chinese in one second. The system uses a built-in

Chinese-English dictionary and combines the processes of translating and editing. Such systems are intended to facilitate the use of English-language computer files, thereby speeding China's acquisition of information from abroad (A new breakthrough, 1986).

Applying Background Knowledge to the Decision-Making Questions

Consider, now, how the foregoing information about the English and Chinese languages and about levels of computer language can aid us in answering questions 2 and 3 from our decision-making list.

Question 2: What kinds of microcomputers would be best? Our answer is that microcomputers with standard keyboards (rather than touch-screen activated models) would be the most desirable, because (a) efficient software is available for writing in both Chinese and English, (b) such computers could be obtained at lower cost than specialized touch-screen varieties, and (c) they could be used for a variety of tasks in addition to the Chinese/English reading lessons. If the quality of such machines that will be produced within China itself is sufficiently high, then using locally-built microcomputers to promote China's technological self-sufficiency would be preferable to importing computers from abroad.

Question 3: What software (computerized lessons) wold be needed for teaching English to speakers of Chinese? In the foregoing discussion we reviewed four options for transferring computer technology from an English-language culture to China. The first option (programs entirely in English) and the fourth (an English-Chinese translating system) are clearly inappropriate for our purpose of teaching reading and writing of English to adults already fluent in Chinese. This leaves two options from which to select the method we will use. Option 2 uses latinized pinyin symbols, while option 3 requires that Chinese characters be constructed from basic radicals (combinations of pen strokes). We decide to adopt option 2 for three main reasons: (a) our potential students already know pinyin, (b) writing pinyin in a computer is far easier and faster than building up characters from the radicals (an advantage for both the creator of the computerized lessons and for the students who write answers to questions via the keyboard), and (c) lessons written with the pinyin system can be displayed on the computer screen in whatever combinations of Chinese and English the lessons require.

Conclusion

The intent of this chapter has been to demonstrate the way a systematic decision-making scheme can be used for determining what educational applications of computer technology in advanced industrial societies might profitably be adapted to the needs of a particular developing society. To explain our scheme, we proposed a series of decision-making steps and illustrated them with a hypothetical project of teaching the reading and writing of English in the People's Republic of China.

A final question may now be asked about our illustrative case. When this decision-making scheme is carried through completely for the example of teaching English in China, what will be the ultimate form of the English-teaching program? In response, we offer the following course plan:

The length of the course will be one academic year, with the class meeting three times a week. Each session will last one-and-one-half hours. The students will be government employees with no previous knowledge of English but who are fluent in pinyin and are likely to meet English-language documents in their work. In the project's initial experimental stage, 40 students will be enrolled, divided into two classes with 20 attending each class session, so that 24 microcomputers (4 as backups in case of a breakdown of machines) will be needed for the course. The course will be taught in the nation's second largest city, Shanghai, at the Shanghai Institute of Foreign Trade under the aegis of the English-language department. The computerized lessons will be created by three of the department's staff under the direction of a faculty member who earned a doctorate overseas with a specialization in computer applications to language teaching. Classes will open six months after the inauguration of the project, with the six-month lead time dedicated to (1) writing the computerized lessons and (2) preparing methods for evaluating the success of each step in the program.

Finally, we should note that even though our example has been that of transferring computer technology, the same general decision-making process can be applied equally well to the transfer of any other type of educational technology.

References

(Items followed by an asterisk are originally in Chinese, translated into English for present purposes by the senior author of this chapter.)

A new breakthrough in the application of computers: The processing system of Chinese-English has passed the evaluation. (1986) *People's Daily*, October 7.*

A new method of processing Chinese in computers. (1985) *People's Daily*, December 11.*

Chen, W. D. (1939) New development trend in the Chinese language since the latter years of the Ming Dynasty. In *Papers on the Romanization of the Chinese Language*. Hong Kong (?): Romanization Publishing Co.*

Hu, Y. S. (1979) *Modern Chinese*. Shanghai: Shanghai Educational Press. The fourth national conference on the application of microcomputers was being held in Beijing. (1985) *People's Daily*, September 15.*

The system of inputting *pinyin* is successfully completed. (1986) *People's Daily*, January 4.*

Thomas, R. M. (1980) Providing research literature to developing nations: a computer-search approach. *Aids to Programming UNICEF Assistance to Education.* Paris: UNESCO, pp. 13.

Wu, Y. Z. (1955) On the simplification of Chinese characters. In Wu, Y. Z. (ed.), *The Problem of Simplifying Chinese Characters.* Beijing: China Book Publisher, Ltd.*

Zhou, Y. G. (1978) *Reforms in Chinese Characters.* Macao: Er Ya Publishing Co.*

ZN 26-key stroke codes for computers. (1985) *People's Daily*, December 18.*

PART II: RADIO AND TELEVISION

An Example of Lessons Learned

Since prehistoric times, people have believed that mysterious, unseen forces operate in the universe. Many religious traditions include speculation about what these forces might be and how they influence events. In parallel to religious views, secular philosophers have added their own estimates about invisible powers. And in recent times it has been a principal task of empirical science to describe the nature of unseen forces and to employ them for human ends. As a result, one of the most notable scientific discoveries since the eighteenth century has been the revelation that our atmosphere is criss-crossed with an immense traffic of wave-like impulses. People are normally unaware of most of this traffic, since the human eye and ear are attuned to no more than a small part of the wide spectrum of impulses that flow about the universe. Because humans cannot directly perceive X-rays, ultraviolet rays, infrared rays, cosmic rays, radio waves, and the like, inventors have needed to create machines that intercept the atmosphere's imperceptible stirrings and translate them into human sights and sounds. Thus, thanks to science and invention, we now are able to use radio and television equipment to exploit a portion of the airways' unseen waves for the instantaneous, long-distance transport of pictures, words, and music. And such transported material can obviously be of educational value. It is this educational use of broadcast media that sets the focus for the pair of chapters in Part II.

As explained in Chapter I, each of this book's four parts adopts a different perspective toward the analysis of conditions affecting the development and cross-cultural transfer of educational technology. The perspective represented in Part II is a *lessons-learned* viewpoint. In other words, the discussion of educational radio and television in both Chapter 4 (advanced industrial societies) and Chapter 5 (developing societies) is built around a series of lessons or generalizations abstracted from the experiences of nations using radio and television for educational purposes over the past few decades.

The three aims of this introductory essay are (1) to identify key events in the evolution of radio and television over the past century and to suggest conditions that contributed to such development, (2) to illustrate the pattern of present-day access to radio and television broadcasts in representative nations of the world, and (3) to compare ways that informal and formal education are promoted by broadcast media and by the recording systems associated with those media.

Stages in the Development and Use of Radio and Television

In a pattern typical of general scientific progress, radio and television technology progressed over the past century by slow and halting early stages, then by accelerated middle stages between the two World Wars and, finally, to the very rapid advances of recent decades. This pattern reflects the changes occurring in the organizational structure of scientific discovery from the early 1800s to the present. Throughout the nineteenth century, most scientific research and invention were still the province of individuals, rather than organizations. Furthermore, scientific study was typically pursued as an avocation by men either with independent financial means or with another occupation as a source of funds. Some were professors in academic life. Others, like Benjamin Franklin and Thomas Jefferson, were amateurs, financing themselves by business ventures, agriculture, or government service. They pursued invention as a hobby.

But in the late nineteenth century, a type of organization known today as the *research and development center* was born. It was a collection of scientists, inventors, and engineers who labored full-time to use scientific principles and their own ingenuity for creating products of practical use. A well-known example was the laboratory of Thomas Alva Edison (1847-1931) at Menlo Park, New Jersey, U.S.A., a center established in the 1870s to create inventions in a wide variety of fields. Edison employed hundreds of engineers and technicians who deserve credit for much of the work that went into the 1,200 patents that he was eventually granted by the US Patent Office. Among his discoveries that would subsequently contribute to the field of radio and television were the microphone, electric dynamo, systems of electric transmission of power, the predecessor to the motion picture camera (kinetographic camera), motion-picture film, a transmitter, and receiving apparatus for radio sets.

During the twentieth century, research-and-development centers have grown at a rapid pace. In the area of electronics they are of three main types: (1) industrial organizations that manufacture electronic equipment and thus maintain research divisions to devise innovations that can keep the manufacturer ahead of competing companies, (2) research units in university departments of physics and electrical engineering, and (3) independent research companies that either work on development

problems of their own choice or else receive commissions from manufacturers to investigate particular problems. Most of the advances in radio
and television of recent times have emerged from one or more of these
types of centers.

Events in the Evolution of Radio Technology

A feature of technological progress occasionally overlooked is the fact
that no significant advance in the field has been the product of a single
theoretician or inventor. Instead, any important development has resulted from an accumulation of diverse discoveries that coalesce to
produce a notable innovation. This feature is illustrated in the case of
radio technology. The Italian inventor and electrical engineer Guglielmo
Marconi (1874-1937) has been widely acclaimed as the originator of the
radio—or, as it was originally called, of the wireless telegraph. However, Marconi did not singly originate the theory and all the mechanical
devices needed for wireless message transmission and reception. Rather,
his contribution was that of devising ways to combine earlier discoveries
so as to make wireless communication possible. For instance, an En-
glishman, James Maxwell, in 1864 had first predicted the existence of
radio waves. But not until the 1880s did a German professor of physics,
Heinrich Hertz, demonstrate that electricity could be transmitted in
electromagnetic waves with the same rapidity as light, the waves showing the same features of refraction and polarization as light waves. Then
Marconi in the 1890s combined Hertz's discoveries with a variety of
existing inventions in wireless telegraphy to perfect the first appliances
used in space telegraphy or radiography. Progress in the field was
hastened by the invention of the first vacuum tube in 1904 by an English
engineer, John Fleming. His device was improved two years later by
Lee Deforest, an American employed by the Westinghouse Company,
thereby permitting the transmission not only of telegraphic signals but
also of the human voice. On Christmas Eve 1906, radio operators on
ships at sea would hear the first voice radio broadcast—a man speaking,
a woman singing, and a violin playing.

Radio as a scientific curiosity attracted the interest of a corps of
hobbyists during the early years of the twentieth century. And in North
America and Europe, numbers of these amateurs would enter the armed
services during World War I, serving as the early experts in the use of
radio for military purposes. Wartime radiotelephony involved both
ground-to-plane and ship-to-shore connections. However, most early
radio communication during the first two decades of the century was
limited to ships at sea and to amateurs exchanging messages.

Following the war, the commercial, entertainment, and hobby poten-
tials of radio stimulated rapid progress in the field as the opportunity to
hear entertainment and information through the air caught the fancy of

the public. The first commercial radio station in the United States, KDKA in Pittsburgh, issued presidential-election returns during its initial broadcast in November 1920, an event which stimulated the establishment of eight more commercial stations the following year. The rush of the public to own radio receivers was so great that by the close of 1922 there were 564 licensed broadcasting stations in the country. Meanwhile, amateur radio enthusiasts in the United States—known as "ham operators"—formed the American Radio Relay League which, along with its counterpart organizations throughout the world, today includes thousands of licensed members.

Developments in North America were paralleled by similar events in Europe. The first successful transmission of the human voice across the Atlantic occurred in Great Britain in 1919, followed by nearly a year of two daily half-hour programs of speech and music broadcast from a six-kilowatt transmitter in Essex. By 1921 nearly 4,000 radio-receiver licenses and 150 amateur transmitter licenses had been issued by the British government.

As more and more transmitters entered the broadcasting field, it became obvious that chaos in the airways would result unless regulations were established for the use of the various bands of radio frequencies. Therefore, national governments set up regulatory bodies and joined in an international coalition to control the assignment of broadcasting frequencies so as to minimize the extent to which one broadcaster would interfere with another. Licensed amateurs were assigned one range of frequencies, airlines a different set, such emergency agencies as the police and fire department still another, commercial stations other ranges, and so on. Today, national and international agencies monitor the airways to ensure that broadcasters operate within these rules.

The period between the 1920s into the mid-1980s has witnessed the continued refinement of radio technology and rapid growth of broadcasting facilities, principally in advanced industrial societies. Of particular importance have been such technological innovations as printed circuits (instead of the hand-wiring and soldering together of a radio's internal elements) and transistors (instead of vacuum tubes). These advances have greatly reduced the size and cost of radio receivers while, at the same time, increasing their sensitivity and the quality of their sound. As a consequence, by the latter 1980s there were more transmitters, more hours of radio programming, and more radio receivers in the world than ever before.

Events in the Evolution of Television Technology

Television, as a more complex technology, developed at a somewhat slower pace than radio, but much in the same general pattern. Like radio, TV was made possible by electronic discoveries in the late nineteenth and early twentieth century, with scientists and inventors in both Europe and North America responsible for significant contributions. A German named Paul Nipkow in 1884 patented a scanning disk for sending pictures by wireless, but the resulting pictures were no more than crude shadows and thus showed little promise of being of much practical use. In 1888, W. Hallwachs showed that photoelectric cells could be used in cameras. In 1907, Boris Rosing in Russia and A. A. Campbell-Swinton in Great Britain independently proposed using cathode rays for producing a televised image in a TV receiver, thus suggesting the basic system in use today. In 1923, Zworykin sought to patent a TV camera tube, the inconoscope. A Scot named John Baird and an American named Charles F. Jenkins in the mid-1920s experimented with a mechanical-scanning-disk and with vacuum-tube amplifiers and photoelectric cells in an attempt to produce a marketable television system. However, the miniature orange-and-black pictures their devices yielded were too small and uneven for public acceptance. As the result of additional refinements, in 1926-7 the Bell Telephone Laboratories could send an experimental TV program by wire from New York to Washington. The next year, radio station WGY in Schenectady, New York, broadcast the first television drama.

By the latter 1930s, new developments were following rapidly one on the other. In the United States in 1937 there were 17 experimental TV stations in operation, along with the first mobile unit. In 1939, President Roosevelt was shown on television opening the World's Fair. That same year the first baseball, football, and professional boxing matches were telecast.

Also in 1939, the *Milwaukee Journal* filed the first application to engage in regular commercial TV broadcasting. However, because there was as yet no standardization of transmitting and receiving systems, the US government postponed the licensing of commercial stations until mid-1941, after agreement had been reached within the television industry on standards of operation.

One of the standardization issues was the question of precisely how the images on the TV screen should be formed. For example, in black-and-white television, the viewed image is produced by a tiny beam of electrons inside the receiver that scans the screen at high speed from left to right (like the human eye reading a printed page) to produce line after line of light-dark patterns. This scanning of the entire screen with tiny dots is repeated 60 times a second, with each pair of scannings interlaced to create 30 pictures or "frames" of 525 horizontal lines each second. The human brain does not see the screen as dots or lines or as 30 separate pictures. Instead, just as with motion pictures, the brain interprets the separate frames as representing the same flow of movement observed in daily life. Thus, in 1941 the US government, in cooperation with television manufacturers, needed to agree on how many horizontal lines per frame and how many frames per second would become the US standard. The agreement reached was the 525-line, 30-frame standard (Gillingham, 1966: 249-250). When color transmission and further engineering improvements were proposed, the federal government again was obliged to select which of a series of alternative systems would be adopted for standard use. The fact that the same standards (such as in the number of lines on the screen) have not been adopted by all nations has caused some difficulty in the interchange of programs between countries and in the production of television receivers that can be used in more than one group of nations.

While the pioneering developments in TV technology took place primarily between the two world wars, it was not until the 1950s that the astonishing expansion of television as a mass-communication medium began. As in the case of radio, progress in television technology in recent decades has consistently improved the quality of both the visual images and the sound (including stereophonic reception) while reducing the cost of television receivers. At the same time, television sets have become increasingly varied in size (from wristwatch miniatures to theater-screen dimensions) and more convenient to use, featuring remote controls and battery-operated units that can be carried anywhere.

In the 1980s, the most popular additions to the growing array of television devices have been the videotape recorder and videotape camera. A video-recorder attached to a television receiver enables anyone to record television programs on magnetic tape for later viewing. Furthermore, in cities and towns throughout the world, great numbers of stores now rent or sell taped educational and entertainment programs, with well-known motion pictures, past and present, featured on many of the videotapes. A videotape camera equips anyone to produce school or home television programs on magnetic tape, with the program immediately ready for viewing on a television receiver that is connected to a videotape recorder. The video-camera, lightweight and battery-operated, can be carried anywhere for photographing scenes indoors or out, in dim or bright light.

Still more recent is the invention of the videodisc recorder. A laser videodisc resembles a long-playing phonograph record. Each side of the videodisc can contain up to 54,000 frames of still images (such as photographic-slide pictures, graphs, or drawings), 30 minutes of moving video, or a combination of both still and moving pictures. When a laser videodisc machine is connected to a microcomputer and a TV-type touch-screen monitor, the system permits a user to turn to any frame on the videodisc in seconds merely by touching the screen. The program can be played at normal speeds, high or low speed, and forward or reverse.

Along with the technological innovations in television recording, additional problems of standardization have arisen. A program on a video-disc cannot be used on a videotape recorder. Neither can a program produced on one videotape system (Betamax) be played on a recorder from a different system (VCR). This lack of standardization yields not only consequences of convenience for the consumer, but also economic and political consequences for the society. Manufacturers of each system seek to capture the market through advertising and by convincing government regulating agencies to establish their particular system as the one the public must adopt.

In summary, as the past century of invention has demonstrated, each decade has witnessed the creation of new marvels in the realm of audio and video technology, suggesting that the future will bring additional inventions whose nature and potential usefulness in the field of education are now only dimly perceived.

The Worldwide Availability of Broadcast Technology

One measure of the educational significance of broadcast technology is the extent to which people have radio and television programs available. Obviously, these media can effect far greater changes in a population's knowledge base when nearly everyone can receive radio and television broadcasts than when only a segment of the population has such access. Tables II.1 and II.2 illustrate the extent of access by showing the numbers of radio/TV transmitters (Table II.1) and radio/TV receivers (Table II.2) in selected nations in the early 1980s.

TABLE II.1. *Numbers of Radio and TV Transmitters for Public Broadcasting* (Public, Government, & Commercial Stations, Early 1980s)

Nation	Radio (All bands)	Television (UHF & VHF)		Radio (All bands)	Television (UHF & VHF)
AFRICA			*ASIA*		
Egypt	154	74	Japan	1,217	11,439
Algeria	55	44	Indonesia	301	231
Cameroon	19	?	Iran	193	478
Chad	7	?	Malaysia	82	38
Sudan	20	6	India	?	19
			Saudi Arabia	12	?
			Burma	7	?
THE AMERICAS			*EUROPE*		
Brazil	1,325	137	Great Britain	488	1,643
Canada	1,226	1,163	West Germany	471	3,424
Mexico	676	385	Soviet Union	?	2,882
Cuba	150	58	France	610	?
Haiti	48	?	Belgium	41	31

(Source: UNESCO, 1985, pp. X5-X25)

The numbers of transmitters can suggest in a general, somewhat imprecise way the variety of broadcasts available and the geographical coverage of broadcasts. In other words, we would expect in such a nation as Japan, with 1,217 radio and 11,439 TV transmitters, that the variety of programs and the geographical saturation would be far greater than in a nation like the Sudan, with 20 radio and 6 TV stations.

Even more important, from the viewpoint of people's ability to receive broadcast material, are the data in Table II.2 indicating the numbers of radio/TV receivers per 1,000 inhabitants. As the figures show, while there is a continuing increase throughout the world in the percentage of people owning receivers, there are also great contrasts between advanced industrial societies and developing nations in the availability of both radio and television. In the United States by 1983 there were more than two radios per person and nearly 8 TV receivers for every 10 people in the population. In contrast, India had only 61 radios and 3 TV sets per 1,000 inhabitants. In certain countries—such as West Germany and, to a lesser extent, Belgium and the Soviet Union—the popularity of television sets was beginning to approach the popularity of radios.

TABLE II.2. *Radio and TV Receivers per 1,000 Inhabitants*

NATION	Radio Receivers			Television Receivers		
	1965	1975	1983	1965	1975	1983
AFRICA						
Algeria	?	179	215	?	30	65
Sudan	?	73	246	1	6	49
Egypt	92	138	174	?	15	33
Cameroon	19	31	89	?	?	?
THE AMERICAS						
USA	1,235	1,857	2,043	362	560	790
Canada	?	743	761	279	413	463
Cuba	150	194	316	?	64	168
Brazil	128	162	386	?	100	127
Mexico	208	260	290	30	80	111
ASIA						
Japan	207	520	713	183	237	253
Malaysia	46	119	437	6	38	96
Iran	55	61	180	4	51	55
Indonesia	12	37	138	0.4	2	22
Mainland China	?	?	?	?	?	7
India	11	29	61	?	1	3
EUROPE						
Great Britain	600	698	993	248	361	479
West Germany	303	342	401	193	311	360
Soviet Union	318	481	514	68	217	308
Belgium	318	397	468	162	269	303

(Source: UNESCO, 1985, pp. X5-X25)

It seems clear that such marked differentials among nations in the provision of transmitting stations and receivers bear important implications for the educational influence these media exert on their respective societies.

Types of Education and of Broadcast Modes

If radio and television, along with such accouterments as audio and video-recorders, are increasingly available to the world's societies, then what educational functions do they perform? This is the question we now consider before turning to the "lessons" of Chapters 4 and 5.

It is important to recognize that throughout the following discussion a very broad meaning is applied to the term *education*. In the present context, *education* is not limited to formal schooling. Instead, any presentation of information that expands people's knowledge or affects their skills or attitudes is regarded as educational. Under such a definition, radio and television news broadcasts, advertisments, travelogues, quiz shows, drama, music and dance, sporting events, cooking demonstrations, fashion shows, advice to farmers and homemakers, and political campaigns can all qualify as educational material. When such presentations are not part of a curriculum but are simply available to the public, so that people can freely choose whether or not to tune in, then the resulting education can be labeled *informal*. However, when the material is organized as a course of study in which students enroll, with their progress evaluated and a certificate of accomplishment awarded, then the experience qualifies as *formal education*. And when learning opportunities combine certain features of both informal and formal education, they can be labeled *nonformal*.

Informal Education via Broadcast Media

When the above distinctions are drawn among informal, formal, and nonformal education, we recognize that by far the largest amount of radio and television education is informal. Nearly everything broadcast over the airways has potential for altering people's knowledge, skills, or attitudes. It is also apparent that the sort of influence broadcasts can exert differs from one society to another, since the amount and patterning of programming, as well as people's access to broadcasts, varies markedly among nations. Such diversity is illustrated by the examples in Table II.3 of the annual total of radio/TV broadcasting hours and the percentage of different types of programs in 10 selected nations. For example, the total annual hours of radio programming in Japan by the early 1980s was 16 percent greater than in Yugoslavia, 61 percent greater than in France, 10 times greater than in Czechoslovakia, and 45 times greater than in Afghanistan. While most countries broadcast more

R. Murray Thomas

hours of radio than of TV, Japan offered 33 percent more hours of television than radio. And while the populations of France and Italy by the early 1980s were similar in size (around 55 million), France offered two-and-one-half times more radio hours and 50 percent more television time than did Italy. The diminutive British colony of Hong Kong, with its highly developed motion-picture and electronic industries, broadcast

TABLE II.3. *Annual Hours of R/TV Broadcasts and Patterning of Programs*
(Early 1980s)

Nation	Total Annual Hours	Percent of Types of Programs						
		Infor-mation	Instruc-tion	Culture	Reli-gion	Enter-tain	Adver-tise	Other
Japan								
Radio	448,921	13	6	20	–	58	1	2
TV	599,204	14	12	24	–	48	1	1
Yugoslavia								
Radio	385,399	18	4	2	–	68	5	3
TV	22,734	31	8	–	–	36	3	22
Great Britain								
Radio	278,745	13	2	41	1	37	6	–
TV	17,377	19	15	18	1	37	3	7
France								
Radio	129,953	18	1	9	1	70	1	–
TV	30,461	27	3	10	1	54	.5	4.5
Hong Kong								
Radio	63,329	17	2	1	1	72	–	7
TV	24,068	10	6	1	.1	73	8	1.9
Italy								
Radio	48,412	22	3	34	3	36	2	–
TV	19,257	38	3	22	–	32	2	3
Czechoslovakia								
Radio	42,975	16	4	19	–	47	.4	13.6
TV	9,650	27	10	3	–	53	2	5
Sweden								
Radio	19,112	22	4	7	2	61	–	4
TV	4,691	34	–	–	1	48	–	17
Afghanistan								
Radio	10,044	6	9	11	1	33	2	38
TV	752	36	5	2	3	54	–	–
Ethiopia								
Radio	8,569	50	6	4	–	40	–	–
TV	1,250	39	33	6	–	21	1	–

(Source: UNESCO, 1985, pp. X27-X42)

more radio and television hours than Sweden and Italy together. Finally, TV hours in Japan were nearly five times greater than the total hours of the other nine nations combined.

Program patterning also differed somewhat from one nation to another. Although the general trend in the 10 sample countries was for entertainment programs to dominate the air time, and for information programs (news and other informative broadcasts) to be in second place, the percentages of these two types varied among nations. In Ethiopia, half of the radio programs and over one-third of the television broadcasts furnished information, while in Great Britain only 13 percent of radio and 19 percent of TV programs did so. In general, only a small portion of broadcast time in the illustrative nations was dedicated to "education" in the sense of direct instruction related to a specific curriculum or to rural development and vocational preparation. In Great Britain a substantially higher percentage of television (15) than radio (2) was instructional, perhaps because such institutions as the British Open University have made extensive use of television. But in Afghanistan, more instruction was provided via radio (9 percent) than via television (5 percent).

In conclusion, relatively little radio and television programming available to the public is "educational" in the sense of intentional, formal, direct instruction, even though all sorts of programs do alter people's knowledge, skills, and attitudes. Hence, most of the educational effect of broadcast media occurs informally.

Formal Education via Broadcast Media

Even though most of the educational influence of radio and television has been informal, the two media have also been used extensively in formal teaching.

Instruction by radio has been offered in two forms—broadcast and audiotape. The principal advantage of broadcasts from a central transmitter is that lessons can be followed by anyone who has a radio available. Hence, teaching can reach large numbers of students simultaneously in diverse locations. Teaching by radio is most often provided via FM (frequency modulation) stations dedicated principally to public-service and educational broadcasting. However, commercial FM and AM (amplitude modulation) facilities are also occasionally used for instruction, particularly in nations where radio transmitters are operated by the government or philanthropic agencies.

Not only are radio lessons beamed through the airways, but they are frequently recorded on magnetic tape so students have the lessons available on tape-cassettes for use at times they find convenient. In many instances such lessons do not begin as a broadcast but, instead, are directly recorded on tape, then distributed to schools, to inservice-education agencies of business and industry, and to individuals for study at home.

Instruction by television is available in three modes—broadcast, closed-circuit, and video-recording. As with radio, most instructional broadcasts are transmitted from stations specializing in educational and public-service programming. A small percentage of TV lessons are also broadcast from commercial stations.

The term *closed-circuit television* (CCTV) identifies a system by which programs are transmitted to TV receivers through wires rather than through the open airways. Closed-circuit systems are typically used for sending lessons from an educational system's central television studio into a variety of classrooms within a single school or in a series of schools. Compared to broadcast television, closed-circuit TV has two main advantages. It does not depend for available time on crowded broadcast channels, and the teacher's desired selection of programs can be sent to the classroom at the exact time the material best fits the teacher's instructional plan. A principal disadvantage of closed-circuit systems is that they are expensive to construct and maintain.

Video-recordings. like audio-recordings, can either be taken from television broadcasts or else produced directly on tape for use in schools, in business or industrial settings, or at home. By the latter 1980s, video-recording equipment had become widely available among educational institutions in a growing number of nations.

The content of instructional broadcasts and recordings has been very diverse, covering virtually all subject-matter fields and all levels of the life span from the nursery school through postgraduate studies and adult education. In effect, both radio and television have been, and continue to be, important media in fostering formal education, with their influence evident not only in advanced industrial societies but in Third World nations as well.

Conclusion

The foregoing review has been designed as a backdrop against which the contents of Chapters 4 and 5 can be interpreted. Both of the chapters have been written in the form of "lessons learned," meaning that they are organized around generalizations about conditions affecting the development and use of educational radio and television in both technologically-advanced and yet-developing societies.

References

Gillingham, George O. (1966) The ABCs of Radio and Television, in Charles G. Steinberg (Ed.), *Mass Media and Communication*. New York: Hastings House.
UNESCO (1985) *1985 Statistical Yearbook*. Paris: UNESCO.

CHAPTER 4

Educational Radio and Television—Their Development in Advanced Industrial Societies

R. MURRAY THOMAS

The following 16 "lessons" are offered as a series of generalizations derived over the past four decades from educators' experience with radio and television, with the generalizations drawn from those Western industrialized nations which have pioneered in the creation and application of broadcast technology. The sources of the lessons are both published research studies and personal accounts of the experiences of educators who have been intimately involved in the use of the two media. Each lesson is accompanied either by examples of the generalization in practice or by an elaboration of causal conditions related to the lesson.

The contents are organized under 7 headings: (1) economic conditions, (2) political conditions, (3) combined technical and political conditions, (4) organizational conditions, (5) additional factors influencing decision-makers to adopt the technologies, (6) conditions limiting educators' adoption of broadcast media, and (7) conditions promoting the success of broadcast media. It will be apparent as the discussion develops that these categories are not mutually exclusive but, instead, they often overlap.

Economic Conditions

It is clear that without substantial financial resources, the expensive equipment and technical skills required for producing radio and television programs would not be available to educators. Thus, a variety of economic factors influence the extent to which a society's educational institutions will utilize radio and television.

Lesson 1: The Purchase of Equipment

Periods of economic prosperity hasten the adoption of radio/TV by providing both the general society and schools with funds for the purchase of equipment, the training of personnel, and the dissemination of information on how to use the media to improve instruction. Societies with strong economies that generate income well beyond the basic food, shelter, health, and national safety needs of the populace are best able to adopt educational radio/TV.

A simple way to suggest the degree of relationship between a nation's economic strength and the quantity of TV technology available is by comparing countries in terms of (1) their per-capita gross-domestic-product (GDP) and (2) the number of television receivers per 1,000 inhabitants. Table 4.1 displays such figures for 20 selected countries in 1983. The correlation between GDP and TV receivers is high (rho = .86), although the relationship is less than perfect because of cultural factors. For example, Saudi Arabia has one of the highest per-capita GDPs, yet the country does not have as many TV receivers per 1,000 inhabitants as do a variety of European nations with lower GDPs. This is perhaps accounted for by the fact that Saudi Arabia's wealth is very new, resulting from oil exports that have become significant in size only during the past three decades. At the same time, Saudi Arabian culture and the population's expectations, which are both seated in Islamic tradition, have only recently been affected by advanced technology, in contrast to such nations as the United States, Finland, and Great Britain, which have a century or more of adopting technological innovations. Yet, compared to other Middle-East Islamic nations, Saudi Arabia is now progressing very rapidly in adopting advanced technology.

In conclusion, then, while a nation's economic strength is a good general indicator of people's access to educational radio and television, cultural traditions also influence the degree to which economic conditions will affect the availability of broadcast technology.

TABLE 4.1. *Relation of Gross-Domestic-Product to Number of TV Sets in 20 Nations*

Nation	Per-Capita GDP	TV Sets per 1000 people	Nation	Per-Capita GDP	TV Sets per 1000 people
Switzerland	15,229	365	Soviet Union	2,674	306
United States	13,152	631	Brazil	2,232	122
Saudi Arabia	12,094	248	Cuba	1,563	154
Sweden	11,903	387	Bolivia	1,054	59
Denmark	11,015	364	Swaziland	893	3
Australia	10,988	380	Nigeria	825	6
Finland	10,015	414	Egypt	711	40
Netherlands	9,616	301	Ghana	688	6
Great Britain	8,495	411	Tanzania	253	0.4
Spain	4,778	254	Bangladesh	139	1

(Source: United Nations, 1985, pp. 1-85)

Lesson 2: Progress in Radio and Television Technology

Advances in the educational application of radio/TV technology are fostered by economic competition among producers of both hardware and software. Competition within an industrialized society and between such societies, as motivated by a desire for profits, fosters the creation of new and improved radio/TV products. Such competition also stimulates efforts on the part of each producer of radio/TV equipment both (1) to discover other manufacturers' production techniques and (2) to prevent others from learning the producer's own techniques.

A key feature of competition in the electronics industry by the 1980s was the extent of sophisticated methods used to learn the production and trade practices of competitors. Experts specializing in ways to discover trade secrets conducted seminars, wrote textbooks (such as Porter's *Competitive Strategy*), offered consultant services, and sold computer data bases on the topic. Legal—though perhaps unethical—methods of discovering trade secrets were often referred to as "hard-headed business practices," whereas illegal ones were labeled "industrial espionage." Methods of discovering others' trade practices include (a) hiring knowledgeable employees from competing companies, (b) interviewing a competitor's former employees, (c) paying freelance management consultants to reveal information they acquired when consulting for a competitor, (d) hiring someone to tour a competitor's plant to gather information about production techniques, (e) purchasing a competitor's TV or videotape recorder and disassembling it to learn how it works ("reverse engineering"), and (f) bribing a competitor's employees to provide design diagrams, customer lists, and marketing techniques (Flax, 1984: 30).

While competition does, indeed, foster creativity and innovation, the opposite effect can result if manufacturers see their inventions pass too freely into the hands of their competitors. As Ross (1983: 42) has warned, "If companies cannot protect their discoveries—whether these are processes or products—then they will ultimately lose their motivation to invest in research and development."

Lesson 3: The Promotion of Television Sales

Manufacturers and sales representatives of radio/TV hardware and educational software aggressively promote their products for purposes of economic gain.

Producers of equipment and programs typically picture the advantages of their own products in unduly optimistic terms while neglecting to mention the products' limitations. They advertise their products in educational journals, in brochures mailed to schools, and at curriculum workshops and professional conferences. They also seek to influence legislators and school-board members, who are influential in determining educational policies and expenditures. Sometimes a company will provide one piece of equipment—such as a television receiver or a video-recorder—to a school system free-of-charge. The purpose of the gift is to have administrators and teachers learn first-hand the instrument's advantages and, with their appetitite now whetted, to purchase more such items for widespread use in the schools.

Political Conditions

The word *political* in this context refers to people's attempts to gain and maintain control over other people or over a society's production facilities and markets. People act politically in order to promote their own beliefs and to enhance their own position in the society's hierarchy of power, prestige, and privilege.

Lesson 4: The Politics of Information Control and Dissemination

Individuals and groups (including governments) typically employ radio and television to disseminate information among the populace and to solicit widespread acceptance of the group's beliefs. Educational broadcasts are examples of such efforts.

From a great host of examples we might use to illustrate this lesson. I have selected two instances of radio school-broadcasting in Japan, one instance during World War II and the other directly after the war. Educational broadcasting in Japan began on a very modest scale early in the 1930s in Osaka, but before the decade was over school radio had been adopted on a national scale in the form of daily broadcasts to be used in schools. By the beginning of the 1940s, the content of broadcasts had become warlike and nationalistic, a result of military officers gaining control over the preparation of both textbooks and radio broadcasts:

> The children were taught that Japan was a divine land, . . . that their emperor was a living god, . . . that the war in China was a just war, and that it had the support of the gods. . . . In response to the frequent air-raid drills, auditory education in recognizing types of aircraft by their sound was carried out during the time for music in the art courses (Nishimoto, 1969: 47-48).

Such a pattern continued until the war ended in August 1945. Then Allied military authorities who occupied Japan stopped educational broadcasting until, late the next year, they could adapt school radio to their own ends. At the close of 1945, Allied authorities had announced that the traditional school subjects of morals, Japanese history, and geography—which had been deeply embued with militarism, ultranationalism, and Shintoism—would be abandoned until new textbooks could be prepared. But until such texts could be produced, the ministry of education, under the direction of Allied occupation authorities, sought to use radio as a rapid method for retraining teachers and instructing students in the social studies. An announcement distributed to the nation's school administrators in October 1946 explained that:

> School broadcasting will be re-established to prepare for the new educational trends and the re-education of teachers necessary to conform with recent conditions, and at the same time to furnish educational materials for democratic education which are to be handled in the same manner as textbooks and used as materials for actual instruction (Nishimoto, 1969: 71).

Lesson 5: The Politics of Educational Leadership

The extent to which a new administrator in an educational-leadership position may significantly change existing policies toward educational radio or television depends on several factors, including (1) the leader's relationship with the former holder of the position and (2) his perception of the cost-benefit of radio and television.

From more than four decades of observing educational administrators' reactions to educational technologies, I would propose the following generalization about the policies a new administrator will adopt regarding educational broadcasting. If the new appointee to an administrative post has won the position in competition with the former holder of the post (as in the selection of a new minister of education or superintendent of schools), then this new leader will tend to adopt educational-technology policies that deviate from the policies initiated by the previous office-holder. In other words, such a change in policy is often motivated by the new administrator's desire to display a dramatic difference between his regime and that of his predecessor. However, if the new leader had been a close ally of the former encumbent and was chosen by that encumbent as the "rightful heir to the throne," the new leader will less likely alter educational-technology policies.

Lesson 6: The Politics of Program Production

The form and content of educational broadcasts are strongly influenced by who has access to, as well as who has power to influence, program-planning decisions.

The pattern of political influences on program production will vary from one educational setting to another, depending on the number of

people involved, the organizational structure, and the talents and personalities of the people in that structure. This matter of the internal
politics of program production is illustrated in Ettema's (1980) study of
the Children's Television Workshop, which produced *Sesame Street* and
Electric Company programs. Ettema identified two stages in program
decision-making: (1) determining curriculum content and sequence and
(2) planning the exact form of programs in order to achieve the curriculum goals. Each stage was the responsibility of a CTW planning team.
Ettema found that more people had ready access to participating on the
curriculum-planning team than had access to the program-production
team. In effect, curriculum planning was "open-shop" and program
production was "closed-shop". A key question about the internal politics
of such program planning is: What will be the optimum number of
people (and what talents should they have) that should participate at
each of these levels of decision-making to ensure the highest quality
programs? From his analysis of the Children's Television Workshop,
Ettema (1980: 192) concluded that:

> It does seem to be the case that OPTIMUM [meaning the most
> effective number and type of participants] is not necessarily the
> same as MAXIMUM. In the project under study here, it may well
> be argued that the curriculum planning process . . . was too accessi-
> ble, and that the widespread participation was often disruptive and
> counterproductive. Certainly, the curriculum planning team was of
> this opinion. A counter argument could be built on the idea that
> participation in curriculum planning must be widespread (i.e.
> democratic) even if efficiency is sacrificed. In regard to production
> of the television shows, it may be argued that the decision-making
> process was not accessible enough, and that the educators and
> researchers were denied several important opportunities for parti-
> cipation. Some of the educators were of this opinion. The executive
> producer disagreed, however, arguing in essence that at times the
> television professionals must simply be left alone to create.

In effect, within the Children's Television Workshop structure, different people enjoyed different opportunities to have their views determine the final form of programs.

Combined Technical and Political Conditions

Lesson 7: Assignment of Air Space

The fate of educational radio/TV is significantly affected by a government's policies regarding the assignment of air-space to broadcasters.
Such policies, in turn, are influenced by both (1) the availability of

different types of broadcast frequencies and (2) the activities of political pressure groups.

This lesson can be illustrated by the case of broadcast-licensing policies adopted by the US Federal Communications Commission in the early 1950s. Blakely (1979: 3), in recalling licensing conditions immediately after World War II, identified several reasons that the future of educational broadcasting at that time looked quite bleak. First, the history of AM (ampitude modulation) educational radio was discouraging. Of the 202 educational-institution stations granted AM licenses between 1922 and 1950, all but 30 had ceased operation. And by 1950 all available AM frequencies had been filled with commercial stations. Although there still was room for new stations on the FM (frequency modulation) band, the number of people owning FM radio receivers was very limited. And while the prospects for educational radio stations looked dim, there was even less likelihood that TV channels would be allocated for educational purposes.

By late 1948, the FCC had awarded licenses to a total of 108 TV stations, nearly all of them commercial. As a host of new applicants sought licenses, it became clear that the VHF (very high frequency) airways were already overcrowded. Consequently, the FCC stopped further licensing until a more satisfactory policy for allocating channels could be worked out. For more than two years the licensing freeze continued as the FCC conducted public hearings on how best to divide licenses among types of applicants. During most of this period, educators showed little inclination to press the FCC to assign TV channels for educational and public-service purposes. Then, shortly before the final hearings in December 1950, seven national educational organizations formed a Joint Committee on Educational Television to persuade the FCC to reserve TV channels for educational stations. The Committee presented such a convincing case that in March 1951 the FCC proposed that 209 VHF (very high frequency) and UHF (ultra high frequency) channels be reserved for noncommercial broadcasting, with this number later increased even further. Blakely (1979: 3), in seeking to account for this triumph of the educational coalition in the face of strong opposition by commercial-television interests, proposed that:

Four factors explain the sudden vitality of organized education that resulted in the formation and persuasive performance of the JCET.

First, a cadre of able leaders emerged in educational broadcasting. Second, the National Association of Educational Broadcasters began to develop into an effective organization. Third, at two seminars . . . educators and educational broadcasters visualized a new role for educational broadcasting and for the kinds of programming it could do. Finally, a new member of the FCC, Frieda B.

Hennock, came forth as a powerful champion of reserving television channels for educational stations.

The success achieved by the united educational activists stimulated an increase in public television stations to over 275 by the end of the 1970s. Programs were then reaching more than 30 million homes a week, with the viewership comprised of nearly a representative cross-section of the American population. There were also 200 qualified public radio stations reaching more than 4.3 million listeners each week (Blakely, 1979: 192). Such an achievement was, in effect, the consequence of coordinated political lobbying by educational organizations to win the assignment of broadcast bands for educational and public-service use.

Lesson 8: Control Over Program Use

The types of R/TV programs available to educational bodies is influenced both by public policy regarding who has the right to record R/TV programs for reuse and by the government's ability to implement the policy.

With the rapidly growing availability of both audiotape and videotape recorders in recent years, there have been increasingly serious problems of who is allowed to copy and distribute recordings of radio and television material. Program producers, on the one hand, wish to receive fair compensation for the money and expertise they invest in creating programs. Members of the public, on the other hand, have facilities to record broadcasts for reuse or to record borrowed or rented audio and videotapes without paying a copying fee or royalty to the producers of the material.

In recent decades, copyright laws that were originally designed to protect print matter have been expanded to protect audio and video material as well. Such laws have increasingly differentiated between copying material for educational use and copying for commercial distribution. That is, copyright regulations increasingly have allowed educational institutions to reproduce and distribute broadcasts that individuals or commercial bodies are not allowed to copy and disseminate.

The way such educational privilege can vary from one nation to another is demonstrated with examples from seven European countries (Internationales, 1979). In Denmark, copyright laws for years had limited audio-visual centers and schools to making audiotapes only of school radio programs for classroom use. Then in 1977 the copyright act was revised to legalize this same practice for educational television programs. In West Germany, school broadcasts can be recorded for instructional use, but the tapes must be erased before the end of the current school year. East Germany has allowed the recording and instructional use of radio and television broadcasts free of charge in every respect. Finnish copyright law freely permits recording school broadcasts for educational purposes, with the State Audio-Visual Center, municipal centers, and individual schools all producing recordings. In France, broadcasts have been recorded and used in schools, but without a clear policy about the conditions under which the use of such recordings should be permitted. Great Britain allows the recording of both radio and television programs for schools, with the use of a given recording limited to a period of three years. Norway permits broadcasts to be recorded, provided that the tapes are used only on the school premises. However, this provision "does not cover recordings made direct from gramophone records or sound tapes produced for commercial purpose. Nor does it cover recordings for dancing schools. . . . Regardless of the character or composition of the programs, the institution pursuing such activity on a professional scale must pay permanent fees per produced copy" (Internationales, 1979: 59).

Establishing copyright regulations is far easier than implementing them. To ensure that the copyright law is followed, a nation needs personnel to monitor recording practices and a way to apply sanctions to people who fail to abide by the regulations. Such implementation is difficult enough within a given nation, but it can become impossible across national borders. In the first place, not all countries are signatories to any universal international copyright agreement. As a consequence, nations that have not been a party to a copyright pact feel no obligation to prosecute its people for freely copying and distributing R/TV fare from other nations. In fact, some governments openly copy material from abroad without permission. In the second place, even signatories to a copyright agreement may choose to overlook, or be unable to monitor, breaches of copyright regulations. As a consequence, in recent years there has been a growing practice of "pirating" broadcast, audiotape, and videotape materials across national borders, including educational materials.

In summary, then, a nation's copyright practices influence what sorts of broadcast materials will be available for both formal and informal education.

Organizational Conditions

Lesson 9: Professional Organizations

As professional organizations grow in strength and number in the field of broadcast technology, the greater the amount of radio/TV equipment that will be purchased by educational bodies and the greater the variety of ways educational radio/TV will be used.

Professional organizations in the fields of broadcast media and of educational practice hasten the adoption of radio/TV technology by means of conferences and publications through which manufacturers exhibit their products and educators describe applications of the technology to instructional and administrative tasks. Such bodies also contribute to the increasingly selective application of technology through (1) stimulating theory construction, empirical research, and analytical reviews of research results and (2) disseminating research and development results by means of publications, conferences, and networks of personal interaction among researchers and users.

The diversity of organizations—in terms of purpose, size, and sponsoring agencies—is reflected in the following description of nine representative educational-broadcasting publications, nearly all of them quarterly or monthly periodicals.

The *EBU Review* (circulation 2,000) is published in Switzerland by the European Broadcasting Union to disseminate information on programming, legal, and administrative aspects of radio/TV worldwide.

Media in Education and Development (formerly called *Educational Broadcasting International*) is not issued by a professional society but, rather, by the British Council, which is the educational/cultural arm of the British Foreign Office. The journal provides information about broadcast media in formal and informal education for 1,500 subscribers. Also in Britain, the International Council for Educational Media distributes *Educational Media International* (formerly *Audio-Visual Media*) to 1,200 subscribers.

In the United States, the 5,500-member Association for Educational Communication and Technology publishes *ECTJ*, a journal of theory, research and development formerly called *AV Communication Review*. The 534-member Society for Applied Learning Technology sponsors the *Journal of Educational Technology Systems* (circulation 3,500). The Broadcast Education Association of 2,000 members publishes scholarly research in its *Journal of Broadcasting and Electronic Media* (formerly *Journal of Broadcasting*).

An American publication with far greater circulation (31,000) is *ITV* (formerly *Educational Television*), a monthly periodical of information about how to use television for teaching and training. Even larger (80,000) is the *T.H.E. Journal* issued by the California-based Technological Horizons in Education. And a 25,000-member consumer group, Action for Children's Television, dedicates its periodical, *RE:ACT*, to promoting greater diversity in TV programs and to reducing commercialism and violence in broadcasts directed at children.

In summary, a growing number of broadcast-education professionals have been joined by concerned members of the public to disseminate information about educational applications of radio and television.

**Additional Factors Influencing Decision-Makers to Adopt
Radio/TV**

Lesson 10: Evidence of Instructional Effectiveness?

Educators do not adopt radio or television for instructional purposes on
the basis of research evidence that attests to the general instructional
superiority of these technologies. Rather, educators adopt such media
mainly for other reasons.

Recent studies of the comparative effectiveness of such media as radio
and television continue to support Campeau's (1974: 31) observation of
more than a decade ago when she assessed research studies on media
used in post-school instruction:

> What is most impressive about this formidable body of literature
> surveyed for this review is that it shows that instructional media are
> being used extensively, under many diverse conditions, and that
> enormous amounts of money are being spent for the installation of
> very expensive equipment. All indications are that decisions as to
> which audio-visual devices to purchase, install, and use have been
> based on administrative and organizational requirements, and on
> considerations of cost, availability, and user preference, not on
> evidence of instructional effectiveness.

Lesson 11: Potential for Solving Current Problems

Educational R/TV are more readily adopted by educators when these
media—by the nature of their characteristics and their advocates'
enthusiasm—give promise of solving a variety of persistent educational
problems.

During the 1950s and 1960s, the most vocal apostles of educational
broadcasting sought to promote the widespread adoption of instructional
television by convincing school administrators that television would provide the solution to some of their most troublesome problems. Such
problems included overcrowded classrooms, a shortage of certain types
of teachers (such as in the sciences, mathematics, and specialized subjects), poorly prepared teachers, and students inaccurately learning concepts because classroom teachers' instruction depended too heavily on
abstract verbalism. Educators were told that television could solve all of
these difficulties. For instance, televised science lessons, taught by skilled scientists, could directly show students chemistry experiments, mic-
roscopic objects, archeological sites in diverse regions of the world, the
inner workings of the human body, and far more. These superb, highly

polished lessons could reach large audiences, whether broadcast over the airways or distributed by cable to a variety of schools or sent through a closed-circuit system to various classrooms within the same institution. And if the lessons were videotape recorded, they could be used over and over, available at whatever times best suited a school's teaching schedule.

Many educational administrators, inspired by such visions of educational television's potential, purchased the equipment and employed the personnel necessary for making broadcast-TV and video-recording an intimate part of the school's instructional system.

Lesson 12: Nature of the Subject-Matter and Learning Goals

The instructional effectiveness of broadcast media is influenced by the particular learning objectives students are to pursue.

For instance, a host of scientific phenomena can be explained far more accurately and in a shorter time via television than via a traditional lecture or a description in a textbook. Television enables students to witness complex laboratory experiments, obtain an enlarged view of tiny objects, see rapid actions reduced to slow motion, and inspect such simulated processes as movements of the solar system and electron exchange in chemical reactions. Television is also effective in vocational education for acquainting learners with the work environment and with the skills required for success on the job. In the humanities, dramatized historical and literary events on radio or television can be more realistic and often capture students' attention more adequately than do such events as described in books or in a lecture. Furthermore, an understanding of the arts—painting, sculpture, the dance, handicrafts—can readily be taught by means of television. And both radio and television are valuable media for teaching musical forms.

In contrast to the usefulness of broadcast media for teaching the foregoing types of knowledge in the physical and social sciences, humanities, and the arts, neither radio nor television provides students practice in skills of speaking, writing, painting, dancing, playing games, conducting research, manipulating materials, constructing objects, and the like.

Factors Limiting Educators' Adoption of Broadcast Media

Lesson 13: Teachers' Changed Instructional Roles

Teachers' resistance to altering their traditional styles of instruction serves as a strong barrier to their integrating audio and video technologies into their teaching. Such resistance can result from a combination of factors, including teachers' inertia, satisfaction with present methods of teaching, dislike for outside interference in planning instruction, unwillingness to yield center-stage to mechanical devices, a misperception of the complexity of the technology, and fear of making embarrassing errors when attempting an unfamiliar instructional technique.

Inertia and Satisfaction

To adopt a new educational approach requires that a teacher exert special effort, particularly when the approach requires marked change from current practice. Such marked change can be required when radio or television is incorporated to a significant degree into a teacher's instructional style. Not only must lesson plans be changed, but equipment must be obtained, operated skillfully, and kept in repair. If the desired program is broadcast and not available on tape, then the teacher's instructional schedule must be adjusted to the broadcast time. Because of these conditions, teachers who adopt radio or TV must exert extra effort to overcome the inertia of continuing along their established instructional path. Many are not willing to do so.

Part of teachers' unwillingness to use radio and television more often is their relative satisfaction with their current teaching techniques. Unless broadcasts or tapes can promise significant improvement in pupils' motivation and learning, adopting the electronic media seems not worth the bother.

Dislike for Outside Interference

In Evans' (1968: 153) study of college professors' resistance to instructional television, he concluded that "the degree of acceptance of an innovation by professors may partly depend on whether they viewed the innovation as being instituted or imposed by the university administration or whether they felt that it originated within their own academic departments as a result of their own planning." In effect, when teachers are themselves actively involved in initiating the adoption of a new medium of instruction, they are more likely to accept the medium.

Yielding Center-Stage

Many teachers—perhaps all—are pleased at being seen in students' eyes as a font of knowledge. And the traditional role of a teacher (giving lectures, leading discussions, posing questions and responding to answers) supports this view of the instructor as the star actor in the daily classroom drama. Hence, transferring the source of knowledge and expertise to an electronic device, such as a television receiver or computer, can be so ego-deflating for teachers that they are unwilling to yield center-stage to the device.

Conceptions of Complexity

Electronic equipment may frighten teachers with its apparent complexity. At least part of this fear comes from the expectation that something may go wrong during the lesson, causing the instructor the embarrassment of appearing inept, unable to control the teaching situation. Evans (1968: 153) found at the university level that:

> To utilize ITV [instructional TV] many professors seemed to think that much training, equipment, and general re-evaluation of teaching goals and activities would be required. Furthermore, evidence seems to indicate that if a complex innovation can be broken down into "palatable bits," at least partial acceptance will be more rapidly effected. Thus, ITV appeared to be more acceptable to our respondents if they viewed it as an adjunct to present traditional teaching methods—in other words, that it be adopted only for certain courses or be used in conjunction with small discussion groups, much as traditionally large lecture sections have been used in many universities.

Lesson 14: Individual Differences in Learning Styles

The fact that the substance of a radio or television lesson is presented in a predetermined sequence and at a constant pace means that the presentation may not be well suited to students' individual learning styles.

There are several ways that broadcast lessons can fail to meet students' learning needs. First, the producers of a TV program have assumed that the viewers already have a particular background of knowledge on which the program will build. However, some learners may lack that background so that they will fail to understand part, if not all, of the lesson. Next, the sequence in which the program introduces events and concepts may not be the sequence which best matches certain students' patterns of thought, resulting in students gaining a distorted notion of what the program was designed to communicate. Finally, radio and TV broadcasts are time-bound, in that each word and picture marches past at a set speed, so that any learner who fails to grasp each phrase and image cannot turn back time to try it again.

It is also the case that students learn some things best when they actively interact with the source of the material they are studying. This interaction may be oral (a class discussion or a question-answer session), written (working mathematics problems in class), or in physical movements (dribbling a basketball under a coach's guidance). Radio and television tend to place the learner in a passive-receptive role.

Educators have created a variety of techniques intended to minimize these shortcomings of broadcast media. If a program is recorded on tape, it can be replayed for students who failed to understand parts of the lesson during its first presentation. To ensure that students engage in active learning during the program, the instructor—prior to the program—can assign students' questions whose answers are to be found in the program.

If a lesson is being transmitted live, rather than broadcast from a recording, then a talk-back system may be arranged so that students can ask questions of the instructor during or after the presentation. A talk-back system not only allows listeners to ask for clarification of vague aspects of the lesson, but it also permits the instructor to pose questions for students and thereby encourage their active participation. A talk-back microphone in each classroom is a common feature of closed-circuit TV systems. The Schools of the Air in remote regions of Australia provide such teacher-student communication by means of two-way radio. In Canada, live instruction is transmitted along telephone lines from a student on the campus of the University of Calgary to 20 distant centers throughout the province of Alberta. Students gathered in each center have available an audio receiver, microphone, and TV screen on which computer graphics and text can be displayed.

Typically, an instructional session will consist of: presentations by the instructor, during which students may interrupt and ask questions; discussions and activities within and among centers; and reports about homework assignments completed between classes (Winn *et al.*, 1986, p. 19).

However, none of the talk-back systems employed in radio and television can equal the freedom of discussion offered by the direct face-to-face relationships of the regular classroom.

Conditions Promoting the Success of Broadcast Media

Lesson 15: An Inherent Characteristic of the Media—Distance Spanning

Natural characteristics of radio/TV make these media more suitable for certain instructional tasks than for others. The most obvious inherent advantage broadcast media have over other technologies is their ability to disseminate instruction over great distances to large numbers of widely dispersed learners simultaneously and at a low cost. As a consequence, radio and television have become particularly valuable vehicles for distance education. The following six examples illustrate contributions of broadcast media to distance-education in various parts of the world.

The British Open University was inaugurated in 1971 with nearly 24,000 students. By the end of the 1970s over 33,000 people had graduated with bachelor degrees, and 78,000 working adults were currently enrolled. The university has no campus, so that all students study in their own homes, at their own pace, and at their own convenience. Courses offered by the institution have usually consisted of 65 percent reading materials, 10 percent radio and television broadcasts (mostly over British Broadcasting Corporation channels), 15 percent individual and group tutoring and counseling (including summer schools), and 10 percent assignments and evaluations. Thus, broadcasts are not the sole teaching medium, but serve as one component of the instructional package. The Open University has been a marked success, continually expanding its offerings. For example, in 1984 the nation's Science and Engineering Council provided funds (two million pounds) to create courses for retraining graduate engineers, scientists, and technical managers in specialized aspects of manufacturing and in industrial applications of computers. The stimulus behind this effort was the declining strength of British industry. "If Britain is to remain a competitive force in terms of new products, processes, and markets, skills shortages cannot be allowed to stifle innovation" (Martin, 1986: 25). By mid-1986 over 1,000 postgraduate students had enrolled, and more than 370 companies were using the new courses as an integral part of their training programs.

Impressed by the Open University's popularity, the British government in 1986 planned a College of the Air, scheduled to open in late 1987 with television courses at basic-education and pre-university levels aimed at the entire population over age 16 (Approval, 1986: 25).

In contrast to the success of the British institution was the fate of an American version of the open university, the University of Mid-America, which began in 1971 as a consortium of four universities (Nebraska, Iowa, Missouri, Kansas) that intended "to bring the opportunity of a complete college degree directly into the homes of residents" (McNeil & Wall, 1983: 48). The alliance had expanded to 11 institutions by the late 1970s, offering a dozen or so courses taught mostly through broadcast television. By 1981 UMA had provided college studies for over 20,000 adult students in America's mid-western plains states. However, in 1982 UMA closed down, its demise brought on by a variety of factors, including insecure federal funding, over-concentration on teaching via TV while neglecting other potentially valuable media, poor coordination among technical teams, lack of clarity about who held decision-making authority, and lack of expertise in marketing the courses (McNeil & Wall, 1983: 52).

Canada's Athabasca University in Alberta Province was granted permanent status in the mid-1970s as an undergraduate provincial version of Britain's Open University. Anyone over age 18 could enter at any time of the year. By the early 1980s, 3,500 students were enrolled. Home-study courses were self-instructional units depending heavily on textbooks, study guides, and workbooks. However, television programs were important elements of some courses, with the programs available on local channels, often on cable.

Portugal's *Telescola* (Television School) is a system providing televised lessons beamed to *reception posts* that are chiefly located in rural areas. A post may be a school room, a village hall, or an abandoned shop that can accommodate 15 or 20 pupils. Telescola was created in 1966 to offer two years of postprimary education to pupils who had completed the four-year primary school but lacked opportunities for further study, usually because they lived in a remote region. Under the Telescola system, during each period of the five-hour school day, Monday through Friday, the teacher-monitor in charge of the reception post first supervises pupils as they view a 20-minute televised presentation. Then the teacher-monitor "exploits" the broadcast by guiding students as they engage in activities representing applications of the televised lesson, with the activities specified in a teachers' guidebook and pupils' texts. By the end of the 1970s, Telescola was delivering postprimary schooling in all subjects of the official curricullum (except physical education) to more than 50,000 children (Taylor, 1981: 103-126).

The Western Australian Correspondence School, since its establishment in 1918, has served the schooling needs of pupils spread across a vast, sparsely populated region of Western Australia. While much of the pupils' study involves the use of self-instructional reading packets, an important component of the distance-learning plan is a series of Schools of the Air, which are small radio-broadcasting units located in regional towns. The units are classed as primary schools, each staffed by one or two teachers to provide direct communication through a two-way radio system to 55 percent of the families that have children enrolled in correspondence courses.

Only primary students may enroll in these schools. Groups of five to ten pupils from each year level have a half-hour lesson each day, during which time they may listen and talk to their teacher and to each other. This enables more rapid feedback than the mail system, and children gain a group identity. In addition, parents' queries, oral reports, and examination of selected students may occur (Angus, *et al.*, 1981: 159).

In a similar manner, New Zealand maintains a correspondence-school system for pupils in remote locations. To supplement the system's printed assignment lessons, the correspondence school broadcasts for twenty minutes every morning of the school year through a medium-wave network of Radio New Zealand. The broadcasts include: (1) school assembly (current affairs, matters of general interest), (2) music, (3) languages (English, French, Maori, German), (4) speech training and poetry, and (5) secondary-school science and social studies. Audiotape cassettes of these programs are mailed to pupils whose locations are such that the broadcasts cannot be adequately received (McVeagh, 1981: 221-222).

Lesson 16: A Key Characteristic of Radio—It Requires Listener Imagination

The fact that radio provides only sounds means that listeners must imagine the appearance of the objects, people, places, and events depicted in broadcasts.

The ability of radio to stimulate listeners' imaginations can contribute to the educational goal of developing students' visual creativity. Even more important from the viewpoint of program production, the creators of radio programs are freed of the necessity of furnishing pictorial material so that a radio program can be produced faster, at far less cost, and with far less trouble than a television program on the same topic.

However, radio's lack of pictorial content also bears the potential of miseducating the listener, since the listener can mentally create a mistaken image of what a radio program intends to teach. Therefore, producers of school radio broadcasts are alerted to giving "advance consideration to what ideas ought to be stimulated, how to prevent ideas which—although they suggest themselves—are not wanted, and how to illustrate abstract subject material" (Internationales, 1979: 129).

Conclusion

This chapter has offered only a sampling of lessons about radio and television in education. A variety of further generalizations could be drawn as well from educators' experience with broadcast media over the past half century. For instance, the extent to which the media are used for educational purposes is affected as well by such conditions as (1) the difficulty of creating a particular kind of program, (2) the talents of the personnel involved in program development and program use, (3) the language in which programs are cast, (4) the advent of such new technologies as computers and videodiscs that compete for instructional funds, (5) the growing availability of local educational facilities, such as a new junior college in the community, so that distance-education opportunities are no longer needed, (6) the appearance of new, higher-quality broadcast programs to replace earlier versions, and others.

References

Angus, M., Williams, M., Hillen, R. & Diggins, G. (1981) Putting the outback into the forefront. In Jonathan P. Sher (ed.). *Rural Education in Urbanized Nations.* Boulder, Colorado: Westview.

Approval for college of the air. (1986) *Times Higher Education Supplement.* (713), p. 25.

Blakely, Robert J. (1979) *To Serve the Public Interest.* Syracuse, New York: Syracuse University Press.

Campeau, P. L. (1974) Selective review of the results of research on the use of audio-visual media to teach adults, *AV Communication Review,* **22** (1) spring, pp. 5-40.

Ettema, James S. (1980) *Working Together.* Ann Arbor: University of Michigan Institute for Social Research.

Evans, Richard I. (1968) *Resistance to Innovation in Higher Education.* San Francisco: Jossey-Bass.

Flax, Steven (1984) How to snoop on your competitors, *Fortune,* **109**, May 24, pp. 28-33.

Gillett, Margaret (1973) *Educational Technology: Toward Demystification.* Scarborough, Ontario: Prentice-Hall.

Internationales Zentralinstitut fur das Jugend und Bildungsfernsehen. (1979) *School Radio in Europe.* Munchen: K. G. Saur.

Martin, Guy (1986) A shot in the arm, *Times Higher Education Supplement,* (713), July 4, p. 25.

McNeil, D. R. & Wall, M. N. (1983) A personal postscript, *Change,* **14**, (4), pp. 48-52.

McVeagh, Hector (1981) The New Zealand correspondence school. In Jonathan P. Sher (Ed.). *Rural Education in Urbanized Nations.* Boulder, Colorado: Westview.

Nishimoto, Mitoji (1969) *The Development of Educational Broadcasting in Japan.* Tokyo: Sohia University.

Ross, Irwin (1983) Who's stealing the company's secrets, *Reader's Digest,* **122**, (2), February, pp. 35-42.

Schramm, Wilbur (1977) *Big Media, Little Media.* Sage: Beverly Hills.

Taylor, L. C. (1981) Schooling with television in rural areas: Portugal's Telescola. In Jonathan P. Sher (Ed.). *Rural Education in Urbanized Nations.* Boulder, Colorado: Westview.

United Nations (1985) *World Statistics in Brief.* New York: United Nations.

Wiinn, B., Ellis, B., Plattor, E., Sinkey, L. & Potter, G. (1986) The design and application of a distance education system using teleconferencing and computer graphics, *Educational Technology,* **26**, (1), pp. 19-23.

CHAPTER 5

Educational Radio and Television—Their Transfer to Developing Societies

CLAUDINE MICHEL

Over the two decades following World War II, most regions of the world that previously were under colonial rule now attained political independence. However, independence did not ensure that newly sovereign peoples would soon become economically self-reliant. Nor did independence dispel the widespread poverty and high levels of illiteracy they suffered. Confronted with these problems, political leaders generally agreed that universal primary schooling and significant increases in secondary and higher education were essential instruments for achieving the nations' social-welfare and economic ambitions. However, the hope that universal schooling could be achieved in the near future was dimmed by the shortage of teachers and lack of school buildings, shortages exacerbated by high population growth rates. Virtually all such developing societies made a valiant effort to increase the pace of building schools and training teachers, but they still could not accommodate all children and youths of school age. And even for those young people who did find a place in school, the quality of their education often suffered because teachers were poorly trained, textbooks were in short supply, and the curriculum was not relevant to the learners' needs in the world outside the classroom. Furthermore, parents often were unconvinced that formal schooling was essential for children, so they let their sons and daughters stay home and help on the farm or in the shop. All of these factors served to limit enrollments and to increase the rate of pupils dropping out of school before they finished even the primary grades.

In numbers of developing nations during the 1960s and 1970s, educational leaders became increasingly discouraged about their inability to provide formal education for the entire school-age population. Hence, they welcomed the suggestion that broadcast radio and television might go a long way toward solving some of their most distressing instructional problems. Broadcast lessons of high quality, taught by expert instructors, could be sent to thousands of learners all over a region. And even where classroom teachers would provide the majority of the instruction, special programs on radio or television could enrich the learning fare that pupils were served. In effect, radio and television promised to equip a country's educational establishment to reach a broad audience with lessons that:

1. Teach both children and adults such skills as functional literacy and writing as well as functional numeracy in mathematics.
2. Foster a scientific viewpoint toward natural phenomena, in contrast to a traditional unquestioning acceptance of magical, supernatural explanations of events. This scientific outlook would include information about such practical matters as health, sanitation, nutrition, and food storage and preparation.
3. Provide information about raising a family and operating a household.
4. Promote knowledge and skills for earning a living at specific occupations and for general trade skills.
5. Explain ways of participating in civic and political affairs.
6. Acquaint learners with the social and scientific world beyond their community, district, and nation.
7. Introduce forms of the arts—drawing, painting, the dance, sculpture, singing, instrumental music, drama, handicrafts—from the local area, other parts of the nation, and abroad.
8. Teach national and world history.

A further advantage that broadcast media offered was the ability to teach all age groups in the population. Television programs could introduce preschoolers to reading and numbers, expand their vocabularies, and acquaint them with natural science, social events, and moral values. Both radio and TV lessons bearing on all aspects of the school curriculum could be broadcast into the schools as well as to school-age listeners in remote locations who are not in school. And both radio and television programs could reach adults in their homes.

A question may now be asked about how widely educational broadcasting has been adopted in developing societies over the past three decades and about how much success such broadcasting has achieved. The answer is that some educational radio and television has been attempted in most nations, at least on a modest scale, most frequently as informal education rather than formal instruction. Among the developing nations that have adopted broadcast media for formal or nonformal education are a number which have attracted widescale international attention. Of particular note have been the experiments with instructional television in American Samoa in the Pacific (Schramm, Nelson & Betham, 1981), the Ivory Coast and Niger in Africa (Blume &

Schneller, 1984), and El Salvador in Central America (Young et al., 1980). Also well publicized are the cases of instructional radio in such countries as the Dominican Republic, Nicaragua, Thailand, and Kenya (Friend, 1985; Meadowcroft, 1985). Assessments of these projects have indicated that educational applications of television and radio in developing societies have met with mixed success. For example, evaluations of teaching by radio in several societies have shown that pupils who studied mathematics, English as a second language, and reading in the indigenous language succeeded better than did pupils taught by those societies' conventional methods of instruction (Meadowcroft, 1985). However, other research demonstrates that the effects of broadcast media are not the same for all types of learners; such factors as students' cultural and socioeconomic status influence how well learners succeed under television or radio instruction (Batmaz & Wagner, 1985). And in a number of cases, educators' early enthusiasm for educational radio or television motivated them to make a major commitment to teaching by broadcast media; but after the use of radio or television had been adopted as a principal mode for delivering instruction, its use subsequently diminished markedly or was dropped entirely (Blume & Schneller, 1984; Thomas, 1980). A diversity of causes account for such varied patterns in the use and success of educational broadcasting, and it is to these causal conditions that we turn our attention in this chapter.

In keeping with the style of Chapter 4, the influential conditions are described in the form of 15 lessons learned in developing societies over the past three decades. Each lesson is first identified by a title, then described in the form of a generalization, and finally illustrated with either case material or an elaboration of factors that bear on the condition. The lessons are organized under 6 topics: (1) relationships between exporter and importer societies, (2) sociopolitical conditions, (3) personnel availability, (4) economic factors, (5) goals and expectations, and (6) guidelines for broadcast education in developing societies.

Relationships Between Exporter and Importer Societies

In the transfer of technology, the nations that originally develop the technologies are traditionally in Europe and North America, with these nations more recently joined by Japan. Such countries, which serve today as the exporters of educational technology, share several characteristics in common. They are highly industrialized, enjoy high rates of literacy and levels of schooling, and were the controllers of colonies in the less-industrialized regions of the world until after World War II. From the eighteenth century through the first half of the twentieth century, they not only gained colonial control of nearly all regions of Africa, Asia, Latin America, and the Pacific Islands, but they used these regions as sources of raw materials and as markets for the sale of their manufactured goods.

Over the two decades following World War II, nearly all formerly colonized regions gained complete political independence or at least a measure of self-governance. However, most of them remained dependent on the former colonial powers for models of socioeconomic planning, for expertise in modern business and industrial practices, for manufactured goods, for funds to support development projects, and sometimes for food. They also continued to depend on Europe, North America, and Japan for educational aid—administrative practices, curriculum planning, teaching methods, and instructional technology. Hence, these developing societies have continued to be the importers of educational technologies.

Key factors in this relationship between the exporting and importing societies that have influenced the application of broadcast technology in developing nations are reflected in our initial 5 lessons.

Lesson 1: Modes of Transfer

There are several common ways that educational broadcast technology is introduced into a developing society, with each way carrying particular implications for how the technology will be accepted by the importing society.

For convenience of discussion, modes of transfer can be identified with 3 kinds of people who initiate the transfer: (1) missionary zealots, (2) interested officials in combination with willing helpers, and (3) learners abroad.

Missionary zealots are members of advanced industrial societies who are intent on vigorously disseminating educational broadcast systems to developing societies. They seek out key members of developing nations' political and educational hierarchies with the intention of convincing those officials to include radio and television in their country's instructional system. The zealots may be either sales representatives of electronic manufacturers or educators whose enthusiasm for broadcast media has stimulated them to pursue this mission.

Interested officials are members of a developing society who are seeking ways to solve their nations' educational problems, particularly the problem of furnishing widespread, high-quality educational opportunities to their populations at a reasonable cost. *Willing helpers* are educational-broadcasting specialists in industrialized nations who do not initiate the transfer of instructional radio and television to other societies but, when invited by representatives of those societies, will serve as consultants.

Learners abroad are either students from developing countries who are in long-term study programs in high-technology societies, or else they are short-term visitors to high-technology nations. When they return home, they attempt to introduce broadcasting into their own societies.

A variety of means may be used by these purveyors of technology to acquaint people of the developing society with the characteristics of educational radio and TV. The principal means are demonstrations (either live or on videotape) and verbal/pictorial descriptions of the educational uses of radio and television (orally or in books, magazines, journal articles, or brochures).

Two characteristics of technology's advocates that influence how educational broadcast media will be adopted in a developing society include: (1) the advocates' apparent level of expertise regarding both the technology and the recipient society and (2) how truthful and well-intentioned these enthusiasts appear to be.

Sometimes the transfer is not directly from an industrialized to a developing society but, instead, between two developing nations. This can be advantageous when conditions in the two Third World nations are similar. For instance, a network of educational radio stations in the mountains of Colombia broadcast lessons one-half hour each morning and evening to teach literacy, numeracy, health, practical vocations, and religion. Supplementing the broadcasts are instructional booklets and teaching-assistants who supervise students who are following the lessons in mountain villages. This ACPO (Accion Cultural Popular) network was started in 1947 by a Catholic priest, Father Salcedo, near the mountain town of Sutatenza, which gave the network its name, Radio Sutatenza. As the system has grown over the years, educators from other Latin American countries have come to see how such distance-education operates, and they have adopted those aspects of the Colombian project that appear to suit the needs of their own regions (Young *et al.*, 1980: 149-162).

Lesson 2: Exporters' Motives

People from the exporting societies who participate in transfer efforts can be motivated by different intentions, some of which are philanthropic and others very self-serving.

The most self-serving people are the aggressive producers of equipment and programs in industrialized societies who wish to profit financially from selling their goods in Third World nations. The danger in this desire for profit is that the suppliers of equipment tend to "oversell" their products. Their glowing claims about the virtues of their goods are unrealistically optimistic, so that naive officials in the recipient nations are misled about the cost-benefits they can reasonably expect.

Another group of broadcast-media enthusiasts in technologically-advanced societies truly have the welfare of Third World peoples at heart. They often are representatives of international organizations (Unesco, Unicef), of the foreign office of a government (the British Council, US-AID), of philanthropic foundations, or of religious orders. In a humanitarian spirit, they advocate the adoption of radio and television because they are convinced that these media will promote educational progress in developing societies.

Lesson 3: Importers' Motives

People of the importing societies who participate in technological transfer can be motivated by intentions that foster educational progress or by motives that hinder progress toward the nation's educational goals.

In many cases, the leaders in Third World countries adopt broadcast media out of a sincere desire to expand educational opportunity and improve the quality of instruction for the populace. In other instances, their motive for importing broadcast technology is that of enhancing the political power of the current government. As a result, educational use of the media becomes an accidental by-product of the political goal. This point is illustrated by the case of the Haitian government, which constructed two well-equipped—ostensibly "educational"—radio and television stations in 1970. However, the real intent was to broadcast propaganda in support of the "Baby Doc" Duvalier regime. Most of the programing funds were dedicated to this end. Although a few programs legitimately qualifying as "educational" were broadcast, the government did not start them. Instead, the initiative came from volunteers in the educational community. The government's lack of interest in using broadcast media to pursue educational goals was reflected in its low-level of technical support for educational programming and its unwillingness to pay educational personnel who produced the broadcasts.

When the original impetus to import radio or television into a society is not political, it is likely the desire to provide public entertainment. However, in some instances the original motive has been educational, with entertainment and political purposes secondary. This is what occurred in American Samoa, where broadcast television was introduced in the early 1960s as a means of upgrading the quality of education in the islands' public schools, and evening entertainment programs were subsequently added almost as an afterthought (Schramm, Nelson & Betham, 1981).

Lesson 4: Exporters' Knowledge

The more that exporters know about the culture and goals of the recipient nation, the more appropriate and efficient the transfer of broadcast technology will be.

The literature on educational broadcasting in the Third World contains numerous examples of inefficiency in educational broadcasting
because foreign consultants lacked sufficient knowledge of the local
peoples and their society. However, for all of the examples that have
gotten into print, there must be hundreds more never published because
the people responsible for such projects would prefer that their bad
judgment remain unpublicized.

The problem of lack-of-cultural-understanding can result from a variety of causes. One of the most frequent is the inadequate acquaintance of
a consultant with a culture. A foreign expert in educational technology
arrives in a Third World nation to make a two-week or one-month or
six-month survey of the country's educational needs. The expert, by the
end of the visit, is obligated to write a report of findings and recommendations and submit it to both the host nation and the organization
sponsoring the trip—a United Nations agency, a foreign government, a
philanthropic foundation, or an international lending bank. Such consultants typically feel compelled to offer rather specific suggestions in order
to justify the money spent for their visit and to exhibit their expertise.
As a result, they are prone to make proposals that reflect an ignorance
of important conditions in the developing nation.

An example of lack of cultural knowledge base is the case of a British
educational-TV expert sent in 1968 as a short-term Unesco adviser to
the Indonesian Ministry of Education. At that time, Indonesia was
newly emerging from a period of civil strife and attempting to extend
primary schooling as rapidly as possible to the entire population, which
was distributed across more than 1,000 islands. The adviser did not
speak the Indonesian language, and he spent most of his time in the
capital city, conversing almost entirely with other foreigners and
English-speaking Indonesians in the ministry of education. In his final
report, he recommended that the ministry abandon its current effort to
publish millions of textbooks and, instead, to put television receivers in
all the nation's schools so that excellent lessons beamed from a central
studio could be transmitted to the entire population of pupils. The
educational television system could take advantage of the nation's new
communication satellite to solve the problem of transmitting programs
to distant locations. The Indonesian minister of education (a political
appointee not well grounded in educational analysis and methodology)
seriously considered instituting the adviser's plan until professional educators farther down in the ministry hierarchy pointed out the impossibil-
ity of the scheme. The cost of supplying schools with TV receivers
would be enormous, there was no skilled staff to develop high-quality
programs, there was no electricity in a great many villages, electronic
equipment deteriorated rapidly in the humid climate, villages would
soon wear out the TV receivers by using them to view entertainment

programs when school was not in session, and there were no facilities for repairing electronic gear except in a few large cities. Therefore, the expert's advice was not adopted, and the ministry continued its textbook-publishing program.

In summary, the advice of foreign consultants, such as expatriates who work in developing areas, is more trustworthy if the consultants have lived in the developing society for an extended period, if they speak the local language, and if they spend much of their time in close communication with the local educators rather than existing principally in an enclave of foreigners.

Lesson 5: Importers' Knowledge

The more that decision-makers in an importing nation know about the educational advantages and disadvantages of broadcast technology, the greater the probability that broadcast technology will be adopted in a form that enhances the educational efficiency of their society.

A danger faced by representatives of Third World education systems when they visit abroad is that they marvel at the educational broadcasting they witness but fail to recognize the complexities of equipment, personnel, program preparation, and funding that are involved in airing educational fare of high quality. Failing to understand the details of creating and transmitting programs, they are apt to set up broadcast plans for which their society is ill prepared. Therefore, educational leaders are served best by advisers on their own staff who have studied broadcasting overseas in some detail and by foreign advisers who are experienced in educational broadcasting and have worked in the developing society for a substantial length of time.

Sociopolitical Conditions

When political power is defined as the ability of one segment of the population to gain greater privilege than another segment, then it becomes clear that educational radio and television can serve as an important tool of political power. The following four lessons illustrate ways that such political influence can be exercised.

Lesson 6: Maintenance of the Political Power System

In at least two important ways, educational broadcast media—particularly television—serve to maintain the existing political power structure: (1) through the control of the content of programs and (2) through offering selected segments of the population greater access to information and education.

(1) Many developing nations operate in a state of political instability, in the sense that the control of the government currently in power is somewhat tenuous, vulnerable to attack from opposing forces. Therefore, it is common practice for government officials to monitor the information and entertainment programs (newscasts, dramas, interviews, debates) and instructional broadcasts to ensure that the people in power and their policies are cast in a favorable light.

(2) Whereas advances in electronic technology have made transistor radios very inexpensive so they can be bought by many people in developing societies, television receivers are still expensive items. Furthermore, AM radio waves reach beyond the horizon so that a program hundreds or thousands of miles distant can be received on a radio receiver. In contrast, FM frequencies that carry television and FM radio transmissions do not extend far beyond the horizon, so that without mountain-top relay stations or communication satellites, people outside of major urban areas in Third World nations cannot receive television and FM-radio programs. Consequently, the more affluent, urban inhabitants of a nation enjoy access to both informal and formal educational broadcasting that is not available to the poor and to distant rural citizens of the country. Hence, the wealthy urbanites' greater access to information and instruction translates into special political power.

Lesson 7: The Language of Instruction

Decisions about the language—or languages—in which broadcasts will be offered influence who in the society receives favored educational opportunities.

In such a nation as Korea (both North and South), the question of what instructional language will be used in schools and in broadcasts is not an issue, since everyone speaks the same language. But in most developing countries, more than one language is spoken. Therefore, the people whose home language is the same as that used for instruction and public communication have an advantage over those who must be schooled in a second or third tongue. Political groups can use this factor of instructional and broadcast language to further their own ends.

A useful example is that of Malaysia. In terms of ethnic background, the population of Malaysia today is around 55 percent Malay, 34 percent Chinese, 9 percent Indian, and the remaining 2 percent other stock (Aziz and Chew, 1980: 101). Under British colonialism, which ended in the early 1960s, primary schooling was available in either English, Chinese, Malay, or Tamil. The medium of instruction in secondary and higher education was chiefly English. Likewise, the language of government and commerce was English. This same pattern obtained throughout the decade of the 1960s until racial riots at the close of the decade stimulated the Malay-controlled government to hasten its program of transition to a nationally-unifying language, which was designated as Malay. Hence, throughout the 1970s and 1980s, the medium of instruction in schools above the primary level changed gradually to Malay, while English was virtually eliminated as the language of instruction at all levels. Radio and television broadcasts reflected this same pattern of transition to the Malay language. As a result, the superior position in educational attainment enjoyed by Chinese and Indian students who attended English-medium schools prior to the 1970s was intentionally diminished by the government's language policy, a policy founded on a rationale which proposed that: "(1) Malays deserve special educational opportunities to compensate them for disadvantages suffered under British colonial rule and (2) the most reasonable source of a unified culture for the nation is the culture of the dominant indigenous ethnic group of the region—the Malays" (Thomas, 1986: 411).

This concern over the political effects of the language—or languages—used for different types of radio and television programs has been a matter of key concern in a wide variety of countries, including the People's Republic of China, India, Angola, Algeria, Somalia, and Thailand (Fry, 1985).

Lesson 8: A Source of Values

One result of the increasing availability of broadcast media has been the change that the media can effect in people's values and expectations.

Whereas skill is reading in required for gaining information from a book, a person need not be literate to learn through radio and television what life is like in other parts of the world. Therefore, radio and TV, whether commercial or educational, often have the effect of raising people's expectations for social improvement, expectations that can stimulate them to action. As one example, the increased availability of radios and TV receivers in developing nations has contributed to an increase in rural-urban migration, as village youths envision a bright future in the city based on their impression of urban life depicted in radio and television programs. And when opportunities in the city are not available to fulfill these newly aroused hopes, social disorder can result. This likelihood of social unrest frequently motivates those who control the content of broadcasts to design programs emphasizing the desirability of the status quo.

Lesson 9: Nationalism versus Regionalism

The centralization of media production tends to socialize individuals into a national culture by downplaying local identities and values.

Most developing nations experience tensions between the central government and the regions, tensions that are often seated in ethnic and language differences, in conflicting urban-rural viewpoints, in religious differences, and in discrepancies in how well the central government meets the needs of diverse areas of the nation. As a consequence, a country's broadcasting policies can influence the balance achieved between national-unity needs (or the interests of the ruling elite) and satisfying regional desires and traditions.

Availability of Personnel

Lesson 10: Sources of Personnel

The source of personnel to operate a system of educational broadcasting, along with the types of knowledge and skill displayed by the personnel, affects the success of the system.

A difficult problem faced by Third World nations has been that of training indigenous personnel to perform the operations required in educational broadcasting. The problem has been more acute for television than for radio because of the greater complexity of both the television equipment and the medium's programming demands. The typical pattern of staff development has been one of importing expatriate specialists to fill key positions during the early stages of the plan, then gradually replacing the foreigners with local poeple trained either abroad or within the Third World nation itself. Developing societies usually have found this task of effecting a satisfactory transition from expatriates to indigenous personnel to be quite troublesome.

One source of difficulty has been the expatriates' ignorance of the societies' customs so they say and do things which offend the local people with whom they work. Or even when they understand the local culture, such as religious beliefs and social etiquette, the foreigners may not sympathize with such practices and thus may reflect their disdain in their behavior.

A further problem can be the foreign specialists' attitudes towards their assignment. Officials in the host nation usually expect the expatriates to train local personnel to take over the expatriates' jobs. However, the expatriates may wish to hold onto their jobs as long as possible, frequently because they enjoy living overseas and they are paid higher wages in the developing society than they would earn at home. Therefore, they resist training indigenous counterparts. This problem is amplified if the expatriates are not skilled teachers, so that even their attempts to train local personnel yield poor results.

Another source of trouble is the pay differential that often obtains between foreign and domestic personnel. The foreigners are frequently sponsored by an international aid organization—such as Unesco or the World Bank—and paid substantially higher wages than indigenous employees who are doing essentially the same work. The local employees often resent this arrangement and may reflect their dissatisfaction by performing poorly on the job or of only grudgingly working with the expatriates.

Such problems as these emphasize the importance for Third World nations and international-aid agencies carefully screening applicants to work in the developing countries' education systems. The screening needs to focus not only on the applicants' technical expertise, but also on personality traits that can affect their relationships with people in the Third World society. It is equally important that the sponsors of the foreign specialists monitor the specialists' performance so as to minimize problems in their adjustment to the job and the local culture.

Inefficiency can also result from the appointment of local personnel to specialist jobs before they are adequately prepared. This can occur when the developing nation cannot attract experts from abroad or else seeks to attain early self-sufficiency by refusing to hire foreigners.

In addition to training local employees on the job, developing nations often send their people overseas to learn skills of educational broadcasting. Again it is important that the agency sponsoring such study screen the educational settings in which learners will be located so as to maximize the likelihood their experience suits their needs.

Lesson 11: Suitable Teacher Education

Successfully incorporating radio or television into classroom practice requires that teachers accommodate their instructional styles to the broadcast technology.

In some developing nations, broadcasting has been assigned a central role in teaching, meaning that the core of daily lessons is conveyed by radio and television. In such cases, the classroom teacher is no longer the chief purveyor of information. To fit properly into this new mode of instruction, teachers must learn to prepare students for each broadcast, to monitor their behavior during the lesson, and after the broadcast to direct them in follow-up applications of the lesson content. Such teachers are also expected to assess pupils' progress and offer remedial aid to those who fail to master the broadcast material.

But not all school systems place broadcasts at the center of the instructional system. Instead, they relegate radio or television to a supplementary position, using broadcasts or recordings only occasionally in selected subject-matter areas (perhaps music on radio, science demonstrations and historical dramas on television). Such subsidiary uses of the media require fewer changes in teachers' traditional roles.

But whether changes in classroom methodology are major or minor, the society's teacher-education system faces the task of preparing both inservice and preservice teachers to adopt somewhat new methods of instruction. And for developing nations, this assignment is typically a difficult one, since their teacher-training facilities are often meager and the quality of inservice of teachers frequently substandard. One method of upgrading the teaching corps has consisted of gathering teachers in regional centers for workshops or short courses. But such an approach is usually expensive and fraught with logistical difficulties. Similar problems are faced with sending teams of supervisors to the schools to demonstrate the new techniques teachers are expected to adopt. But it is here that the nature of broadcast media suits them uniquely for solving the teacher up-grading problem. There is no need to gather teachers in a regional center nor to send teams into the schools when, from a central radio studio, upgrading lessons can be beamed to teachers throughout the nation. It is common practice in a variety of countries to organize the teachers in each school as a listening group that once or twice a week tunes in to a teacher-education broadcast. Following the broadcast, the group discusses how the content of that lesson could improve their own teaching. Even more valuable than radio programs are televised teacher-training lessons that demonstrate by sight and sound exactly how new instructional methods function in a classroom. Furthermore, audiotape and videotape equipment adds flexibility to such programs by enabling educators to record lessons for use at convenient times in the future. Thus, through broadcasts, teachers learn the new roles they are expected to play when radio and television programs are added to their classroom instructional tools.

Economic Factors

Lesson 12: Funding Requirements

Unless a society is prepared to bear the substantial recurring costs of education via radio and television, a broadcasting system cannot operate in an efficient manner.

In high-technology countries and Third World nations alike, the 1960s and early 1970s were the years of greatest enthusiasm for educational television. Among the most active advocates were a variety of international-aid organizations, philanthropic foundations, the foreign-aid offices of American and European governments, and international lending banks. These bodies help finance professional consultants, television transmission equipment, and television receivers for schools in order to get Third World nations started in broadcast education. As the years advanced, these foreign funding agencies expected the recipient nations to assume the continuing costs of those broadcast systems. However, the recipients were often not able, or at least not willing, to allocate the amounts of money needed to maintain the exensive equipment and to pay educational programming costs, much less to expand the facilities to care for additional segments of the population. One important aspect of the problem is that most of the equipment has had to be purchased abroad with foreign-exchange funds that are typically in short supply. Likewise, technical expertise must frequently be imported. Consequently, educational television in such settings has in recent years diminished or, in some instances, been abandoned entirely. For instance, financial problems of this sort contributed to the marked decline of instruction via television in American Samoa during the latter 1970s, as the US government was no longer prepared to supply funds to maintain the expensive broadcast-education system it had constructed in the mid-1960s. For a similar reason, the broadscale experiment with educational television in the African nation of Niger (214 television classrooms containing 9,000 primary children by the year 1975) was constrained by the nation's condition of poverty and by France's withdrawal of financial assistance to the project (Young *et al.*, 198: 54-56).

Lesson 13: Cost Effectiveness

Even when a society can bear the expense of instructional broadcasting, and even if students learn adequately under such a system, educational radio or television may not be adopted if the benefits fail to justify the expense.

This lesson is demonstrated in the case of the Ivory Coast. In the early 1970s that West African nation invested heavily in an educational television system aimed at improving pupils' language proficiency, reforming the curriculum, upgrading elementary-school teachers' skills, and generally bringing quality education to increasing numbers of learners. According to the plan, more classrooms each year would be equipped with television sets until all schools at all grade levels would be fully supplied by 1985. By 1976 over 322,000 pupils were receiving television instruction, a number that more than doubled by 1981 when there were 17,396 television receivers in classrooms, enough to accommodate 80 percent of the nation's 882,928 primary-school pupils. In the early years of the project, directors of the television system had reported that pupils following the televised lessons completed the six-grade primary curriculum far sooner than those following traditional classroom teaching. However, in contrast to this report, a 1981 evaluation of the project financed by Unesco and US-AID concluded that the original purposes of the television plan had not been achieved and that the cost for educating pupils via television was 80 percent higher than via traditional classroom methods. As a result of this disappointing cost-benefit assessment, the Ivory Coast in 1981 abandoned television education for primary-grade pupils (*Europa Yearbook*, 1983: 621).

Goals and Expectations

Two final lessons about conditions that influence the role assumed by educational broadcasting relate to the expectations people hold for what the media will accomplish.

Lesson 14: The Magnitude of Educational Progress

Proponents of educational broadcasting for developing nations may defeat the constructive role such broadcasting can play if the outcomes they promise are unreasonably optimistic.

An examination of the most publicized, broadscale applications of instructional television in developing nations suggests, at first glance, that generally they were failures. And, indeed, when compared with the visionary hopes their advocates held for the projects at their outset, many of the ventures did fail. The error in many of these cases was that the sponsors of the projects proposed massive changes in a nation's entire educational operation without sufficiently recognizing the magnitude of problems that would be faced. Such an error is not uncommon when the changes being suggested will require large expenditures and major disruptions of traditional administrative and instructional arrangements. In order to convince high-level government officials to provide the funds and accept the disruptions, the promoters of educational broadcasting are apt to exaggerate (either through poor foresight or mendacity) the benefits to be realized. When the predicted benefits do not appear, the resulting disappointment may cause officials to abandon educational broadcasting. Such apparently was the case in Niger, where originators of the television instructional scheme declared that within ten years of the project's inauguration, 30 percent of the nation's primary-age children would be taught by TV. But after ten years, only 10 percent of the children were receiving TV schooling (Young et al., 1980: 54-55). The Ivory-Coast plan likewise failed to fulfill the unduly optimistic promise that its formulators had predicted and was thus abandoned.

When such educational broadcasting projects are judged by less demanding standards than the original goals set for them, we may find that benefits did derive from the ventures and that they were not complete failures. For example, in a retrospective appraisal of the Niger program, Young (1980: 54-55) and his colleagues observed that:

> In 1964, 22 pilot classes started work. . . . By 1972, 510 of the original 800 children had graduated from primary school without ever having a face-to-face lesson from a trained teacher [since paraprofessional "monitors" rather than fully trained teachers supervised the television classrooms]. This proved that the system worked. Also remarkable was the children's attitude to learning. In traditional society in Niger the elders have authority, and children are expected to ask no questions; these children were taught to question, to find out for themselves, and were soon doing so enthusiastically. One of the things that made this possible was that the curriculum was closely tied to the children's environment. . . . the themes of the television programs fitted in with what was actually happening in the villages.

Therefore, if self-direction and initiative were among the objectives the plan was designed to foster, then to that extent the project was a success. (Of course, educational television is not the only medium through which such objectives might be achieved. A regular classroom teacher using an inquiry approach to instruction could also achieve such ends. Still, this does not negate the fact that television instruction in Niger did deserve credit for promoting pupil initiative.)

Lesson 15: A Transitional Role for Educational Broadcasting

The success of an educational broadcasting project may be found in its contribution to the evolution of an education system rather than in how permanently it dominates the instructional process.

In other words, the current condition of an education system may call for the use of radio or television as the central instrument of instruction. But as the educational system evolves, the welfare of learners may be better served by a new combination of instructional media that relegates radio and television to a subsidiary role.

This lesson is illustrated in the case of American Samoa, where the US government in the early 1960s attempted to immediately improve the islands' ramshackle elementary schools that were staffed by poorly trained instructors teaching an unsuitable curriculum. The government built 26 new elementary buildings equipped with television monitors that received lessons in virtually all subject-matter fields from a central studio on Pago Pago Bay. The television system was used not only as the dominant medium for teaching the children but also as a vehicle for upgrading the skills of classroom teachers. In such a pattern, education via television reached its height at the end of the 1960s. Throughout the 1970s its use declined until by the 1980s it served only occasionally to supplement the classroom teacher's instruction. Some observers of the Samoan experiment concluded that educational television had failed, because it did not continue permanently as the principal medium of instruction. However, when viewed from an historical perspective, television could be judged a success for its transitional functions. By the 1980s, few if any members of the Samoan educational establishment seemed to think that installing the instructional television project in the 1980s had been an error.

> The system furnished islanders with far better opportunities for learning English and better models of teaching, planning, and evaluating than they ever had before. The system also stimulated controversies about educational goals and methods—controversies that brought to Samoa additional teaching methodologies that could be compared with instructional television for their appropriateness in the Samoan setting. Numbers of these alternative approaches in science, mathematics, health education, the language arts, and bicultural education have since been adopted. . . . [Although] many innovations now in the schools have no necessary connection with instructional television, they are in the schools as a result of a catalytic function of the educational television experiment . . . (Thomas, 1980: 166).

Guidelines for Broadcast Education in Developing Societies

Our review of lessons derived from developing societies' experience with instructional broadcasting has suggested several guidelines that educators might adopt to better ensure the wise employment of radio and television in Third World nations. I am proposing that educational planners can profitably:

— Examine critically the assumption that broadcast media can drastically reform a country's educational system. But if broadcast media are to be adopted, they first should be tried out in a small-scale pilot project so that the development problems can be worked out at low cost and with as little disruption of the broader education system as possible.

— Offer modest predictions of what outcomes might be expected, and describe the project as an experiment rather than as a venture which is bound to produce startling educational results.

— At the outset, establish methods of evaluating each step in the development process as well as methods of determining the cost effectiveness of the broadcast media.

— Estimate the diverse ways that educational radio or TV might be combined with other educational resources to achieve the country's educational goals, including ways that alternative uses of these technologies might suit the needs of different populations in the society.

— Assess the short-term and long-term impact of the imported technology on the cultural, economic, and political autonomy of the country, including the overall effect of these media in raising and fulfilling expectations of the populace without disturbing the country's sociopolitical stability.

References

Aziz, A. & Chew, T. Y. (1980) Malaysia. In T. Neville Postlethwaite & R. Murray Thomas (eds.). *Schooling in the ASEAN Region*. Oxford: Pergamon.

Batmaz, Veysel & Wagner, Daniel A. (1985) *The Effects of Television Exposure on School Achievement: A Moroccan Case Study*. Paper presented at the Comparative and International Education Society's annual conference. Stanford University, April 18-20.

Blume, Wilbur T. & Schneller, Paul (1984) *Toward International Tele-Education*. Boulder, Colorado: Westview.

Europa Yearbook (1983) London: Europa Publications.

Friend, Jamesine E. (1985) *Teaching Reading by Radio in the Dominican Republic*. Paper presented at the Comparative and International Education Society's annual conference. Stanford University, April 18-20.

Fry, Mary (1985) *Development, Languages, and the Radio*. Paper presented at the Comparative and International Education Society's annual conference. Stanford University, April 18-20.

Meadowcroft, Jean H. (1985) *Teaching by Radio: Mathematics, Language Arts, Science, and Community Education*. Paper presented at the Comparative and International Education Society's annual conference. Stanford University, April 18-20.

Schramm, Wilbur, Nelson, Lyle M. & Betham, Mere T. (1981) *Bold Experiment: The Story of Educational Television in American Samoa*. Stanford, California: Stanford University Press.

Thomas, R. Murray (1986) Malaysia, *Education and Urban Society*, **18** (4), pp. 399-411.

Thomas, R. Murray (1980) The rise and decline of an educational technology: television in American Samoa, *ECTJ*, **28** (3), pp. 155-167.

Young, Michael, Perraton, Hilary, Jenkins, Janet & Dodds, Tony (1980) *Distance Teaching for the Third World*. London: Routledge and Kegan Paul.

PART III: EDUCATIONAL PRINT MATERIALS

An Example of Diverse Perceptions of Technology Transfer

The practice of using the written word to serve educational purposes goes back thousands of years. Ancient people graved historical records, genealogies, and laws into stone tablets. Then, beginning at least 4,000 years ago, the Egyptians wrote on papyrus, a writing surface they manufactured by gluing together thin layers of the filmy inner stem of papyrus reeds in order to produce long scrolls. In other cultures, historical accounts and business transactions were recorded on bark. In the Indonesian archipelago, literary works and the lineage of kings were written on lontar leaves. And, according to legend, the Chinese wrote on flat pieces of bamboo or on silk fabric until an emperor around 100 AD ordered one of his courtiers, Ts'ai Lun, to discover a more convenient writing medium. Ts'ai Lun is said to have fulfilled his commission by matting together the beaten fibers from the inner bark of the mulberry tree, thereby inventing paper. Although the types of fibers and the machinery for making paper have changed over the past two millennia, the basic principle of paper manufacturing remains the same today (Boyce & Every, 1959: 258).

In these early times, the primitive state of technology necessarily limited the educational use of written products, since reading materials were available only to a few scholars. Books had to be copied by hand, a laborious process that made reading matter very expensive, and the copying process often resulted in inaccurate reproductions of the original works. Not until movable type was adopted for book production in fifteenth-century Europe did the possibility of widespread literacy and dissemination of knowledge become a reality.

Johann Gutenberg (1400?-1468?) of Mainz, Germany, has been credited with playing a major role in bringing the mass printing of books to fruition. It was Gutenberg who achieved the practical application of the idea of movable type. Prior to his time, block printing had been practiced to a limited extent in Europe, such as in the production of playing cards. The face of a flat wooden block would be carved to form a card's image; and when ink was applied to the carved surface, the image could be printed time and again to produce identical cards. However, individual blocks were never assembled to form a page of print until Gutenberg applied the block-printing principle to creating individual letters of the alphabet. Each letter was carved on the top of a small block or *punch*, with all the small blocks cut to an identical height. The resulting *stamps* or *type letters* could then be used over and over again, reassembled in different sequences to produce each new page of print.

The Koreans and Chinese had already experimented with wood, pottery, and tin for producing printing blocks that could thus be assembled to form a printed page. However, their Oriental movable-type technology was never put to great use because so many blocks were needed to represent the thousands of ideographs in Chinese writing, and the Chinese never developed a suitable ink nor an efficient press for printing in large quantities (Denman, 1959: 593).

The success that Gutenberg and his colleagues achieved in launching modern-day mass printing was due not simply to the invention of movable type. It was due also to the confluence of a series of related technological achievements—the creation of a sufficiently tacky ink, of a way to apply ink to the type face, of a suitable printing press, and of a means for positioning paper on the type. Then, from the mid-fifteenth century on, the book-printing industry spread quickly through Europe. Improvements in type-face design, the casting of type, the construction of printing presses, the manufacture of paper, and the binding of books contributed to an accelerated dissemination of literacy and, consequently, to the spread of knowledge. As a result, mass education as we know it today was made possible by the advances in print technology.

The Advent of the Textbook

The earliest printed books were the Bible, religious tracts, law codes, histories, geographies, essays on philosophy and natural science, and works of biography, poetry, and drama. All of these had an educational function. But not until the sixteenth century did the progenitor of the modern-day textbook appear in Western culture. Westbury (1985: 5235) has identified two periods in the history of textbooks. The first appeared in the sixteenth and seventeenth centuries "when the technology of the printed textbook and vernacular instruction emerged and found a relatively fixed form."

Writers such as Comenius (Komensky) (1592-1670) developed textbooks which used pictures and carefully developed layouts to support equally carefully developed instructional text. His *Orbis sensualium picturs* (1658) remained in print for more than 200 years as a basic school textbook. The overall forms of these textbooks are still widely used. At the same time numberless primers were developed for basic catechetical and secular instruction; again, the basic form of these texts was to remain constant for 200 or more years and came to define the nature of the modern primer (Westbury, 1985: 5235).

Subsequently, during the second historical period, covering the nineteenth and twentieth centuries, textbooks established themselves as the chief determinants of the structure of curricula and teaching. As national education systems evolved, the pattern of instruction in elementary schools was set by graded textbooks in an ordered sequence. Likewise, in secondary schools a rather limited number of texts standardized the subjects to be taught and their content. Today, textbooks continue to be the dominant form of educational print material. However, a variety of other print media also play a role in teaching and learning.

One common variant of the traditional textbook is the workbook or worksheet that requires students to write the solution to problems posed about the subject they are studying. Frequently the workbook assumes a supplementary role to a textbook; information about a subject is first explained in the textbook, and then students apply this information by performing tasks presented in the accompanying workbook. The advantages of the workbook over the traditional text are that the workbook requires students to practice what they have studied, and their solutions to the workbook problems reveal how well they have mastered the learning goals.

Other print media use for instruction include newspapers, magazines, technical journals, pamphlets, how-to-do-it handbooks, dictionaries, atlases, encyclopedias, collections of short stories, and novels. One advantage that teachers in more affluent societies have over teachers in less-developed regions is the greater availability of print materials that can extend students' learning resources beyond the basic textbook.

The Uneven Availability of Print Media

Some notion of the discrepancy among different regions of the world in the availability of printed material is reflected by the number of different book titles—including textbooks—published each year. The top section of Table III.1 shows the number of new titles by regions for representative years. The middle section shows the number of titles per one million inhabitants. The bottom shows the discrepancy in number of titles between developed and developing countries. As the figures indicate, for the world as a whole during the 1955-1983 period, there was a steady increase in both the absolute number of titles available and the number of titles per one million people. There were 187 percent more titles issued in 1983 than in 1955. However, because of the rapid population growth over this period, the number of titles per million inhabitants increased only 26 percent. Over this same twenty-eight year span the developed nations continued to be far ahead of developing ones on book titles. However, the rate of increase in developing regions (334 percent) exceeded that in the developed regions (158 percent) in the total number of titles. But because of the higher population-growth rate in developing countries, the increase in titles-per-million-people in developed countries (96 percent) was more than double the percentage of the increase in developing nations (45 percent).

TABLE I.1. *Book Production by Regions of the World*

| | Number of Titles | | | |
	1955	1965	1975	1983
World Total	269,000	426,000	572,000	772,000
Africa	3,000	7,000	11,000	13,000
Northern America	14,000	58,000	92,000	105,000
Latin America	11,000	19,000	29,000	47,000
Asia	54,000	61,000	88,000	176,000
Europe (inc. U.S.S.R.)	186,000	260,000	343,000	419,000
Oceania	1,000	5,000	9,000	12,000

| | Number of Titles per Million Inhabitants | | | |
	1955	1965	1975	1983
World Total	131	168	184	165
Africa	13	23	27	25
Northern America	77	271	389	405
Latin America	60	77	89	121
Asia	64	57	65	64
Europe (inc. U.S.S.R.)	307	385	471	551
Oceania	68	286	428	500

| | Developed versus Developing Countries | | | |
	1955	1965	1975	1983
Numbers of Titles				
Developed Countries	225,000	366,000	484,000	581,000
Developing Countries	44,000	60,000	88,000	191,000
Per Million Inhabitants				
Developed Countries	249	357	431	487
Developing Countries	38	40	45	55

Source: *Statistical Yearbook*. (1985) Paris: Unesco, p. VI-11.

Thus, as the variety of books available in the world has grown steadily over the past few decades, the more advanced industrial societies have continued to experience far greater advantages in the availability of titles than have the less developed nations.

Educational Uses of Print Media

Textbooks, like other printed material, can play various roles in the process of instruction. The most common conception of a textbook, in the eyes of both teachers and students, is that it contains authoritative knowledge. The text's contents are not only true, but they are of such great value that learners should commit them to memory. A second conception of textbooks is that they offer records of prior events which will influence future events, so textbooks can help learners envision the future. From a third perspective, a textbook reflects a particular viewpoint or set of values from which to perceive life. As a consequence, the task of learners becomes that of analyzing the contents of the text in order to estimate how the contents could have been different if the book had been written from a different viewpoint or based on a different set of assumptions and values. Whichever of these three perspectives a teacher adopts will clearly result in quite different ways that learners use printed materials in studying national and world history, the social and physical sciences, health education, religion, art, music, and the like.

Not only are there differences between more-developed and less-developed societies in the amount and diversity of print media, but there are also differences in the extent to which teachers use print materials in varied ways. Professional literature about teaching methodology suggests that in such countries as Great Britain, Sweden, and the United States teachers more often use texts and supplementary reading matter in a greater variety of ways than do teachers in typical developing societies. This difference would appear to be not only the result of greater amounts of diverse reading materials in the more developed areas, but also a result of greater impetus to create new uses (new *operating systems*) in the more-developed nations than in less-developed ones.

The Modern-day Revolution in Publishing

If the word *revolution* is used to mean extremely sudden change, then the term is properly applied to the present-day state of the publishing industry. The kinds of changes in publishing over the past century, and the resulting implications for the conduct of education, can perhaps best be illustrated by our inspecting the process of publishing a book or a periodical during four representative years: 1888, 1968, 1988, and 2008. Of the changes that appeared over the 1888-1988 period, the most dramatic came in the 1970s and 1980s as computer technology was applied to all stages of the publishing operation.

For each of the four representative years, we will describe the basic steps in book publishing and distribution that were regarded as the *state of the art* of the times—with the phrase *state of the art* referring to the most up-to-date practices in common use by the more progressive publishers in advanced industrialized societies. Of particular importance in this chronological review is the fact that some place in the world today, publishing practices typical of each of the first two representative years are still found. In other words, there are publishers today who still employ technology typical of 1888 and 1968 and of the years in between. And as might be expected, the older publishing practices are more prominent in developing nations than in advanced-technological societies.

For each of the four time points we will identify how the following twelve steps of the book publishing-and-distributing process would typically be carried out:

1. *Author Creates.* An author (or authors) writes and corrects the draft of a manuscript.
2. *Manuscript Submitted.* The author prepares the manuscript in the form suitable for submission to the publisher.
3. *Editor Consults Experts.* At the publishing company, an editor sends a copy of the manuscript to experts from the author's subject-matter field in order to learn the experts' opinions about the contents and style of the manuscript.
4. *Manuscript Revised.* If on the basis of the editor's and experts' opinions the manuscript should be improved, the manuscript is sent back to the author for revision.
5. *Manuscript Copy-Edited.* After the revisions, a copy-editor at the publishing company makes any improvements that seem necessary in the manuscript's organization and phrasing. The copy-editor also marks the manuscript with symbols that inform ·the printer of the desired kinds of headings, sizes of type, and placement of the printed material.
6. *Manuscript Cast in Type.* The copy-edited manuscript may be returned to the author for his or her approval before it is be sent to the printing plant to be composed in type, ready for printing. Or else the manuscript is sent directly to the printer.
7. *Proofs Printed.* After it is composed in type, the material is printed in a tentative form called galley proofs (continuous printing of type, not yet divided into pages) or page proofs (the material arranged in the numbered pages that will appear in the final book). The proofs are sent to the author to correct any mistakes made during the typesetting process.
8. *Book Printed.* After the page proofs are corrected, the book is printed on a press.
9. *Book Bound.* The printed pages are put in proper order, and the

book is bound in either a hardback or a paperback cover.
10. *Book Advertised.* Before the books were yet printed and bound, the publisher's advertising department had already informed bookstores, educational institutions, and individuals that such a book would soon be available.
11. *Book Distributed.* Books are shipped to bookstores and schools that have ordered them.
12. *Readers Receive Book.* Readers obtain the books by purchasing them at the bookstores or directly from a publisher. Or, in the case of students, the books may be obtained from the school or a library.

Consider now how this 12-step process would typically be carried out in each of the four selected years.

Book Publishing in 1888

During this era authors submitted handwritten manuscripts to publishers, outside reviewers sent the publishers their handwritten opinions of manuscripts, and editors marked the manuscripts by hand. As a result, the printer who would set the material in type worked from handwritten copy. Typesetting was a laborious process, requiring that the printer choose each letter by hand from a type case and place the metal letters one by one in proper sequence in a small hand-held container. The resulting lines of individual letters were subsequently locked within a metal frame to form a full page of type, and a tentative *proof print* was made and sent to the author so that any errors could be repaired. When the corrected proofs were received from the author and further corrected by the publisher's proof readers, the pages of type were placed in a printing press, ink rolled onto the type faces, and the pages printed onto paper. To produce a book, the printed pages were next arranged in order, the pages bound together by sewing and gluing at the book's spine, and a cover attached.

As a means of distributing books, publishers advertised their wares by brochures sent in the mail, by announcements in the public press, and by the visits of travelling sales representatives. Books were then shipped to bookstores, educational institutions, and individual purchasers by mail, by train, or by horse-drawn wagon.

The 1880s witnessed the advent of three machines—the typewriter, the linotype, and the monotype—that would significantly affect the publishing industry over the coming decades. However, none of the three were in widespread use by 1888. The Remington Arms Company in America barely began selling typewriters commercially in the 1880s, so that typewriters were still a rarity in the world of publishing. The linotype machine was invented in 1886, enabling an operator to compose entire lines of metal type simply by entering the contents of a manuscript at a keyboard. The Lanston monotype was introduced at the same time for the assembly of justified lines of individually-cast type characters. But because linotype and monotype machines were not generally available by 1888, the single pieces of type respresenting individual letters still had to be set by hand.

Publishing in 1968

By the mid-twentieth century, authors were expected to submit manuscripts to the publisher in typewritten form. Many authors now used a typewriter to compose the original drafts of their work. Many others, however, still wrote their original drafts by hand, then had a stenographer prepare a typewritten version for the publisher. Outside reviewers of manuscripts submitted their opinions to the publisher either in typewritten or in handwritten form. Copy-editors added their own handwritten revisions to the manuscript before it was sent to the printer. A linotype operator set the bulk of the manuscript in type, while special pages—such as the title page—could be set by hand in a special size or style of type. A compositor in charge of the book's *layout* next arranged the lines of type, plus such illustrations as photographs or drawings, to form each individual page, and placed the pages in order. Proofs were mailed to authors, with the request that they write their corrections by hand in the margins of the pages. When the proofs were returned to the publisher, any errors in the typesetting were corrected. The pages were subsequently printed on a press, which could be one of several varieties—a flatbed letter press, a cylinder letter press, a rotary press, or others. The pages were finally bound, ready for the market.

The methods of advertising a book in 1968 were basically those used in 1888, although they had become far more sophisticated. Brochures and catalogues were sent through the mail, announcements were published in the public press (even on radio and television in modest measure) and in professional journals, and travelling sales representatives visited bookstores and schools. In addition, book fairs and exhibits at publishing conventions and educational conferences had become a popular mode of informing potential buyers of a book's or periodical's availability. Readers then bought the print materials from stores or through the mail.

Compared with the late nineteenth century, publishing a book or journal in 1968 was far faster, resulted in a higher-quality product, and involved somewhat less hand work. Typesetting was mechanized, and printing technology offered more options, such as full-color illustrations.

Publishing in 1988

Remarkable innovations in publishing practices during the 1970s suddenly appeared, then increased at an accelerating rate in the 1980s, principally because electronic computers and laser technology were applied at
so many stages of producing and distributing books and periodicals. By
1988 authors had two main options for bringing their works to the
reading audience: (1) sending their manuscripts to a publisher and (2)
printing the material themselves by means of *desk-top publishing*. We
shall inspect the process that each of these options typically involved.

New Processes in Professional Publishing

Up-to-date authors no longer wrote by hand or with a typewriter.
Instead, they composed their works on a microcomputer that utilized a
word-processing program. This provided the author the freedom of
writing a manuscript in bits and pieces which could be quickly assembled
in any desired sequence as the work developed. Paragraphs were easily
shifted from one place to another, sentences rephrased, spelling checked
automatically, the bibliography and footnotes assembled in proper order
as the manuscript evolved, an index created, and tabular material and
illustrations inserted. Each day's work on the manuscript was stored
magnetically on a small disk that could hold the entire contents of a
textbook or an entire issue of a professional journal. The author then
could print out the final result as a flawless document, with as many
copies as desired.

Authors using word-processing programs on their desktop computers
could then choose among three main ways of submitting their manuscripts to the publisher. One was simply to send a typescript, as hereto-
fore, except that it would have been produced by a computer printer (as
a print-out) rather than on a typewriter, and it might appear in a form
which more nearly resembled the desired end (typeset) product because
of the greater flexibility of the computer printer. A second alternative
was to send the manuscript on a computer disk, along with a print-out
for verification and error checking. A third way was to transmit the
disk's contents over the telephone line, directly from the author's computer into the publisher's computer. In the latter two instances the
purpose was to provide the document to the publisher in a "machine-
readable" form so that the typesetting process could be expedited and
might also be more economical.

At the publishing house, more and more editors began to work with
computers to help them with their editing functions. While manuscripts
were still read and marked, often with inks or pencils of different colors
to indicate different readers or different editing steps, computer-aided

editing capabilities were also being relied upon to perform such functions as spelling checks, syntax analysis, and tests to ascertain the level of reading difficulty in relation to the requirements of the intended readership. Other functions, such as indexing and word searches (to ascertain whether a new term was properly defined when introduced), were also possible.

Some manuscripts were still presented by the author in a traditional typewritten form. If this was the case, publishers often arranged to convert the typescripts into machine-readable form to facilitate the editing process and/or to reduce the cost of the final typesetting. Such conversion was accomplished by the use of optical character recognition (OCR), a process whereby each individual typescript character is identified and encoded, often by a machine and program sufficiently powerful that it would be trained to recognize typescript characters of varying designs and perhaps also to identify different type styles and to preserve such distinctions for appropriate treatment in the typesetting process.

The publisher also had several options available for obtaining an opinion about the manuscript from experts outside the publishing house. The most common method in 1988 was still that of mailing a photocopy of the document to the outside evaluator, but facsimile transmission via the telephone line was also possible, so that a manuscript already containing editors' markings could be received by the reviewer who, in turn, could make his or her own marks, and "fax" back a copy of the document. Or, alternatively, the document, in machine-readable form, could be transmitted to the reviewer who could change it (identifying his or her comments and corrections with agreed-upon encoding) and send it back to the editorial office in the same fashion from the reviewer's own desktop computer.

With documents in machine-readable form, publishers also had more options for the preparation of galleys and final pages. Instead of relying upon trade typesetting houses, many publishers found it advantageous to produce final typeset pages, again sending to authors computer-produced galleys or page proofs for review. Various typesetting options were available, with coarser and more economical imaging sometimes used for review/approval stages (proofs), and high-resolution output selected for final reproduction. Moreover, various forms of illustrative material, prepared by the author or skilled illustrators, could be incorporated into the output and "typeset" by raster-imaging devices at the same time that letters and words were formed on the paper or on film intended for the printing plate-making process.

And yet one other option was available, which was to bypass the traditional printing process altogether—especially for smaller quantities for limited readerships—and to create the final images (both the type and illustrations) directly upon the sheets of paper that would be bound into pamphlet or book by a process in which the imaging device could produce multiple copies, in consecutive page sequence, with sufficient speed and economy to avoid recourse to the printing press.

More and more emphasis was placed by publishers on the machine-readability of the author's and illustrator's material. This was true for several reasons:

1. It would be easier and more economical to update and revise the document at a later date, without having to go through all of the earlier, preparatory stages.

2. Simultaneous or subsequent publication could take place in several formats (different page sizes, different type faces and sizes, or in condensed or enhanced versions), again without the need to re-key, proof-read, correct, and verify, and with significant reductions in the publication cycle.

3. "Alternative publication" opportunities were also available through storing the document on a computer data base which could be accessed and searched remotely by the scholarly community from their own desktop computers via the phone line, and copies of the document or relevant portions could also be printed out remotely.

4. Increasing use was made, at many levels, in "raster image processing", a technique which permits the output of text and graphics as tiny dots of black laid down across the width of a page, regardless of how the type and pictures are arranged. These images can be inspected on an interactive display screen, manipulated and re-positioned, and then output in print at varying resolutions (fineness of detail), ranging from rough proof copy of 100 to 300 dots per inch to a final highly precise printing image at from 1000 to 3000 dots per inch.

5. And finally, in machine-readable form it would be easier to take advantage of subsequent technological developments not yet practical or in general use in 1988, such as CD Roms or other techniques for the compressed storage of information.

But, on the whole, in the year 1988, no profound changes had as yet been made in the printing, binding, advertising, and distribution of finished products. Publishers were apprehensive that such changes would come about, and they followed developments in the new field of desktop publishing for some indication for what might result from emerging technology.

Desktop Publishing

Just as authors in the 1980s began to find compelling reasons for the use of computers in the preparation of material for publication through traditional sources, so they began to explore the creation of new publishing opportunities. There was a great deal of interest by 1988 in "publishing from the desktop." This concept was poorly defined, but it suggested that writers could now become their own publishers since they would have, on their desktops, sufficient computer power to control all or most of the mechanics of the traditional publishing process. They not only had the power and convenience of "word processing," but also the ability to "typeset" directly on paper, with columns appropriately justified to right and left margins, with proportionately-spaced type, and even with type characters derived from the designs of recognized artists and craftsmen—Helvetica, Bodoni, Caslon, Century Schoolbook, or virtually any of hundreds of faces, sizes, and styles. They also had the ability to create their own art work, to size it, to manipulate it in various ways, and to blend it into attractively designed pages, using computer programs which sought to capture the best of the established traditions of the graphics arts industry.

While many individual writers lacked the interest and skill to take advantage of some of these new tools, small networks or teams could easily be formed, almost spontaneously, and the networking of desktop computers made it possible for people with specialized skills and interests to participate in an interactive publication process, which became both "democratized" and compartmentalized. Publishing thus started to become a relatively informal desktop function rather than an institutional arrangement. It was widely believed that new marketing and distribution arrangements would emerge, but no one was clear about what they would be or about what role the traditional publisher would assume.

There was uncertainty as to what further changes would take place as a result of the influence of "electronics" (computers, lasers, telecommunications, satellite transmission, video recording, and the like) upon traditional publishing activities. For example, would facsimile print-out devices in the home provide the principal method of distributing printed news that would come to the home computer via the telephone line? Would such newspapers be printed on demand? Would they be printed in their entirety or would the reader ask only to see selected items in "hard copy" form (printed on paper)? If advertising provides the revenue source which makes the newspaper profitable or economical, how would these revenues fare if classified and display ads could be accessed only on a selective basis rather than packaged in a newspaper in which the editorial matter constitutes merely the "newshole"? And what about other sorts of learning materials, such as textbooks and workbooks? Could they be "ordered up" piecemeal via the telephone line or satellite from a source remote from the school or home, with the portions needed for this week's lessons printed out on the teacher's or student's microcomputer? Or, would the lesson simply be called-up on each student's microcomputer so there would be no need to print it out on paper?

Publishing in 2008

Trends in publishing in the 1980s appeared to foreshadow what the near future had in store. It is to this task of speculating about advances in educational print media that we now turn. Our guide question then becomes: What might we expect from state-of-the-art print media and other reading matter by the year 2008? And beyond that, what will happen to the entire process of publishing and disseminating educational materials?

First of all, it must be said that we perceive of the 1980s and the early 1990s as representing a turning point not only in the various fields associated with publishing, but in society generally. At least two contrasing scenarios, (A) and (B), seem possible:

(A) In such industrialized nations as the United States and Britain, if present economic conditions continue (involving the virtual elimination of the middle class) due to the decline in domestic industrial production, to competition from abroad, to the growth of a lower-income service sector, and to the increasing concentration of income in the hands of the intellectually elite, we will have a society in which powerful tools for communication, publishing, and education generally will be directed toward a privileged class that can afford the necessary technology. For the larger number in the lower and underprivileged classes, there will be less need for reading and less value imputed to formal education. Encapsulated information programs will be interspersed with the games and circuses of television—or its successor medium—in a form which will make information more or less indistinguishable from commercial advertising.

(B) Alternatively, the Western world, and the United States in particular, could suddenly shift its direction and seek to develop its primary resources—its people—in a fashion that would result in a redistribution of income and opportunity, a change in the concepts of work and individual identity, and a new outlook on the value of continuing education, from birth to the end of a significantly increased lifespan.

Authors writing about the second possibility—(B)—think that option (A) is more likely to be followed. But it is nevertheless the function of the educator to devote his or her skill, persuasiveness, and energy toward the pursuit of the second and more attractive option (B) if, indeed, it is not too late for such an opportunity to exist.

Whether or not the reader agrees with this estimate of the future, it should be evident that technology will be profoundly shaped by the course that our civilization—either by conscious processes or by the absence of policy—elects to pursue. Here are some of the possibilities as we see them:

Computers and other electronic technologies will make it possible for vast quantities of information to be stored on the desktop, including training materials which incorporate text, graphs, and sound in a highly interactive manner.

It will not only be information that is stored, but expert systems will be stored as well. These systems will represent procedures which have been developed over the centuries—questions to be asked in certain circumstances, then investigations to be made depending upon the answers and responses elicited. These systems (involving hardware, but of more importance, software) will be known as "knowledge tools" and will be constantly enhanced and improved so that the latest research findings can be incorporated into a seamless structure that can begin at the lowest level of communication and progress to the highest.

These developments will mean increasing use of mixed media (computers, videodiscs, television, and other newer devices) and teaching and learning systems in which the learner interacts with the electronic media, not only in the formal years of education but throughout the life span.

The human interface with desktop systems will pose no particular problems of "computer literacy," for the ability to use computers as knowledge tools and not merely for hypnotic games will emerge from the relative ease with which system designers make it possible to communicate with other people in a network environment but with the outside world as well.

In general, those who communicate successfully will tend to take advantage of all the facilities which the desktop system can provide. Most published works will be created on desktop systems. Most documents will be stored or accessible through desktop systems, and formal publishing through the print media will rely heavily upon improvements in the speed and resolution of output devices driven by raster image processors that are capable of handling text and graphic material simultaneously, producing multiple copies at significantly higher speeds.

There will be comparable changes in the development of printing presses, so that the distinction between a product which resembles an office copying machine and one which resembles a high-speed newspaper web press will gradually diminish.

Effective means of packaging and binding will lag. But ultimately methods of collating sheets and enclosing them within the covers of a book will encourage and facilitate the printing of small quantities of products at local outlets, such as retail stores. This will be like "demand printing" but will represent some sort of compromise that will deal more effectively with the major marketing problems in today's world, particularly with the matter of how to have books and other published materials available where desired and when needed.

Nevertheless, the tools required to provide these resources will not be inexpensive. It seems to be true that today's poor can afford television sets, at least in the advanced industrialized nations. It is less likely to be true that tomorrow's poor will have access to desktop systems and the supporting communication lines. To provide the continuing education that will be required, other means will need to be created to provide such access. Libraries, schools, clubs, and other agencies of continuing education will become more and more essential. However, printed media will still be widely used because of its portability and general convenience. What will be printed out, however, will be only those portions of documents considered relevant by the learners and their instructors.

Obviously this estimated trend will raise even more profound questions about copyright protection and author and publisher compensation, questions which will need to be addressed in novel ways that somehow reflect the extent of usage of such tools and materials.

Conclusion

The overview offered in this introduction to Part III has been designed to provide a foundation for the matters discussed in Chapters 6 and 7. We have seen how the publishing industry evolved to the level of sophistication achieved by the late 1980s in advanced industrial societies. A question now may be asked about what effect such technological progress may have on the availability of educational print materials—particularly of textbooks—in developing societies. Or, stated another way, what conditions in the relationship between more-developed and less-developed societies influence the transfer of print technology to developing nations? This is the question on which the authors of Chapters 6 and 7 have centered their attention.

As mentioned earlier, in each of the four parts of this volume, we adopt a different mode of viewing the matter of educational-technology development and transfer. The mode illustrated in Part III is that of diverse viewpoints toward technological transfer. The analysis in Chapter 6 is from the perspective of an educator from an advanced industrial nation—Professor Altbach of the United States, who has for some years studied educational publishing in the Third World. The analysis of this same issue in Chapter 7 is from the viewpoint of an educator in a formerly colonized, currently-developing society—Professor Gopinathan of the Republic of Singapore. Their contributions demonstrate the usefulness of viewing matters of technological transfer from diverse perspectives.

R. Murray Thomas and John W. Seybold

References

Boyce, D. W. & Every, D. (1959) Paper. In *The Encyclopedia Americana* (Vol. 21). New
   York: Americana Corporation.
Denman, F. (1959) Printing. In *The Encyclopedia Americana* (Vol. 22). New York:
   Americana Corporation.
Unesco (1985) *Statistical Yearbook 1985*. Paris: Unesco.
Westbury, I. (1985) Textbooks, history of. In Torsten Husen & T. Neville Postlethwaite,
   International Encyclopedia of Education (Vol. 9). Oxford: Pergamon.

CHAPTER 6

Textbooks in Comparative Context

PHILIP G. ALTBACH

In an age of computers and satellite communications, the most powerful and pervasive educational technology is the textbook. Even in classrooms where "computer literacy" is the watchword, textbooks are used, and there is little evidence so far that their influence has declined. For most of the world's schoolchildren, the textbook remains the basic element of education, the essential companion to the teacher. And in many countries, the provision of textbooks is a challenge. This essay reflects on the provision of textbooks, focusing mainly on the Third World in an effort to provide a broad comparative context in which to understand how texts are developed and distributed.

It is generally agreed that textbooks are an essential part of the educational enterprise (Heyneman, *et al.*, 1978). Yet, there has been little analysis of how textbooks are developed, produced, and distributed. The situation is particularly unclear in the Third World, where texts are especially important to effective schooling. In many countries, teachers are poorly trained and texts are essential educational aids. Yet, in the very countries where they are most needed, textbooks are frequently in short supply. The problems are daunting. Creating an effective textbook requires a combination of skills and a knowledge base. Producing textbooks requires technologies which are widespread and relatively inexpensive, yet in short supply in many areas. The distribution of textbooks constitutes another set of challenges. And the effective integration of textbooks into the schools requires that teachers know how to use them. Thus, the "textbook infrastructure" is a complex one (Neumann, 1980).

Textbooks serve several important functions in schooling. It is worthwhile to outline some of them in order to understand their role in the Third World. Textbooks, in many respects, circumscribe a curriculum (Kumar, 1981 and Kumar, 1986). They define what is to be learned, and the teachers must be well trained and well informed to go beyond a text. Textbooks provide essential facts and techniques for learning guidelines for a subject. Textbooks, along with lesson plans, are among the main ways of ensuring that the curriculum that has been designed is actually used in the classroom. Textbooks, in many contexts, provide key supplementary material, including information, tests, bibliographies, and study guides which permit students to go beyond the minimal curriculum.

In the Third World, textbooks are overwhelmingly important (Altbach, 1983). The text is very frequently the *only* book that a student uses, and the goal of one book per student has eluded many countries. The text is the link between the student and the wider world of learning. In situations where the teacher is not well trained and does not have access to additional educational materials, to guidance on teaching techniques, or to up-to-date information, the textbook is a major resource in the classroom. The goal of providing an adequate number of texts to Third World students remains to be achieved. Creating effective textbooks is also a challenge. Curricular, political, and economic decisions go into the development of a textbook. The infrastructures of publishing are also needed, since even the best ideas must be transformed into books, which must then be distributed to the appropriate classrooms (Gopinathan, 1983).

Textbooks are, in a way, an illustration of national will and of national policy in many countries. In fields like history and social studies, texts communicate the polity. Even in scientific subjects, the examples used and the approaches to the curriculum reflect societal elements. Thus, textbooks assume considerable importance and are sometimes the subject of controversy. When Japan altered the interpretation of the World War II in its textbooks, there were protests, and even street demonstrations, in China and South Korea. In the United States, debates about religion and science have affected textbook development (Bernstein, 1985). In the Third World, textbooks provide an opportunity to develop a coherent approach to national history. The content of such books is a matter of concern to educators and politicians, with content issues occasionally erupting into public controversy or even international disputes. Textbooks, in other words, are important far beyond the confines of the classroom.

This essay discusses the complex nexus of relationships that relate to the development, production, and distribution of textbooks. It will consider the international ramifications of text development, the domestic network that is necessary to produce a text, and the current issues of concern to textbook planners. The textbook is an ideal case study of how the development of a key element of the contemporary school is dependent on many forces, within and outside of the educational system.

Third World Textbooks in International Context

International factors affect the development and use of textbooks in the Third World. There is a powerful international knowledge network that communicates research, new educational trends, and information of all kinds. This network includes internationally circulated books and journals (Altbach, 1987). Recently, computer data bases that are transmitted by satellites have also become an integral part of the network. Technical assistance by experts in many fields, including education, is also within the network. The international knowledge network is characterized by considerable inequalities, with the Third World dependent in many respects on the industrialized nations.

On the surface, textbooks are the result of basic decisions within countries and are the result of independent judgments. But realities are much more complex. Many Third World texts are related to international trends in research and curriculum. External forces play a key role in text development. Until fairly recently, many school textbooks were imported from abroad. Such imported books naturally reflected the orientations and values of the country of publication. Frequently, these books were part of the colonial heritage (Kumar, 1986). Very few countries today import school-level textbooks, but elements of the colonial experience remain. The issue of the language, for example, is a difficult one in many Third World nations. Some still use the colonial language for textbooks, although most have gradually, and with considerable difficulty and expense, shifted to one or more indigenous languages. The commitment to provide primary education in the national language or mother tongue is widespread in the Third World, but in the field of textbook development, the implementation of this commitment has been a very difficult one. Even where the language has been indigenized, it is sometimes the case that the content of the books remains "foreign" to some extent. It has not been possible to prepare entirely new books in all fields, and translation with some adaptation to local circumstances has been widespread. As books are revised and updated, the indigenous content and orientations are strengthened and books are becoming more relevant to local needs. Nevertheless, the colonial heritage has had a lasting influence throughout the Third World (Kumar, 1986).

In the contemporary world, many of the innovations in currculum and in instructional design emanate from the industrialized nations. These ideas are communicated through the major internationally circulated journals and are frequently stressed by the international aid agencies. Some of the innovations have proved to be less than successful, such as the "New Math" or instructional television. Yet, they were quickly communicated to the Third World and adopted in some countries because they were seen as the most modern innovations to be developed by the world's educational leaders. Many other innovations, of course, were much more successful and were worthy of adpatation to Third World needs. The point here is that many major curricular developments originate in the industrialzed nations and are exported to the Third World. Such curricular innovations have major relevance to textbook development, as they are quickly incorporated in instructional programs and into textbooks as well.

New trends in textbook design and development also occur in the industrialized nations, and they are quickly incorporated by publishers in order to serve local school systems (Apple, 1984). This frequently means that Third World nations, in order to take advantage of innovations, must obtain permission from Western publishers for the use of materials. This permission is sometimes difficult to obtain and often requires the payment of fees. International copyright regulations make it difficult to quickly move on a textbook project. The "compulsory licensing" stipulation in international copyright has eased the process of using foreign materials in Third World textbooks, but there are both time and bureaucratic problems involved (Altbach, 1986).

The most advanced printing equipment and photocomposition equipment is produced in the industrialized nations and must be imported by Third World nations. This equipment is particularly useful for textbooks, which must often be printed in large quantities and could benefit from the economies of scale and also the innovations in book color and design made possible by the most modern presses. Yet, the high cost of the machines and the difficulties of maintaining them put them beyond the reach of many Third World publishers. Indeed, some smaller Third World nations still have textbooks printed abroad because of the lack of modern printing equipment at home.

While an increasing number of Third World nations have curriculum development centers and have built up expertise in the writing and design of textbooks, it is nonetheless fair to say that the centers of curricular innovation, instructional design, testing and evaluation are all in the industrialized nations. This means that basic concepts are inevitably imported from abroad, even if the books are actually written within the country. The fact that many of the curriculum designers in the Third World are trained in the West adds to the problem.

The basic concept of the modern textbook is Western, although there have been many adaptations to meet the needs of Third World nations. The idea that books should be printed on high quality paper, that they should have illustrations, and that optimally there should be at least one textbook per pupil in class all stem from the experience of the industrialized nations and on research done in them. Recently, some experts have indicated that one textbook for two students might be just as effective for learning (Heyneman and Loxley, 1983). The use of "disposable" workbooks and supplementary written material is also stressed in the West, where lavish use of color and pictures is common, and the idea that textbooks should be used over and over so that they should be sturdy is generally accepted. Western textbooks for the primary and secondary grades, lavishly and expensively produced, are generally provided free of charge to pupils. In the Third World, such textbook policies may be impractical, yet the Western orientation is seen as that which is best. It is sometimes not possible to provide books free to students, and thus it is important to produce books at the lowest possible cost. Further, textbooks which are printed on newsprint and kept by the student may provide important reading material in the home. It is frequently impossible to use expensive quality paper, which often must be imported. In short, the "gold standard" of textbook design and development of the industrialized nations may be inappropriate for the Third World. Yet, the idea that Western styles of textbook development are best remains powerful and another indication of the impact of the industrialized center on the developing periphery.

While textbooks are increasingly written, designed, and produced in the Third World, there is an international culture of textbooks that is dominated by the industrialized nations in almost every respect. Control of technology and design, the international copyright system, the flow of experts, and many other factors are part of the equation that creates centers and peripheries. Yet, there is also growing independence as indigenous needs are stressed and a knowledge and technology basis built up.

The Textbook Nexus

The creation, production and distribution of textbooks is a very complicated process, involving considerable expertise and a number of steps of policymaking. It is important to understand the key actors as well as the policy and educational concerns that relate to textbook development. This discussion focuses largely on the realities of the Third World, although the processes are similar everywhere. It is possible to separate out the policy decisions that relate to textbooks from the more technical aspects, including design, production and distribution.

Policymakers and Textbooks

A variety of decisions enter into the development of a textbook. In most countries, the basic decision-makers are in the educational bureaucracy—from the level of the ministry of education to curriculum experts to school administrators and sometimes to teachers at lower levels in the system. The educational system has the basic expertise and is aware of the needs for specific kinds of books in particular subjects and grades. However, in many cases, political leaders are also involved. The allocation of funds for large textbook projects often takes place at the political level. In some subjects, such as history and social studies, decisions about the orientation of the curriculum and of textbooks may involve discussions of social values, the interpretation of national history (a particularly sensitive topic in nations which achieved independence recently and which are trying to create a sense of nationhood), and political loyalties. In some cases, international aid agencies may also be involved in basic textbook decisions as they may allocate funds for text development as part of a broader educational assistance program.

The decision to stress textbooks as part of an educational development plan is one that has long-term implications and which involves the commitment of considerable sums of money. Even the creation of a textbook in one subject field requires major expenditures of money and energy. Typically, a textbook development effort is a multi-year project just to get the books produced and into the hands of the students. Fiscal and personnel resources must be allocated on a fairly long-term basis and decisions such as the size of the printing and the nature of the distribution mechanism must be made (Pearce, 1982).

A series of more basic decisions concerning textbooks must also be reached before any large-scale program can be started. The question of whether books are to be expensively printed or issued on newsprint, and whether they are to be illustrated, must be answered. Decisions concerning how textbooks will be produced must also be made. Some countries produce textbooks through private sector publishers, while many have "nationalized" the production of textbooks, creating agencies within the ministry of education. The distribution of textbooks is also a political decision. Some countries distribute textbooks free to students directly through the schools. Others sell textbooks through local booksellers. Each of these crucial decisions is complicated and is very important to the nature of the textbook industry in the country and has implications for publishing, bookselling, and intellectual life. Issues of economics, philosophy, ideology, and assessments of the ability of various sectors of the economy to fulfill specific responsibilities are all part of the background to making these basic decisions. If wrong decisions are made at any step of the process, the success of a particular project may be jeopardized, and the basic structure of the textbook industry may be damaged.

The Process of Creation

Once a textbook has been sanctioned by the appropriate authorities, the challenge is to produce it and ensure that it is placed in the hands of the students. The beginning of this process includes the creation of the actual content of the book. There are many ways in which textbooks are created.

The basic decisions on what should be covered in the book in terms of the curriculum is generally made by curriculum-development authorities in the ministry of education or by agencies sanctioned by the ministry. Such issues as how the material articulates with other grade levels in the same subject, the difficulty of vocabulary, decisions about tests to be used (since books frequently articulate with testing programs) and, of course, the basic philosophy and approach to the subject matter must be stated so that those doing the actual preparation of the book know how to proceed with their work. These kinds of decisions are complex and often controversial. Disagreements among educators concerning the educational philosophy to be used in a book or the best testing program may be intense. Different agencies are frequently involved in the process, and there are sometimes disagreements among them. For example, the curriculum development division in the ministry may have a different perspective than the testing and examination unit. Text plans are often submitted to teachers and other education professionals at the "grass roots" for further input, and additional disputes can arise. Then, once the basic approaches to be used in the book are agreed to and the subject matter to be covered is stated, textbook writers are called in to prepare the volume.

The actual writing of a school textbook can be done in many ways. Frequently, a team of teachers is asked to write the book. Sometimes a single individual is commissioned to do the writing. In some countries, an agency devoted to curriculum development also has the responsibility of writing textbooks. Private sector publishers are sometimes asked to prepare books on the basis of specific outlines, and it is the responsibility of the publisher to locate writers and produce the book. In the United States, the preparation of a school or university textbook aimed at a large potential market has become a process that can cost several hundred thousand dollars. Well-known educators are asked to assist in the process and lend their expertise, but the actual writing is frequently done by professional authors (Whitten, 1975). In the Third World, there is seldom money available for such a complex process (Loveridge, *et al*, 1970).

Once the text is written, and this stage can take up to two years to complete, it is generally carefully evaluated before it is published. Curriculum experts and others must approve the content. Books are sometimes pretested in the schools to see how effective they are in the classroom. In many subject areas, government agencies (usually the ministry of education) have to evaluate the book for its content relating to national history and related matters. Decisions concerning illustrations and the use of charts are made; and if such items are to be included, they must be designed. Once the text is completed and approved and all ancillary materials are also prepared, it is ready to go into production.

The Process of Production

Publishing a textbook is not very different than publishing any other kind of book, but there are some variations. For one thing, in most countries, textbooks are not sold in the open market and thus the economic calculations needed for textbook publishing are different than for general books. The potential audience can be fairly accurately predicted for a textbook, although there may be competition for that market. The physical process of production, however, is similar.

Textbook publishing requires an infrastructure. Personnel with needed publishing skills are required. A publisher is a coordinator of the elements of the publishing process, and thus managerial skills and knowledge of the various elements of book production are essential. Specialized skills such as book design, editing, preparing manuscripts for printing, costing the process, and the like are also needed. For many textbooks, illustrators need to work closely with production personnel.

In some countries, textbook publishing is a function of a ministry of education or other government agency, while in others publishing is left to private sector or parastatal publishing enterprises. It is the case that publishing done directly by government ministries is usually more costly and less efficient than when done outside of official channels. Countries like Nigeria have established parastatal publishing firms with public funds but operated with the principles of private management as a means of increasing the efficiency. It has also been found that non-govenment publishers are generally able to provide quicker service. Nevertheless, textbook publishing is handled by a variety of agencies in the Third World.

In general, textbooks are produced with some kind of subsidy, direct or hidden, in order to keep the prices low. In Malaysia, the Dewan Bahasa dan Pustaka (Literature Agency) is responsible for many textbooks (Ahmad, 1986). It is funded by government and handles both preparation and the publication. In addition, some books are produced by private sector publishers. In India, the National Council of Education Research and Training (NCERT), an agency of the national government, works to develop textbooks and publishes some of them (Rastogi, 1976). The NCERT also works with education ministries and semi-governmental agencies in the states to produce books. In some states, private sector publishers also issue texts although the bulk of the market is dominated by government agencies for the primary and secondary levels in the Indian languages. In short, practices differ, but in general there is a considerable government involvement in the production of print media below the post-secondary level in most of the Third World.

In addition to the skills of the publisher, the physical capability to produce books is necessary. While the composition, printing and binding of books is not "high technology" and the book industry is fairly widespread throughout the world, the Third World faces special problems in terms of book production. For some of the smallest countries, even the basic elements of a book industry are lacking, so it is necessary to import textbooks. For much of the Third World, book production facilities do not reflect the latest Western-developed technologies. "Low-tech" printing may, in fact, be an advantage, since it can be cheaper in terms of some Third World economies, where wages are low and the cost of importing new technologies is high. The skill levels of the local labor market may also be fairly low, making older and simpler manufacturing processes more efficient in the short run. Costs using outmoded machines may actually be lower. In India, for example, hand binding of books is still somewhat less expensive than machine binding. The books produced, however, are not as attractive and cannot provide the level of illustrations and other educational aids that books produced with the most modern equipment can provide. Choices must be made in composition and printing technologies, and it is not necessarily the case that the most modern is the best in some Third World contexts. It is also the case that it may be more efficient to import books or to have indigenously designed books printed abroad than to design and print all books domestically, regardless of the political consequences.

Textbook production includes three basic steps—composition, printing and binding. The most dramatic technological innovations in recent years have taken place in composition and to a lesser extent in printing. Computer-assisted composition has dramatically lowered the costs of book composition and has permitted a much higher level of choice and sophistication in printed materials. Other related innovations have made it possible to include quality illustration and a wider range of graphs and tables than was previously the case. These new technologies need not be very expensive, although they are all based on equipment imported from the industrialized nations and it may be both expensive and difficult to obtain in some Third World nations. Printing has also seen some important technological innovations in recent years. Photo-offset printing has permitted inexpensive short-run publishing, but this is not particularly important for textbooks, where printings are usually large. Modern web presses have greatly increased the speed and efficiency of large-run books. These new presses, however, are also produced in the West and are very expensive. In order for them to operate efficiently, they must be kept busy constantly, thus requiring a considerable market for books and the ability to maintain the equipment efficiently. To utilize these new technologies, it is often necessary for there to be cooperation between the public and private sectors to make most effective use of the most modern equipment. The final step of the production process, binding, has not seen great technological change, although the latest binding techniques using effective glues can make textbook production cheaper. Again, in the Third World context both the equipment and the raw materials may have to be imported, thus increasing the cost considerably. Traditional stitched or sewn bindings may be the most effective, but for many books the cheapest binding may be stapling. This may be particularly useful when the book is printed on newsprint and not intended to last long.

The choices of composing, printing, and binding technologies relate to the kind of book being printed, the use intended for the book, cost factors, available facilities, and sometimes pedagogical considerations as well. A choice of paper, as an example, may involve a variety of considerations. Paper, in the Third World context, is one of the most expensive parts of book production while as a proportion of the total cost of a book, paper is less important in industrialized nations. Many factors go into the choice of paper. Book ("cultural") paper is frequently imported from major Western producers and is therefore expensive in the Third World. Domestic paper is often newsprint that is unsuitable for books that are intended to last long. Paper is also frequently in short supply. Thus, textbook publishers may have a variety of constraints on the choice of paper. What might seem to be a simple matter is constrained by issues of price, availability, and potential use.

Textbook production in the Third World does not require high technology but it does need a necessary minimum of personnel and manufacturing resources. In some countries, these facilities are in short supply and in many the cost is high. Choices of manufacturing techniques, paper and the like are necessarily linked to broader considerations of cost, use, and availability.

The Process of Distribution

Once textbooks are sanctioned, designed and printed, they must reach their intended users. In the Third World, distribution can be a problem; and even where the mechanisms exist, choices must be made. In the West, textbooks are generally distributed through commercial or quasi-commercial channels. Educational authorities (at various levels) order books from commercial publishers to be distributed to the appropriate sites. In some instances where pupils purchase their books, commercial booksellers have a role in textbook distribution. Third World nations frequently face more daunting problems in terms of textbook distribution. In some countries, it is not so easy to physically supply books to schools. This is particularly the case where most schools are in rural areas which are not effectively served by modern transport services, and such is the case for much of the Third World.

There has been a lively debate concerning whether to supply textbooks free to students or to ask them to pay for books. The extent of subsidies from the government is also a subject of controversy. Policies differ in the industrialized nations, although the trend is toward providing free textbooks in government-operated schools. In the Third World, the constraints against providing free books are considerable. Chief among them is a lack of money for such subsidy and the need to use available funds to produce the largest number of books. Yet, many pupils cannot afford to purchase books because of levels of poverty, so that the lack of free textbooks will mean that drop-out rates will dramatically increase. Hence, Third World countries face a dilemma in terms of textbook distribution policies. Some countries also face problems in getting books to students in remote areas. In effect, distributing books, which might seem to be the simplest part of the textbook nexus, is in some ways among the most difficult. Distribution involves decisions concerning who should pay for books, how books can be physically transported to the users, and how the distribution process can be coordinated with educational needs.

Textbook Debates

With the recognition that textbooks are a key element in the educational equation, important not only for effective schooling but also for literacy campaigns and the maintenance of reading skills once basic literacy has been achieved, textbooks have become a more controversial part of educational decision-making. I will raise here some of the main policy issues which are now being debated among educators, among government officials and, in some contexts, among international experts and aid officials.

Who Should Produce?

It has earlier been pointed out that a variety of agencies produce textbooks. The multinational publishers still play a major role in both Third World and industrialized nations, although they have come under increasing criticism. Government agencies publish textbooks. Domestic private sector publishers play a role, as do parastatal enterprises. While there has been an international trend toward government production of texts in the Third World, there has also been increasing criticism of this policy. It is pointed out that textbooks are the most important part of the book industry in most nations (including the industrialized countries) and that if the government dominates textbook production and sales, it is depriving the private sector (which is generally responsible for general and scholarly publishing) of one of its main sources of profit. In short, removing the text market from the private sector may damage the viability of the book industry generally. Some have argued that government textbook publishers do the least efficient job of publishing and that alternative means need to be found to ensure prompt, effective, and economical publishing of books.

Alternatives have been posed, but no consensus has been reached; and it is likely that national variations will determine the most effective form of textbook publishing on a country-by-country basis. Clearly, what is most effective in a centrally planned economy may be different than in a market situation. Choices in a decentralized educational system may also differ from those in a highly centralized situation. Textbook production policies in a small nation will differ from those in a large nation. The desire of ministry of education officials to keep control over the entire process of textbook development may tend to keep the government in the textbook publishing business. Whatever the choice, the publication of textbooks is an important element of a nation's book industry and the location of text publishing will significantly affect the publication of other kinds of book. In addition, choices will determine the cost of books and sometimes publication time.

Choices

In some countries, education authorities at the local or regional level have choices concerning textbook adoptions. More than one book is available for possible use for a particular subject matter at a specified grade level. In general, in such situations private sector publishers are allowed to publish textbooks (often conforming to curricular guidelines) and then to compete in the educational marketplace. In other countries, there is only one book produced to meet a particular need, and all schools must use that book. Centralized decision-making and text publishing may be necessary in small countries where it would not be viable to produce more than one volume for a particular market. Yet, the long-term benefits of textbook competition on prices, curricular alternatives and different approaches to a subject may be beneficial. For much of the Third World, textbook planning tends to be centralized and choice is very limited.

Indigenization

It is generally agreed that textbooks should be written for the specific needs of a country and should reflect indigenous realities. This is particularly true for history, civics, and the social sciences, where texts play a key role in shaping a national consciousness in many Third World nations. Yet, external influences are widespread. Curricular trends from the West are frequently incorporated into textbooks throughout the world. Methodological innovations are also used. Third World textbook writers and curriculum planners are sensitive to the balance between indigenous content and orientations on the one hand and the impact of new educational ideas from abroad on the other. A key element of indigenization has been the use of local languages, particularly in the primary grades. The increased use of mother-tongue education necessitated the preparation of textbooks in those languages, a major task in itself. While some books were simply translated, there was a good deal of original thinking and writing done in order to prepare relevant textbooks in local Third World languages. The problems of indigenizing textbooks in science, mathematics, and other fields are more difficult— in part because there are debates about the nature of "indigenous science" and in part because the creation of new and original material is difficult. Without question, the debate about indigenization is one of the most important for Third World textbook planners and publishers.

The Economics of Textbooks, or Who Should Pay?

Seen in the total context of educational expenditures, textbooks are only a minor part of the education budget. In the Third World, in fact, textbooks are typically underrated as a part of expenditures. However, books are costly where funding is very limited. Textbook development and preparation is an additional expense. Thus, there is a good deal of debate about how textbooks should be paid for. Some of the costs are in fact hidden, since the development expenditures are frequently part of the budgets of curriculum development units, academic institutions, or occasionally private publishers. When foreign assistance is used or books are adapted from overseas publications, development costs are further reduced (Aprieto, 1983).

Because textbooks are produced in relatively large quantities and it is possible to fairly accurately predict the market, the uncertainties built into publishing other kinds of books is generally absent from textbook publishing. Textbook publishing, when done on a "for profit" basis can be a lucrative undertaking and, as noted earlier, is frequently the economic mainstay of many publishers in the West. The economics of textbooks in the Third World is determined not only by the cost of producing books, but also by decisions concerning who will market them, how they will be distributed, and who should pay for them. Where books are provided free to students, the entire cost falls to educational authorities and ultimately to the government. In some countries, books are sold at subsidized prices to pupils, thus reducing the burden on public funds. In some instances, the full cost of the books is borne by the students, but this is unusual in the Third World. The arguments concerning who should pay for the books impinge on the ability of very poor populations to afford books, even at subsidized prices, on the overall funding pattern for education, on the philosophy of education held by the political and educational authorities and, on the availability of external funds (from agencies such as the World Bank, which has provided funding for textbook development and publication in several Third World nations).

What is a Textbook?

Directly related to the economics of textbook publishing is the issue of defining a textbook, since a cheaply printed book will cost less to produce than one which uses high quality paper and lavish illustrations. The policy decisions that go into defining a textbook and thus determining its cost are complex. Should books be printed to last for a number of years and lent by schools to pupils? Or should they be disposable, so that the student who uses the book can keep it? Should there be one book per student or should students share books? Some reasearch indicates that sharing books among two or three students does not diminish learning, and nations strapped for funds may find that sharing books is a necessary policy. Some countries have simply adopted Western ideas about the nature of textbooks, while others have been searching for an indigenous model that will conform to fiscal realities and still provide the needed books.

Distribution

The simple act of getting textbooks from publisher to user is quite complicated. Book distribution assumes an infrastructure of transportation and shipping that many Third World nations do not possess. Problems are especially acute in the rural hinterlands, which account for 80 percent or more of Third World populations in many instances. Timely provision of books to schools in rural areas is a problem. Further, distribution is frequently related to other decisions relating to textbook publishing. In some countries, for example, commercial booksellers are involved in textbook distribution, and this permits the utilization of established transportation channels and also permits the book trade to obtain some benefit from the sale of textbooks.

Textbooks and the Educational System

Textbooks are an integral part of the educational equation, yet are too often seen as a separate factor, needed by schools but somehow not of the same importance as teacher training or curriculum development (Yadunandan, 1983). In the United States, textbooks are typically developed by private sector publishers in response to what they perceive as a need, or at least an opportunity for profits (Cole and Sticht, 1981). Books are selected by educational authorities on the basis of what is available in the marketplace. In the Third World, with a few exceptions, the marketplace will not be able to produce textbooks because the publishing industry is not sufficiently well developed. Thus, it is important to ensure that textbooks are seen as a key part of any strategy for educational development and to ensure that funds are allocated for textbooks as they are for other aspects of education.

Textbook provision must be part of any educational plan. This means that as a reform is conceptualized, the provision of textbooks and related educational aids must be included in any specific planning that takes place. Textbook staff should be part of any team that works on educational development. Further, the means of publishing the books that are included in the plan must also be considered and included in any strategy for implementation. At present, textbooks are not, in general, part of the basic educational plan and are taken care of in an ad hoc way toward the end of any reform or development effort. Once textbooks are seen as an integral part of any educational development scheme, there will be an improvement in the supply of books. Further, curriculum planners will see the books as integral to the curriculum, and there will be a better articulation between the various elements of the system. Funding will also be included for textbooks as part of the total effort.

Textbooks and the New Technologies

Publishing has been affected by the new information technologies, but it is still possible to produce books by using traditional printing technologies. The current situation is perplexing for those involved in textbook developing and publishing in the Third World, and it is worthwhile to consider the various implications of the new technologies. There is much talk of "computers in the schools" throughout the world, and steps are taken in the major industrial nations to include computer literacy in the curriculum and to ensure that schools have access to microcomputers. But even in these countries, the educational system will remain based on traditional approaches and practices for a long period to come.

It seems certain that computers will be a permanent part of the social landscape and, therefore, part of educational systems in the industrialized nations. And the impact of the computer will spread slowly to the Third World. Yet there will be no dramatic revolution in schooling. Rather, the new tool will be used as an educational device and as an object of study and learning.

From the perspective of textbook development and production in the Third World, the new technologies are important but are not about to bring a revolution. In some ways, the new technologies lock the Third World to those who control technologies in the industrialized nations. In other ways, there is the possibility of increased Third World autonomy. They limit autonomy because control over the manufacture of computers, printing machines, and sophisticated reprographic equipment is in the hands of the industrialized nations, as are the new data bases. The technologies may be beneficial because composition and printing is made quicker and, in some situations, less expensive. Third World nations will have to carefully examine the options and develop appropriate policies.

The new data bases permit curriculum planners and textbook writers quick access to sources of information and to current research on most aspects of education. Third World countries can obtain access to the data bases, although there is frequently considerable expense involved. The data bases reflect Western scholarship exclusively, and this is a factor that must be taken into account. New print composition techniques mean that it is often easier to produce high-quality graphics for textbooks as well as to produce camera-ready copy ready for printing. As noted earlier, these technological innovations are frequently expensive and might, in fact, cause problems for existing typesetting and printing facilities.

Thus, the new technologies are a mixed blessing. For many of the smaller Third World nations, the cost and complexity of the innovations make them beyond reach. For others, investment in new technologies may significantly improve the textbook situation. Indeed, such investment may permit countries like India, Mexico, or Egypt to become major regional centers for textbook production. It is very unlikely that Third World classrooms will be dramatically altered by the new technologies. Outside of a few special schools in the cities, education will remain virtually untouched by electronic technology, and thus textbooks will remain among the most important educational inputs.

Conclusion

Textbooks are among the most important yet ignored aspects of any educational system. Even in the West, research on textbooks is very limited and in the Third World, it is practically nonexistent. There is a need to understand, in much more detail, the elements of textbook development, including the curricular implications, economic factors, and distribution problems. The fact is that textbooks are essential to effective schooling, and that they are even more crucial in the Third World, where they are among the most critical inputs.

Textbook development is no secret, yet it requires a combination of traditional skills that are in short supply—the ability to coordinate the publishing enterprise, knowledge of both the curriculum and of the educational techniques to communicate information to students at differing levels of the educational system, and the needed infrastructures to ensure printing and distribution. These matters are definitely "low tech", but at the same time they are at the heart of the educational enterprise. Textbooks do not require massive expenditures. Rather, they necessitate real commitment to comprehensive educational development. Textbooks must be brought from the periphery of the educational enterprise to its very heart.

References

Ahmad, D. H. (1986) The role of the Dewan Bahasa dan Pustaka in the advancement of indigenous academic publishing in Malaysia. In S. Gopinathan (Ed.), *Academic Publishing in ASEAN* (pp. 150-156). Singapore: Festival of Books Singapore.

Altbach, P. G. (1983) Key issues in textbook provision in the Third World. *Prospects*, **13**, 315-326.

Altbach, P. G. (1986) Knowledge enigma: copyright in the Third World. *Economic and Political Weekly (Bombay)*, **21**, 1643-1650.

Altbach, P. G. (1987) *The Knowledge Context: Comparative Perspectives on the Distribution of Knowledge*. Albany: SUNY Press.

Apple, M. (1984) The political economy of text publishing. *Educational Theory*, **34**, 307-319.

Aprieto, P. N. (1983) The Philippine textbook project. *Prospects*, **13**, 351-000.

Bernstein, H. T. (1985) The new politics of textbook adoption. *Phi Delta Kappan*, **66**, 463-471.

Cole, J. and Sticht, T. (Eds.) (1981) *The Textbook in American Society*. Washington, D.C.: Library of Congress.

Gopinathan, S. (1983) The role of textbooks in Asian education. *Prospects*, **13**, 343-350.,

Heyneman, S., Farrell, J. and Sepulveda-Stuardo, M. (1978) *Textbooks and Achievement: What We Know*. Washington, D.C. The World Bank.

Heyneman, S. and Loxley, W. A. (1983) The effect of primary-school quality on academic achievement across twenty-nine high- and low-income countries. *American Journal of Sociology*, **88**, 1162-1194.

Kumar, K. (1981) The textbook as curriculum. *Bulletin of the Indian Institute of Education*, **2**, 75-84.

Kumar, K. (1986) Textbooks and educational culture. *Economic and Political Weekly (Bombay)*, **21**, 1309-1311.

Loveridge, A. J. et al. (1970) *Preparing Textbook Manuscripts: A Guide for Authors in Developing Countries*. Paris: Unesco.

Neumann, P. H. (1980) *Publishing for Schools: Textbooks and the Less Developed Countries*. Washington, D.C.: The World Bank.

Pearce, D. (1982) *Textbook Production in Developing Countries: Some Problems of Preparation, Production and Distribution*. Paris: Unesco.

Rastogi, K. G. (1976) *Preparation and Evaluation of Textbooks in Mother Tongue: Principles and Procedures*. New Delhi: National Council of Educational Research and Training.

Whitten, P. (1975) College textbook publishing in the 1970s. *Annals of the American Academy of Political and Social Science*, **421**, 56-66.

Yadunandan, K. C. (1983) Nepal: For better planning of textbook production. *Prospects*, **13**, 361-369.

CHAPTER 7

Cross-Cultural Transfer of Print Media

S. GOPINATHAN

The processes and problems inherent in the generation and international transfer of educational technology (more specifically, print media) have been one of the least studied aspects of the internationalization and diffusion of knowledge relevant to education. This has been ignored both in the few studies of international publishing that exist and in the much larger corpus of writing on educational development and reform in the developing countries. This lack of knowledge is indeed surprising considering that the traffic in educational materials is at least as old as colonialism—America's most popular arithmetic text in the 1770s was Thomas Dilworth's *The Schoolmaster's Assistant*, a reprint of an English text. Yet research in this field is important if we are to understand better the relationships between Western educational models and paradigms, curriculum and technology, and the processes of educational development and change in the developing world. Studying the roles of such varied agencies as the examination syndicates in the United Kingdom, national and international aid agencies, and transnational publishing houses should illuminate our understanding of patterns of ideological, educational, and commercial influence in the cross-national transfer of print media.

Part of the reason for a lack of scholarly attention may be due to the assumption by educationists that pedagogy was neutral and therefore unproblematic and because attention was focused on school-society relations: gaining control over private sector education, expansion of facilities, and access for minorities were typically the types of problems that merited attention. Some attention was paid to medium-of-instruction issues but even here discussion dealt not so much with in-school issues (such as poor achievement, relevance of policy, curriculum or methodology, and availability of materials) as with questions of national integration and identity.

Recent scholarly work offers new perspectives with which to study educational print transfer in the Third World. Apple (1979, 1985), for example, has explored the assumptions underlying the selection of curricular knowledge and transmission modes. His American-centered

analysis dealt with the links between economic and cultural class dominance and the legitimation of certain forms of curricular knowledge.
This has been extended by Altbach (Altbach and McVey, 1976),
Altbach and Rathgeber (1980), Altbach, Arboleda and Gopinathan
(1985), and Smith (1975), who have discussed the role of publishing
both within the context of national intellectual and cultural concerns,
and within an unequal system of global intellectual relations. This enables us to treat pedagogic curricular-materials issues as significant and
critical, and to place them firmly within a global perspective. However,
if there are strong forces for internationalization, it is true as well that in
the developing countries there is a counter pressure for a more conscious indigenization process, especially in social science knowledge, as a
means of resisting the developing countries' intellectual dependence on
the West (Gopinathan, 1985). This struggle is bound to leave its mark
on how issues of curriculum and pedagogy are treated in the late 1980s
and beyond.

Definitions and Characters of Print Technology

Before we examine in detail the process of transfer, we need to sort out
the various uses of the term "educational technology". As pointed out in
Chapter 1, there is little agreement over what is to be covered by the
term "educational technology". In most cases, educators when asked to
provide examples are likely to mention computers, overhead projectors,
interactive video, educational radio and television, and the like. Very
few are likely to see print matter—and the most common form of print
matter in education is textbooks—as technology, even less so now with
the demise of the programmed textbook. However, if educational technology is understood as a system for meeting educational objectives—an
operating system which conditions the way in which educational processes are determined—then the familiar textbook is very much technology.

Several differences and useful distinctions can be made between print
media and other technologies discussed in this book. Unlike the other
technologies, the important printing process necessary for producing
print has been known for a long time and is universally accessible. It is
cheap, efficient, affordable, and relevant technoloogy for even the
poorest of developing countries. It is the one technology, part of which
could be said to have been spawned in what is now the developing
world. Yet other features suggest themselves. The physical format of the
textbook is now stable, though by no means singular. In terms of
function, the textbook is seen as providing most often instruction for a
whole school year in a given subject at a given level, quite unlike the
way specific information and skills are presented over radio and tele-
vison or computers. In some instances a single author is responsible for

a series of texts within a subject area for a whole school level, such as senior high, and that writers' work thus has an authority and impact that is nowhere matched by existing information sources transmitted via the other technologies. Perhaps most significantly, the intellectual process that print made valuable when it supplanted orality, and which now seems threatened by other forms of literacy, needs closer examining for its educational and cultural potential.

There is at least one sense in which the concept of recency in technological development can be applied to textbooks. Many new developments have occurred at the production and printing level that, while not replacing or radically altering the basic design of the textbook, nevertheless make for changes. One obvious element is the capacity to employ color cheaply in textbooks, which has made whole new extensions and uses for illustrations and graphics. Refinements in paper and ink technology have made possible lighter and more durable print materials, with important consequences for re-use, thus making the provision of this type of educational resource in developing countries more cost-effective. Further, developments in micro-processing now open up cheaper prospects for typesetting and graphics which should further reduce costs.

For the purposes of this essay we define textbooks as organizations of selected, ordered, and simplified content capable of being taught. The term *organization* allows us to see beyond the conventional textbook form to multimedia kits, programmed books, loose-leaf books, modules and other similar innovations to textbook design. *Selection* implies authority and approval, *ordered* and *simplified*, the important notions of grading and sequencing, of integrated and planned divisions of content. Finally *capable of being taught* allows us to focus on the principal user, the pupil, and how a textbook must meet his needs.

The Multiple Roles of Textbooks

Several reasons may be advanced as to why studies of educational technology transfer, more particularly the cross-national transfer of print materials, may be considered of crucial relevance now. One major reason is the continued dominance of this technology in the classrooms in both the developed and developing world, and especially the latter. In terms of accessibility and breadth of impact, the textbook remains, and is likely to remain, the most widely used instructional tool. A further reason is that developing countries, faced with the enormous problems involved in producing competent teachers, especially in a context of expanding enrollments and diminishing resources, are hoping that "teacher-proof textbooks" will solve some of the problems of quality in the education system. It has been argued as well that teacher productivity could be enhanced by the use of textbooks in large classes since textbooks free the teacher to do a variety of tasks other than direct teaching. More positively, however, studies of cognitive achievement in the developing countries show textbook availability to be an important factor. Heyneman, Farrell, and Sepulveda-Stuardo (1978) have stated,

> from the evidence so far, the availability of books appears to be the most consistent factor in predicting academic achievement. It is positive in 15 out of 18 statistics (83 percent). This is, for example, more favourable than the 13 out of 24 (54 percent) recently reported for teacher training.

There are yet other features of textbooks that explain their widespread use. They are flexible in that they can be used in a variety of ways and in a variety of educational contexts. Books are portable, easily handled, cheap enough in many instances to be individually owned, and reusable. Their very commonness makes them non-threatening to teachers. Very importantly, unlike other media, they require no maintenance or additional energy sources.

Given the fact of mass-based education systems, the ability to deliver information in an efficient and cost-effective manner is crucial. Good texts raise standards and require only a relatively small investment of resources. The very growth of the school system has enabled the publishing and printing industries to modernize, since a steady market is assured. In turn, the cost of books is reduced, provided the basic structure of the textbook is retained. Further, advances in textbook production noted earlier make it a cheaper proposition than mixed-media curriculum materials.

Yet another consideration is that the state now intervenes massively in education, and the state has its own views of the value and content of textbooks used in the schooling. Recent controversy over Japanese textbook revision, the insistence on a form of civics or moral education as part of the curriculum in many newly independent countries and the reworking of history syllabuses and curriculum all attest to the symbolic uses of the text. As FitzGerald in her analysis of US history textbooks (1980) and the issues raised by state textbook adoption policies in the US indicate, these are not just concerns at the periphery. As early as 1972 the Canadian report *Canadian Publishers and Canadian Publishing* raised concerns about the influence of US publishers on Canadian curriculum materials, calling it "a valuable cultural resource (in need of) a carefully planned public conservation program".

Textbooks at one level carry the intrinsic values and the historical mirror in which the nation wishes to see itself reflected. The selection and legitimation of content are seen as vital to national needs and therefore production, selection, control, and use are vital to the state. It is also likely that textbooks would come to be established as a major instrument of the schooling process as the state became progressively more involved in education. The increasing numbers to be educated resulted in the need for bureaucratic control, for common standards, and uniformity. Textbook content offers one way of introducing students everywhere, and especially in a developing nation, to common socializing experiences, thus giving texts a vital integrative function. In an equally significant way, because textbooks are the curriculum made explicit, they allowed for the very important function of education evaluation—pupils could now be assessed publicly at a national level. Selection for higher levels could thus be made on the basis of achievement.

Factors Influencing the Evolution of the Textbook Industry in Developing Countries

The Historical Context

Our understanding of the current situation and prospects for the future will be enhanced by first reviewing how the provision of textbooks originated in many developing countries. The dominance of the textbook in Third World education mirrors the dominance of the text in the first world; and it is colonialism in most instances that facilitated its transfer. It is also the assumptions and functions of the education system that has entrenched the textbook and the ways it is used and viewed in post-colonial times. In almost all colonial territories, particularly British, Dutch, and French, textbooks became important only with the advent of a modern-type education system introduced by the colonial authorities. That system in contrast to the traditional system of apprenticeship and mastery of religious texts for a select few was predicated on the assumption of mastery of a body of knowledge in specific subject areas contained in texts, with mastery levels defined by annual examinations. The annual examinations were the gatekeepers to advanced grades where new content had to be learnt, again as set out in textbooks. The point to be noted is that textbooks became necessary in a variety of cultures and societies in the colonized world only upon the introduction and adoption of the metropolitan education system. The new knowledge it introduced, often in the metropolitan languages, differentiated via grade levels and evaluated by examinations is the basis for the evolution of the modern textbook industry in the developing world.

The colonized territories possessed little capacity either for writing or producing textbooks. Few indigenous peoples were educated in the metropolitan language, fewer still had writing skills, and the meager printing capacity was often taken up by newspaper and religious publishing. As a consequence, almost all the books to be used in the system had to be imported. Thus, in many of the ex-Commonwealth countries the major British publishing houses like Oxford University Press, Longman, Heinemann, MacMillan, and Graham Brash among others came to be established, essentially as importers of textbooks then in use in Britain. With some variation, many of the texts in use in the early 1950s, like Durell's *General Mathematics* or Ridout's *English Course* or McKean's *Biology*, were to remain unadapted, but in use, well into independence. Such continued use can be explained by a variety of factors at work—the undoubted superiority of these texts to anything indigenously produced, the lack of writing expertise in the newly independent countries, the continuance in British ex-colonies of the Cambridge University Overseas Examination system, the use of expatriate teachers and headmasters and senior advisors at the ministry of education, among others. It would be fair to say that metropolitan publishers dominated and controlled the textbook market; even when school curriculum began to be nationalized and revised after independence, it was often done with the aid of expatriate advisors. As a consequence, in the first phase after independence, British-produced textbooks with "scissors-and-paste adaptation" continued to be promoted by metropolitan publishers and eagerly accepted. Such were the close links between curriculum advisors and textbook publishers in Malaysia, Singapore, and Hong Kong that in the late 1960s a basic English language course was used with only minor changes in at least three countries.

If metropolitan publishers made vast profits through textbook supply (even today major British textbook publishers depend for their survival on exports) they were responsible as well for introducing the expertise needed. These metropolitan publishers trained the early writers, editors, and illustrators and taught printers the finer points of textbook printing. It must be acknowledged that they took the first steps in general publishing, for their supplementary readers became the earliest children's books and their publishing of post-graduate dissertations was the start of academic publishing. Such was the role played, for instance, by Oxford University Press, Heinemann, and Longman in Malaysia and Singapore. However, only very few publishers paid much attention to general publishing, and even fewer to publishing in non-metropolitan languages. Equally important, the fundamental features of the imported education system were not altered, promising experiments in some African countries notwithstanding, and thus the part played by textbooks remains unaltered.

The entry of government, and in some instances commercial publishers, into textbook publishing was determined by other considerations. Typically, one of several factors acted as a trigger to more extensive government involvement. Among these were decisions when changes in medium of instruction or the introduction of a second language were proposed, when some syllabi were obviously outdated or inappropriate to changed sociopolitical circumstances, when ethnic or regional pressure groups lobbied for changes in curricula and textbooks, when textbook prices and availability became political issues, when supplies to rural regions became a bone of contention, when commercial publishers made few efforts to improve quality, or when commercial publishers were seen as indulging in corrupt practices. The motives were many, some honorable, some forced by political and economic expediency. Note also that even when governments decided to intervene more frequently, it did not always imply the need to create an indigenous capacity or technology; in Ghana and other countries, governments made deals with metropolitan publishers that often were harmful to national publishers.

A major element in explaining changes in the provision of print materials is, of course, change in the education system itself. Curricular transformation is one such example. By the early 1960s many newly-independent countries had begun to recognize the inadequacy of the emphasis on a liberal-arts curriculum and introduced various forms of technical-vocational education. Since such training had to be relevant to the emerging industrial infrastructure in these countries, to materials (such as timber or cane), and to machines available in school workshops, many of the syllabi and accompanying material had to be country-specific. In Malaysia and Singapore some of the early books in the industrial arts for use in schools were written by local teachers. Equally significant were the changes that were made in history and civics syllabi. The degree of change depended upon the particular circumstances under which independence was won. Where independence came as a result of struggle, as in India and Indonesia, the changes made were more extensive. Understandably, the ministries of education were very much involved, and the manuscripts in these subject areas were locally authored and printed.

A third element in curricular change which impacted on textbook writing and production was the recognition of syllabi inadequacy across the board. Often such changes were due to a combination of factors— the availability of new syllabi from overseas examination authorities like health science, major curriculum reform projects in the metropolitan countries as was the case with modern mathematics, and the reform in science education following Sputnik. Also influential were changes in methodology in such traditional subject areas as language teaching, especially of English, with slow changes in literature to include more

material with a local background and the need for subjects to accommodate new clienteles in education. Domestic science was introduced to
cater to the girls who were entering the education system from the 1960s
onwards in large numbers. Very often the changes were introduced
before the textbooks were available. But most importantly, they provided an opportunity for local writers and publishers to get into the
textbook market.

Another momentous shift in the curriculum area had to do with
changes in the medium of instruction. In some countries there was a
wholesale move to an indigenous medium of instruction (Malaysia, Indonesia), while in others the indigenous language was introduced as a
second language (Singapore). In some instances second language learning was compulsory, in some others not. In some countries the indigenous language was used as a medium of instruction, while in other
countries it was taught as a subject. In nations like the Philippines and
India, it was not just metropolitan and indigenous languages but also a
number of indigenous dialects/languages which were given new school
roles. In countries like Thailand where an indigenous language was
always the main medium of instruction, a recognition of the importance
of English led to a demand for relevant English language texts. In spite
of the variations noted above, what was significant for textbook publishing in these developing countries was that new materials were
needed. Malaysia's Dewan Bahasa, (language and literature agency)
produced between 1975 and 1979 some 743 titles in the national language and was responsible for printing 35 million copies. In some
instances producing books in these languages was a pedagogical problem
as well as a technical one, since scientific vocabularies had to be developed in the "new" languages as well as suitable typefaces to enable
printing to be done.

Cultural-Political Factors

Some of the facts noted above, notably the desire to "set history right"
and to give a valued place to indigenous languages, are the outward
manifestations of a larger understanding of the uses of education in a
developing society. In many developing countries independence presented a huge political challenge in that governments had to fashion a
political and cultural identity out of disparate ethnic groups. It was to
education that these leaders turned. Thus, control over education—and
in many countries that meant control over private and ethnically-
separate schools—was always of importance. The expansion of education in many developing areas was caused not only by a desire to
maximize human potential but as a means of incorporating younger
citizens into the desired national identity. Hence, within the system,
textbooks were seen as efficient and reliable in instilling common histor-

ies and experiences. It was the textbook that spoke to the young of the colonial struggle, the national heroes, the national monuments, and figures from myth and legend. Such uses for texts are, for instance, very clear in the Indian and Malaysian cases. The concern was not, as it was with the Western developed world (secure in their national identities) with maintaining choice and plurality. But rather, driven by political imperatives, the developing nations sought to emphasize the commonalities of the national experience and to encourage knowledge of and sympathy for national goals. This is a desire that has by no means been exhausted in many countries, and the role of print material remains firmly a matter of concern in such societies.

The Technological Factor

In many of the developing countries, the extent to which print-media technology is indigenously generated depends to a large extent on the level of economic development. Thus, even when we characterize print-media technology as cheap and efficient in comparison to other technologies, it is by no means true that all developing countries can afford it in equal measure. Developing countries are themselves quite varied in resources, and it is this factor that primarily determines just how a particular technology is used. In other words, even if there is a desire to use nationally generated print materials, there may be an inadequate infrastructure to produce enough. It may be more realistic to import the needed texts, even if these are quite inappropriate, given the differences in cultural and educational characteristics. In almost all developing countries there is a need to import paper, inks, printing machines, and binders; and all these represent a drain on foreign exchange. Such imports are for a product that is nationally consumed, with the exception of countries like Singapore and Hong Kong whose printing capacity is so advanced that they can export print. Countries like India, China, and other populous nations are so vast that they must of necessity have their own complete infrastructure for producing books. But in many other countries poorly developed infrastructure results in inadequate supplies of a valuable instructional tool and raises questions about standards built upon imported examples.

It is also necessary to bear in mind the fact that while printing books seems less complex than other forms of technology, it relies on a number of elements and processes. It involves writers (who only emerge when an education system itself matures), the school system, technical expertise within the publishing industry, a developed printing industry, access to capital for importing inks and paper and a good distribution system. The fact that developing countries have to some measure mastered the technology should not obscure the fact that it has taken them some two to three decades to develop the expertise. What must be worrying planners is how long it will take to master the newer technologies and how, when one technology has been mastered, another appears to tighten the bonds of dependence on the industrialized countries once again.

The International Factor

As indicated earlier, viewed historically, many ex-colonial territories have been participants in educational exchange for some time. With the adoption of metropolitan educational institutions came the commercial and ideological one-way traffic in educational materials from the center to the periphery. Such traffic has only slightly diminished in intensity. While developing countries have been able to substitute locally-authored materials at the elementary and secondary levels, the general expansion in literacy, income, and higher education has continued to feel a demand for a wide range of imported books. In addition, developing countries continue to rely on the educational expertise available in the metropolitan countries, and often when educational innovations are transferred, such as modern mathematics or inquiry science, it often happens that educational materials are transferred as well.

Another example of internationalism in the production of print materials is the effort by the U.S.A., the U..K and the U.S.S.R. to subsidize the production of low-cost editions for use in higher education in the developing countries. The American scheme resulted in the publication of 12 million copies of US titles in 57 languages, while the U.K. English Language Book Society Scheme resulted in the sale of 1.5 million copies in 1984 alone (Childs, 1986: 72). In 1983 the Soviet Union exported 24 million copies of books in English, and it currently prints more than 2 million books a year in 13 regional Indian languages.

More significantly, there are current major efforts to transfer the technology of print-material production. The World Bank has been a major influence in enhancing the capacity to produce textbooks. Since 1973 the World Bank has financed about 45 projects which have included some provision for textbooks; and it is to be noted that these provisions have resulted in the provision of vast numbers of copies—a total of 350 million for Indonesia, the Philippines and Ethiopia.

Further, the emphasis given to textbooks in World Bank education projects has increased considerably, from 6 percent of all education projects before 1974 to 32 percent in the period 1979-1983. Since growth in overall terms has been greatest in the primary school, most of the projects have been involved in the provision of texts at that level.

In Southeast Asia both Indonesia and the Philippines have faced severe problems in producing and distributing an adequate number of textbooks. In the early 1970s the World Bank embarked on an eight-year $39 million project in Indonesia to develop curricula and produce 138 million copies of texts in core subjects for Grades 1 to 6. In the Philippines, preliminary World Bank studies indicate that in the early 1970s there was only one book for every 9.8 pupils in grades one to four, one for every 11.5 pupils in grades five to six, and one for every 8.5 pupils in secondary schools. A lack of adequate curricular materials was responsible for both low and uneven achievement and high repetition rates. With Bank support, a Textbook Board was created to supervise a US $52 million credit. The project's aim was to produce and distribute some 75 of the 109 new textbook titles and thus reduce the pupil-textbook ratio from 10:1 to 2:1. A recent assessment notes that "during the period, eighty-four textbooks and corresponding teachers' materials were developed and tested, over 33 million copies of the new textbooks were contracted for printing, and 247 million copies actually distributed to the 40,000 schools throughout the country, with more than 252,000 teachers and school administrators given orientation" (Aprieto, 1983). Already it is clear that the economies of scale have lowered costs between 50 and 70 percent. Pupil costs, as a consequence of this program, have increased by less than 1 percent, while student performance appears to have risen 14 percent. The World Bank has been so convinced of the program's utility that it has made available another loan of $100 million for the period 1982-85.

The Present Situation

What, then, is the current situation with regard to print materials in developing countries? It is clear, for example, that great strides have been made in providing Asia's schoolchildren with relevant print materials. As Table 7.1 indicates, most Asian countries have either maintained or improved on the number of new editions produced annually.

The statistics in Table 7.1 must be read with care since there do appear some puzzling figures. It is hard to imagine India producing only about 500 titles. With this caution in mind, some broad generalizations can be drawn from the table. Six of the countries produced between 200 and 400 titles of textbooks in 1983. Newly independent Brunei does not have a large school system nor a developed publishing industry and produced only 25 titles; Japan produced some 1,800 titles while Korea was a major producer with 2,206 titles. It is a bit difficult to locate China within this continuum as the figure 5,029 represents both books and pamphlets.

The second broad generalization is that not many countries have been able to improve on their 1974 performance. Korea, Singapore, and Sri Lanka are among those that have increased the supply of textbooks, but India has only marginally increased the number, while declines have been registered for Indonesia and Thailand. These figures must be cause for serious concern, since they imply that even with general improvements in economic conditions many developing countries provide inadequately for this basic instructional tool.

How does Asia compare with other regions in textbook provision? Table 7.2 provides some glimpses into conditions in Africa and Latin America. Once again the picture is not of steady gain. In Nigeria, one of Africa's most populous countries, textbook production declined, but there were substantial increases in Tunisia and Zambia. The picture is incomplete for Latin America, but again declines are evident for Chile, Uruguay, and Argentina. As with Asia, what must be distressing is the relatively small number of titles produced annually in Africa; more substantial progress seems to have been made in Asia and Latin America. However, what the figures do not reveal is how many titles were reprints and how many new works. All too often in many school systems, textbooks are outdated.

Qualitative improvements have also been made to textbooks. And with the syllabus revision that has been undertaken within many developing-country education systems, many of these books now reflect and relate more closely to national conditions. More illustrations, the use of color, more pedagogically based structuring of content, the production of workbooks and teachers' guides, and the incorporation of study aids within texts have all undeniably made for better texts. However, textbooks in regional languages are not as plentiful as needed. In India, of the 17,158 books published in 1980/81, only 2,225 (12.97 percent) were in Hindi, while titles in English were 7,655 (or 44.61 percent) (Singh, 1985: 114).

Finally, infrastructural facilities have been built up in many countries to decrease dependence on imported textbooks. Almost all elementary-level texts are indigenously produced in Asia, and a large number of secondary-level texts are extensive local adaptations, locally produced.

Within the Third World, particularly in Asia, innovative projects, which involve teachers in their preparation and evaluation and which are closely tied to teacher training, are under way to produce more interesting, relevant, low-cost educational materials. The Asian Program of Educational Innovation for Development (APEID), Bangkok has played a particularly important role in this transformation. The Program's brief is innovation in general, yet it has made important progress both in convincing educators to see beyond the textbook and in promoting and demonstrating the viability of low-cost indigenously produced educational materials. These materials are complementary to the textbook and range from models, charts, puppets, educational toys and games to science and mathematics kits and laboratory equipment.

Pakistan is an example of this. The National Educational Equipment

TABLE 7.1. *Production of School Textbooks in Asia*

Country	Number of Titles	
	1974	1983
Afghanistan	—	108*
Bhutan	10	—
Brunei	—	25**
China	—	5029
Hong Kong	131	538*
India	529	543
Indonesia	476	226
Japan	—	1843
Korea, Republic of	—	2206
Malaysia	240	394
Nepal		—
Pakistan	—	—
Philippines		380*
Singapore	81	389
Sri Lanka	57	111
Thailand	336	298
Vietnam	—	300†

Source: Unesco, Statistical Yearbook, 1975, 1981 and 1985
* Figures for 1981
** Figures for 1982
† Total for books and pamphlets

TABLE 7.2. *Production of School Textbooks in Selected African and Latin American Countries*

Egypt	414 (1977)	
Ghana	27 (1978)	20 (1982)
Kenya	26 (1976)	40 (1981)
Nigeria	583 (1978)	174 (1983)
Sudan	88 (1977)	
Tunisia	69 (1978)	172 (1983)
Zambia	31 (1978)	
Chile	529 (1976)	100 (1983)
Columbia	527 (1980)	670 (1983)
Uruguay	481 (1975)	158 (1982)
Argentina	6674 (1976)	395 (1981)
Mexico	4851 (1976)	
Cuba	726 (1976)	
Peru	925 (1976)	
Venezuela	480 (1975)	

Sources: Unesco Statistical Yearbooks. See also Eva M. Rathgeber (1985) "The Book Industry in Africa 1973-1983: A Decade of Development" and A. E. Augsberger "Publishing in Latin America: An Overview" both in Altbach, Arboleda, Gopinathan (eds.) *Publishing in the Third World*.

Centre produced a primary teachers' tool kit covering science, mathematics, social studies, and Urdu. The kit consisted of 100 items complete with teachers' guides and was supplied to 50,000 schools. In addition, the centre trained 2,200 master-teacher trainers, who will in turn train 200,000 more teachers in the use of the kit. In Bangladesh, Nepal, and Korea various educational equipment bureaus are using local low-cost resources and materials to produce equipment for science and technology instruction. In India the National Centre for Educational Research and Training produces more instructional materials for translation, adaptation, and adoption. Singapore has established the Curriculum Development Institute of Singapore (CDIS) to prepare instructional materials. In the Philippines three curriculum centers were established to coordinate and produce new textbooks. It is clear that in all these countries curricular materials have come to mean more than the usual textbook, and the pride of place commercial publishers once enjoyed has now been replaced by a more national effort, incorporating the ministry of education, curriculum development centers, and teacher-training institutes.

It is important to reiterate that in much of the developing world the production of new, improved curriculum materials has gone hand in hand with large-scale curriculum innovation. Such parallel moves have the advantage of forcing both curriculum planners and text writers to come together to develop materials, a procedure which has more chances of producing text materials which meet curriculum objectives. There are several African examples which illustrate this process (Yoloye, 1986). And it needs to be noted in this context that assistance in curriculum development was available in a number of instances from overseas bodies—the Education Development Center (U.S.A.) and Unesco. Such co-operation is much to be preferred over the wholesale importing (often dumping) of unsuitable texts.

In the mid-1960s the EDC in cooperation with the national ministries of education developed three curriculum projects, namely the African Mathematics Programme (AMP), the African Primary Science Programme (APSP), and the African Social Studies Programme (ASSP). Under the African Mathematics Programme, textbooks and teachers' guides were tested out in about 1,500 classrooms in 10 African countries. The African Primary Science Programme developed the strategy of creating science curriculum centers in 7 countries which then produced materials for testing and use in primary classrooms. These cooperative measures, which have helped African countries cut down the cost of producing relevant materials geared to the national curriculum and local realities, have now lessened the dependence these countries have on imported text materials. The experiences gained from the earlier collaboration were valuable in the formation of the African Curriculum Organization in 1976.

Though in many ways the developments noted are to be welcomed, several cautions may be raised. As with many other educational developments, the concept of the instructional package is itself one developed in the West and founded on the belief that a variety of modes of presenting information would stimulate and sustain learning, be flexible, and even allow for group or individualized learning as needed. In the US the producers of these sorts of materials have not always been the traditional print-oriented publishers but also those able to exploit the new technology, and this suggests a commercial consideration as well behind the innovation.

What is regrettable, however, is that many curriculum-development centers do not undertake an assessment of how the packages are used, how cost-effective they are when compared to the single textbook, and if they do indeed promote the type of cognitive gains claimed for the materials. Unless there is systematic research into the value of certain forms or formats for instructional uses, much effort currently expended in developing these materials might well be misplaced effort.

Towards a Technology of Text Materials

Notwithstanding the above, some crucial issues remain when we address questions about the efficiency of text materials for instructional purposes. We need to address the issue of what it is about textbooks that enhances learning and how such features may be improved to further improve learning. This, however, is easier said than done, since very little research has been conducted on text design in the context of learning; and what exists is both technical (not written with the textbook writer in mind) or else scattered in journals, since they are written from perspectives ranging from reading research, to educational psychology and typography, to mention only a few. One recent research which brings together these diverse perspectives within a coherent framework is Jonassen's (1986) *The Technology of Text.*

The literature on text technology appears to have at least the following foci: a print-orientation in which consideration is given to such details as line length, type characteristics (design and size), spacing, and margins. These are techniques for signaling the content structure of the prose passage via linguistic—but primarily spatial and typographic—cues to the form, function, sequence, content, and importance of segments of a passage. These devices are important (and based on research can be altered and adapted to further enhance learning) because they are linked to text-processing characteristics which in turn determine how well a text is understood, remembered, recalled, and utilized.

The second focus is research dealing with what are termed mathemagenic behaviors, that is, text comprehension processes. These processes are thought to be affected and enhanced by such characteristics as advance organizers, illustrations, inserted questions, adjunct questions, and the like. Such text characteristics are assumed to have different effects, and the challenge is to research how they operate and to build them into text design. In brief, the assumption is that different text characteristics instigate or stimulate different learning processes which in turn lead to different learning outcomes. What research in text technology seeks to do is to find better ways of both structuring the medium as well as the message.

The above issues can be briefly illustrated by reference to the functions that illustrations have in textbooks. Even in developing countries there are few textbooks today that do not have illustrations, if not in color at least in black and white. Conventional wisdom has it that illustrations may be a useful aid in comprehension and make the text more varied and interesting. Considering that it makes the book more expensive when illustrations are included, one would have assumed that the practice had a sound empirical basis. But as Duchastel (1980) points out, the research literature is very muddled (partly because of methodological problems). He noted also that illustrated texts are combinations of verbal and graphic components; so the key to successful illustration would appear to be how well the two elements combine, and that in itself must take account of the characteristics of the content and the characteristics of the learner. Pelletti (in Mitzel, 1982) studied the combination of graphic materials in elementary social studies texts and found that though motivation was enhanced, cognitive achievement did not increase. Duchastel (1980) draws attention to three possible roles for illustrations:

(a) an *attention role*, where an illustration is primarily intended to keep students interested,
(b) an *explicative role*, where an illustration directly assists comprehension by visually clarifying a point, and finally,
(c) a *retentional role*, where an illustration assists later retention of information by being easier to recall than verbal ideas alone.

The explicative role, which can be further subdivided into more specific functions, is the crucial one; but it would seem that very few textbook writers and illustrators in developing countries recognize the nature and functions of illustrations and their relationship to pupil learning. Consider as well the often poorly realized potential of captions for aiding learning. Too many captions are verbal descriptions of the illustration so that very often the opportunity to surprise the learner, to challenge thinking, to extend understanding beyond the accompanying text is lost. A final consideration has to do with the wide variety of illustrations available to the designer, ranging from black and white photographs and detailed drawings to graphs and charts, simple line drawings, and even cartoons. While there is little reliable comparative research into the value of these different types of illustrations for different instructional purposes and reader characteristics, it would seem important to consider the relevance of these types in designing books for more effective instruction.

Other research may be briefly alluded to. Davis and Hunkins (1969: 285-92) analyzed end-of chapter questions in several fifth-grade social studies textbooks to determine what thinking processes they encouraged and concluded that 86 to 89 percent of the questions focused primarily on acquisition of knowledge and almost no questions called for analysis, synthesis, or evaluation.

A considerable amount of research has also gone into issues having to do with readability of text materials. A readability formula provides a simple way to predict the level of difficulty of text through counts of vocabulary difficulty and sentence complexity. Hundreds of readability formulae have been developed over the years. In general, they seem to work reasonably well in predicting learner difficulty but nevertheless need to be used with caution. In the mid-1960s a number of studies were done to the difficulty level of textbooks in mathematics materials, science textbooks, and high school literature anthologies. In many instances the readability level was found to be inappropriate to the needs of students (Hilton, 1969: 1474; Hartley & G. Klare, 1978: 773-775).

While it is important to move on the basis of empirical data towards designing more effective curriculum materials, it is by no means clear that these studies and the findings, valuable as they are, can be utilized without adaptation to a developing-country context. There are many vital differences that one needs to note when one assesses the role of textbooks in developing-country education systems. Such is the urgent need for text materials that one cannot wait for the results of careful studies. Indeed many planners think it preferable to go ahead with imported texts rather than wait to develop indigenous ones. While the principle of a readability formula may be useful, much work will need to be done with a large number of indigenous languages to ascertain the formula's general applicability. Then again one may need to examine how well the principles of text structure and organization which are predicated on Piagetian and Brunerian assumptions translate into different cultural contexts. A considerable body of research in cross-cultural psychology is showing that culture does condition learning styles and strategies.

More importantly, however, planners need to tackle issues relating to the textbook as a dominant learning tool. It needs to be noted that in many cultural contexts the textbook is an alien tool. When one looks at the African context one notes that song, dance, drama, and poetry associated with traditional African rituals and festivals were the primary media of communication. With these media went valuable content-myths, legends, proverbs, and a store of data on the environment, social relations, and a moral code. This national educational resource was kept down during the early years of missionary-sponsored education, but even today there is by no means unanimous support that they should be reintroduced into the school curriculum (Eisemon et al., 1986: 232-246). It would seem relevant, when in the developed countries more attention is being being paid to such a variety of instructional media as video, films, tapes, and computers, that developing countries should also examine the mix these resources offer. Given that the assumptions of Western-style education arose out of a different cultural context and that recall of content as tested by examinations is a major feature of such systems, it may indeed be difficult to promote alternate learning designs. The justification for trying must lie in the possibility that only through such an integration can the textbook move from being an alien tool to an instrument of enrichment.

References

Altbach, P. G., Arboleda, A. A. & Gopinathan, S. (eds.) (1985) *Publishing in the Third World: Knowledge and Development.* New Hampshire: Heinemann.

Altbach, P. G. & Gopinathan, S. (1985) Textbooks in the third world: challenge and response. In P. G. Altbach, A. A. Arboleda, & S. Gopinathan, (eds.) (1985) *Publishing in the Third World: Knowledge and Development.* New Hampshire: Heinemann.

Altbach, P. G. & McVey, S. (1976) *Perspectives on Publishing.* Lexington, Massachusetts: Lexington Books.

Altbach, P. G. & Rathgeber, E. M. (1980) *Publishing in the Third World: Trend Report and Bibliography.* New York: Praeger.

Apple, M. W. (1979) *Ideology and Curriculum.* Boston: Routledge & Kegan Paul.

Apple, M. W. (1985) Making knowledge legitimate: power, profit, and the textbook. In *Current Thought on Curriculum.* Washington, D.C.: Association for Supervision and Curriculum Development.

Aprieto, P. N. (1983) The Philippines textbook project, *Prospects,* **13**, (3), pp. 351-359.

Childs, W. M. (1986) Low-priced books for the developing world. In W. M. Childs and D. E. McNeil (eds.). *American Books Abroad: Toward a National Policy.* Washington: Helen Dwight Reid Educational Foundation.

Davis, O. L. & Hunkins, F. P. (1969) Textbook questions: what thinking processes do they foster? Cited by E. Hilton in R. L. Ebel (ed.). *Encyclopedia of Educational Research,* 4th edition. Toronto: Macmillan.

Duchastel, Philipe C. (1980) Textbook illustration: research and instructional design. In J. W. Brown & S. N. Brown (eds.). *Educational Media Yearbook.* Littleton, Colorado: Libraries Unlimited.

Eisemon, T. O., Hallett, M. & Maunda, J. (1986) Primary school literature and folktales in Kenya: what makes a children's story African?, *Comparative Education Review,* **30**, (2), pp. 232-246.

FitzGerald, F. (1980) *America Revised: History Schoolbooks in the Twentieth Century.* New York: Vintage.

Gopinathan, S. (1986) *And shall the twain meet? Public and private-sector relationships in textbook publishing in less developed countries.* Singapore: Institute of Education (mimeo).

Gopinathan, S. (1984) *Intellectual Dependency and the Indigenization Response: Case Studies of Three Disciplines in Two Third World Universities.* Buffalo, New York: State University of New York (unpublished doctoral dissertation).

Gopinathan, S. (1985) Publishing: transnational influences. In Torsten Husen & T. Neville Postlethwaite (eds.). *International Encyclopedia of Education.* Oxford: Pergamon.

Hartley, J. & Klare, G. (1978) Textbooks. In D. Unwin & R. McAleese (eds.) *Encyclopedica of Educational Media Communication and Technology.* London: Macmillan.

Heyneman, S. P., Farrell, J. P. & Sepulveda-Stuardo, M. A. (1978) *Textbooks and Achievement: What We Know.* Washington, D.C.: World Bank (staff paper 298).

Hilton, E. (1969) Textbooks. In R. L. Ebel (ed.), *Encyclopedia of Educational Research,* 4th edition. Toronto: Macmillan.

Jonassen, D. H. (1986) *The Technology of Text: Principles for Structuring, Designing, and Displaying Text.* Englewood Cliffs, N. J.: Educational Technology Publications.

Newmann, P. H. (1980) *Publishing for Schools: Textbooks and the Less Developed Countries.* Washington, D.C.: World Bank (staff paper 398).

Pelletti, J. C. (1982) The effect of graphic roles in elementary social studies on cognition achievement. Cited by E. W. Warming in H. E. Mitzel (ed.), *Encyclopedia of Educational Research,* 5th edition. New York: Free Press.

Robinson, P. (ed.). (1981) *Publishing for Canadian Classrooms.* Halifax, Nova Scotia: Canadian Learning Materials Center.

Searle, B. (1986) *General Operational Review of Textbooks.* Washington: World Bank (mimeo).

Singh, Tejeshwar. (1985) Publishing in India: crisis and opportunity. In P. G. Altbach, A. A. Arboleda, & S. Gopinathan, (eds.) (1985) *Publishing in the Third World: Knowledge and Development.* New Hampshire: Heinemann.

Smith, K. (1975) Who controls book publishing in anglophone Middle Africa? In *Annals of the American Academy of Political and Social Science, 421,* (September), pp. 140-150.

Unesco-Asia. (1984) *Textbooks and Reading Materials Vol. 3: Textbook Production and Utilisation in Asia and the Pacific.* Bangkok: Unesco Regional Office for Education in Asia and the Pacific.

Yoloye, E. Ayotunde. (1986) The relevance of educational content to national needs in Africa, *International Review of Education, 32,* (2), pp. 149-172.

PART IV: EDUCATIONAL OPERATING SYSTEMS

An Example of Socio-political, Historical Analysis

An *operating system* can be defined as "a persistent, standardized way of doing something." By *persistent* we mean that the method is used not simply on one occasion but, instead, is used over and over so it becomes habitual. By *standardized* we mean that its basic features do not change from one occasion to another but, instead, remain essentially the same over time. When defined in this very broad sense, operating systems are clearly nothing new. People have always adopted persistent, standard ways of carrying out tasks. Furthermore, operating systems are not limited to humans, but animals display them as well, with their systems either dictated by the species' genetic nature—as in the division of labor among ants and bees—or learned through experience—as in a dog's sitting up to beg for food. And if we define *education* as "a planned process for fostering learning," then an educational operating system will be "a planned, persistent, standardized way of promoting learning."

The purpose of this introductory essay is to sketch some principal characteristics of educational operating systems and to offer illustrations of these characteristics. Then the two chapters that comprise Part IV analyze in detail an array of factors that contributed to the development and transfer of the governmental institution known as *the ministry of education*, the most powerful educational operating system in the present-day world. In Chapter 8, Professor McGinn traces the ministry structure as it evolved in France from before Napoleon's time. Then in Chapter 9, Professor Kelly analyzes the transfer of the ministry structure to French colonies in Southeast Asia, where it continues to dominate the administration of education today.

One useful way to comprehend the nature of educational operating systems is to analyze them along a series of dimensions that represent different perspectives. Each dimension offers a particular way to view a system, thereby furnishing diverse insights that enrich our comprehension of the system as a whole. In the following discussion we consider dimensions under two categories—descriptive and causal. Descriptive dimensions answer the question: What is the system's structure, and how does the system function? Causal dimensions answer: What forces or conditions have caused the system to reach its present state?

Descriptive Dimensions of Operating Systems

From the multitude of viewpoints we could adopt for describing an operating system's form and function, we have chosen seven for the purpose of illustration. The seven concern a system's scope, range of tasks, form of organization, procedures, personnel, facilities, and assessment techniques.

Dimension 1: Scope

The term *scope*, as used here, refers to both (1) the type and variety of educational goals encompassed by the system and (2) the number of people involved.

As examples of goal types and variety, consider these three systems— a national ministry of education, a parent–teacher association, and a mastery-learning instructional technique. Of the three systems, the ministry of education is responsible for the broadest range of educational goals, because the nation's entire educational enterprise can come within the ministry's purview. Ministry policies can influence lifelong education from preschool through old age, including formal, nonformal, and informal programs. In comparison, a parent–teacher association in a single school typically focuses on a far more limited range of goals— home-school relations and the kinds of support activities that parents may furnish to help with their children's schooling. Even more limited in scope is the goal of a mastery-learning mode of instruction. The phrase *mastery-learning* has been coined to identify a set of instructional procedures that teachers adopt to reach the goal of ensuring each pupil an optimum opportunity to achieve the objectives of a lesson. A mastery-learning system includes such a sequence of procedures as (a) choosing objectives which the student is reasonably well prepared to pursue, (b) stating the objectives in the form of observable behaviors, (c) offering instruction, (d) frequently evaluating the student's achievement, (e) offering the student ways to correct shortcomings revealed by the evaluation, and (f) continuing this cycle of evaluation and correctives until the objectives have been mastered.

When we compare our three exemplary operating systems in terms of the numbers of people involved, we recognize that the ministry of education has the broadest scope, since it touches the lives of everyone in the nation who is engaged in education, either as a staff member or as a learner. In contrast, a parent–teacher association in a single school affects only a small number of people, and a mastery-learning program in a single classroom influences even fewer. Of course, if a ministry of education adopts a mastery-learning system for all of the nation's junior-secondary schools, then the scope of mastery-learning becomes far greater.

Dimension 2: Range of Tasks Performed

This second dimension focuses on the question: What tasks or activities does the system require for the pursuit of the goals? Answering this question explains how people and equipment are expected to spend their time. In way of illustration, consider the activities required by three additional operating systems—a "new-math" instructional program, a vocational-guidance program, and a test-item bank.

General tasks in the new-math program include those of specifying new-math objectives, obtaining suitable textbooks, training teachers in new-math instructional procedures, and evaluating how well students have achieved the objectives. Each of these tasks can then be analyzed into more specific constituent activities. For example, the activity of obtaining suitable textbooks can include the subtasks of: (a) establishing criteria for textbook selection, (b) obtaining a variety of textbooks to examine, (c) examining the textbooks in relation to the criteria, (d) selecting the text that best meets the standards, (e) determining the number of students who will need the books, and (f) ordering the books so they will arrive by the time they are needed.

One type of vocational-guidance program can involve these general tasks: surveying the vocational needs of the community, acquainting students with key characteristics of different vocations (training requirements, working conditions, opportunity for advancement, income), examining individual students' vocational interests, and engaging students in the task of comparing their interests and skills with the vocational opportunities in the community. Then each of these activities can be further analyzed into its subtasks.

Test-item banking is a method for storing large numbers of test items in a computer so the items are readily available whenever evaluators wish to compose an achievement test. The general tasks required by a test-banking system can include (a) determining the subject-matter areas to be included in the bank, (b) defining the learning objectives for each area, (c) creating and collecting test items focusing on those learning objectives, (d) assessing the quality of the test items (reliability, clarity, validity), (e) devising a computer program that facilitates the storage and retrieval of the items, (f) informing potential users of the services the item bank offers, and (g) establishing procedures for the continuing implementation of these services. Again, each of these functions is comprised of more specific subfunctions.

Dimension 3: Organizational Characteristics

Once the goals and tasks have been identified, it is instructive to learn how the parts of the system fit together. This dimension is sometimes referred to as the *organizational structure* or *administrative hierarchy*. Frequently an organizational structure is presented in the form of a diagram that is intended to reflect the levels of authority and lines of communication that are expected to obtain in the system.

Figure IV.1 displays the general structure of a small North American city school system. The levels of authority are represented as different strata, with the greatest decision-making power at the top and the least power at the bottom. The lines connecting the boxes show the official channels of communication, which are the routes through which messages move up and down among the elements of the system. It should be apparent that the diagram oversimplifies the system's structure, since each of the elements in the diagram has its own more detailed pattern of elements. For example, the school board has five members, one of whom is the president of the board, while each other member has a special assigned role—secretarial, legal, public-relations, or financial. Likewise, each of the assistant superintendents is in charge of a variety of employees who have specialized assignments and levels of responsibility within their segment of the structure.

In addition to diagrams that display intended power and communication relationships, operating systems typically include written regulations describing these relationships in greater detail. The regulations not only clarify the responsibilities and privileges of each unit, but they also describe the relationship of one unit to the rest.

Figure IV.2 displays the structure of a traditional Muslim school in Indonesia, a type of school known as a *pesantren*. It is a school in which students, known as *santri*, study Islamic religious doctrine and traditions under the tutelage of a Muslim scholar (an *ajengan*) and his staff. The school is usually in the countryside, where the students live an ascetic life in simple dormitories. They often work in the ajengan's rice fields or around his home as payment for his instruction. As Fig. IV.2 shows, in this particular school, the scholar is at the top of the authority hierarchy, with his wife and their two adult sons serving as assistant instructors. Four of the more experienced santris function as teaching aides, with the 60 regular santris at the bottom of the authority hierarchy. As the lines of communication indicate, the ajengan and his assistants all

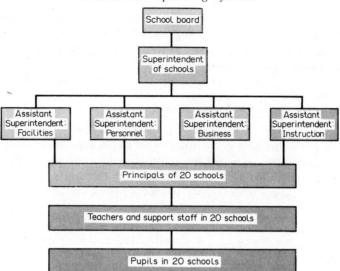

Fig IV.1. Organizational Structure of City School System

communicate directly with the regular students, so that the channels of communication are more direct than in the city school system pictured in Fig. IV.1. Like the city school system, the pesantren has regulations governing relationships among its units. But unlike the city system, the Muslim school's regulations are not written. Instead, they are merely understandings that new students gradually acquire in the form of advice offered by more experienced santri and the instruction staff.

Although such formal diagrams and their accompanying written regulations are useful for describing intended authority and communication relationships, the actual day-to-day operation of the system usually deviates to some extent from the formal plan. For example, in the city school system, a teacher who plays golf regularly with the superintendent establishes a communication link outside the formal structure.

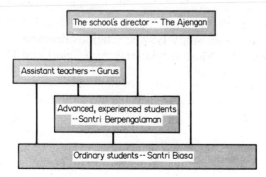

Fig IV.2. Organizational Structure of an Indonesian Islamic Pesantren

Likewise, a student whose mother is a member of the school board acquires potential power not recognized in the diagram. Furthermore, while the formal structure suggests that power flows from the top to bottom, when teachers organize a successful strike, they manage to reverse the exercise of power by exerting pressure which influences the behavior of authorities above them.

Another way that the formal structure falls short in accounting for the complete operation of the system is in its failure to picture forces outside the structure that affect the system's operation. For instance, the Indonesian pesantren is aided by a Muslim philanthropic society which provides funds and textbooks to help support the school. Likewise, the ajengan's two sons have recently taken positions with the regional Ministry of Religion office, so they no longer are available as full-time instructors.

In summary, an important aspect of an educational operating system is its formal structure, including the identification of its units and an explanation of the duties and privileges assigned to each unit, along with the authority and communication relationships among units. However, each system in its daily operation deviates to some degree from the formal description of its units. Therefore, an accurate understanding of the system not only requires an account of its formal structure, but also requires information about how the system-in-practice departs from its formal description.

Dimension 4: Sequence of Operating Procedures

In addition to channels of authority and communication, a proper description of an educational organization also includes a pattern of steps that are followed in carrying out the system's functions. The pattern answers questions of chronology—what happens first, what happens second, which events happen in parallel, which events happen in recurring cycles, and the like. As with authority and communication structures, these steps are often displayed diagrammatically. For instance, Fig. IV.3 depicts the steps that each proposed research project is to follow in a university's educational-research bureau.

Because the formal sequence of steps in a system may not accurately describe the way the system functions in practice, a proper understanding of the steps requires an analysis of the unit's day-by-day operation in addition to the information provided in its formal plan.

Dimension 5: Operating Personnel

The term *operating personnel*, as used here, refers not only to the people who provide educational services but also to the recipients of

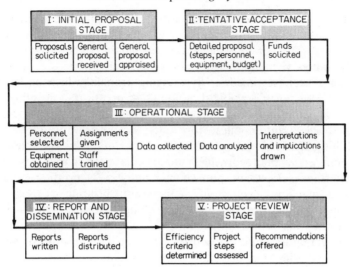

FIG IV.3 Project Flow-Chart for a University Research Bureau

those services. Hence, the operating personnel in a school are not only the administrators, teachers, and support staff, but also the students, since the system cannot operate without students. Likewise, in the case of a curriculum-development bureau, not only are the people who work in the bureau considered to be operating personnel, but also the teachers in the schools who use the curriculum materials are regarded as personnel.

Questions that lead to an understanding of how both the providers and the recipients of services fit into the educational system include: (1) How is each job or role in the system defined? (2) What are the requirements for admission into each role? (3) What responsibilities or tasks are assigned to a given role? (4) Where and how do people acquire the requisites for admission to the role and the skills needed for performing the role? (5) What privileges, rewards, and opportunities does each role provide? (6) How is performance in one's role evaluated? (7) What consequences result from such evaluations—that is, what influence does high-level performance compared to low-level performance exert on the individual's fate, on other personnel, and on the system?

Dimension 6: Facilities—Equipment and Supplies

Facilities are the physical settings and materials employed by the system to carry out its tasks—buildings, furniture, machines, and books as well as such expendable supplies as stationery, chemicals, and the like. Educational operating systems differ markedly in the number and variety of

facilities they need. For instance, a textbook-publishing operation requires a broad diversity of facilities, whereas a budget-and-accounting
operation calls for only a modest number, and a socratic-discussion
method requires virtually none.

The range of items needed by a large-scale textbook-publishing unit
includes the following array: (a) buildings—for offices, a printing plant,
and the storage of equipment, paper, and finished books; (b) transport
vehicles—trucks, automobiles, fork lifts; (c) office furniture—chairs,
desks, tables, file cabinets; (d) office machines—typewriters, telephones,
microcomputers, photocopying units; (e) reference resources—
dictionaries, encyclopedias, publishing manuals; (f) printing facilities—
typesetting machines, composing equipment, printing presses, book-
binding machines; (g) supplies—office stationery, art materials, book
paper, printing ink.

The budget-and-accounting unit of a provincial education department
requires a building for offices, automobiles for transportation, office
furniture, office machines (typewriters, telephones, computers), reference resources (statistical summaries, accounting procedures), and stationery.

A socratic discussion method does not require any particular equipment, because it is simply a special style of dialogue between teacher
and student. The method is named for the ancient Greek sage, Socrates,
whose instructional dialogues were described in Plato's writings (Buchanan, 1948). What distinguishes a socratic approach from other discussion
techniques is the pattern of its questions. The socratic questions a
teacher poses for the learners are designed in such a logical sequence
that, as students answer each query, they carry themselves necessarily to
the ultimate conclusion the instructor wanted them to reach. Such a
teaching method requires no special facilities or supplies. It can be used
at the seashore or on a park bench or in a classroom.

Dimension 7: Assessment Methods

Our final descriptive dimension is defined by the question: What techniques are employed in the system to assess the efficiency of its operation?

Educational systems vary greatly in the ways they evaluate their goals,
their organizational structure, their work patterns, their personnel, their
facilities, and their final products. In the case of a given system, the
attempt to discover these ways can be guided by such questions as:
Which aspects of the system are evaluated, either formally or informally? Against what standards, or according to what criteria, is each of
these aspects compared? Who carries out the assessments? What evaluation instruments or techniques are used? To whom, and in what form,
are the assessment outcomes reported? How are the assessment out-

comes used; that is, what action results from the evaluation reports?

In conclusion, the foregoing seven dimensions illustrate types of perspectives that can be used for describing significant characteristics of educational operating systems. The dimensions are especially useful as the bases on which to compare one system with another. With the descriptive dimensions now behind us, we turn to our second analytical category, that of causal dimensions.

Causal Dimensions for Analyzing Operating Systems

In proposing causal dimensions, we are attempting to provide a scheme for answering questions about what forces or conditions are responsible for a system reaching its present state. Such dimensions have been our principal concern throughout this volume.

There are many patterns in which causal dimensions can be cast, with each pattern or approach providing a different way of analyzing a system. Six of these approaches are briefly described below. The first two relate to time (contemporary factors and chronological sequences), while the last four relate to scholarly disciplines (sociology, political science, psychology, and economics).

Cluster 1: Causes in Relation to Time

A *contemporary-factors* perspective is defined by the question: What conditions at the present time are accounting for the form and function of the operating system?

When we employ this approach for causal analysis, we try to discover what forces currently are bearing on the system, including forces that serve to maintain the system's present state as well as forces pressing to change it. We also try to learn the relative influence or power of the contending forces, on the assumption that some of the factors are more significant than others.

A *chronological-sequence* viewpoint is reflected in the question: What progression of factors or events led to the state that an operating system has reached at a particular time? This is the historical approach, that of tracing the steps by which one event has led to another as the years passed. Historical analysis very often includes some measure of a contemporary-factors perspective in that historians are seldom satisfied with identifying only one causal event that leads to subsequent happenings. Instead, they commonly cite a series of simultaneous forces that have converged at a given time to forge each new linkage in an historical sequence of events. This sort of historical approach appears in Chapters 8 and 9, where the evolution of the ministry of education is followed over a period of two centuries.

206 R. Murray Thomas

Cluster 2: Causes from the Viewpoints of Scholarly Disciplines

Our understanding of causal factors behind educational systems depends not only on the time span included in the analysis but also on which scholarly disciplines are used as the lenses through which the system is viewed. Each discipline focuses attention on its own set of questions.

The field of political science is typically concerned with how power or authority is distributed and exercised in a society. Consequently, the questions political scientists seek to answer include: Who has the power to make what sorts of decisions in the society, and why do such people hold that power? How secure is the authority of those in power? In other words, to what extent do the governed accept the existing authorities as the legitimate governors? What methods are used to gain and maintain power in the society, and why are such methods used? What relationships exist between the education system and the political agencies of the society and why do such relationships obtain?

The field of sociology is concerned with ways people are organized and with how the groups relate to each other. Sociologists ask such questions as: What kinds of groupings of people exist in the society? What determines whether a person becomes a member of a particular group? What are the advantages and disadvantages for the individuals who belong in various groups? Under what conditions can people change their group membership? How do the characteristics of a group influence that group's relationship to other groups in the society?

Psychology, as a scholarly discipline, seeks to explain how individuals think, feel, and act. Psychologists ask: To what extent are an individual's thoughts, feelings, and actions determined by the person's genetic structure and to what extent by environmental influences? Which environmental forces have the greatest influence on the person at different stages of life? To what extent can an individual's beliefs and actions affect the physical environment and exert influence on other people's lives?

The discipline of economics deals with questions about the production, distribution, and consumption of commodities. Consequently, economists inquire about: Who controls the methods of production and distribution, and by what means do they maintain this control? What positions do different people hold in the economic system, and how do they obtain their positions? How do the strengths and weaknesses of one economic system compare with the strengths and weaknesses of other systems?

It is apparent that the domains of these four disciplines blend with each other in complex ways. Such overlapping has resulted in the evolution of such hybrid disciplines as social psychology, political economics, and political psychology. It is also clear that the analysis of educational operating systems is enriched when authors draw on more than one discipline for their explanations of cause. This fact is illustrated in Chapter 8 and 9, where McGinn and Kelly depend heavily on sociological and political perspectives for interpreting the evolution and dissemination of the ministry of education as a social organization. However, they have drawn very little from economic and psychological perspectives to account for the development of the ministry as a form of technology. If the two authors had chosen to concentrate on psychological variables (the influence of particular personalities) and economic forces rather than socio-political factors, the resulting account of the ministry's development would have been somewhat different. Hence, authors' choices of disciplines to apply in their analyses reflect their estimate of which kinds of forces have been the most powerful determinants of the operating system they are inspecting.

Conclusion

The purpose of this introductory essay has been to identify ways that a variety of perspectives can be adopted for describing educational operating systems and for explaining what has brought the systems to their present condition. A different picture of the system will result if an author adopts one set of perspectives or dimensions rather than another. In Chapters 8 and 9, McGinn and Kelly depict the ministry of education in France and in French Indo-China by means of a chronological-sequence approach which features both sociological and political perspectives.

Reference

Buchanan, Scott (ed.) (1948) *The Portable Plato.* New York: Viking.

CHAPTER 8

The Creation and Development of an Educational Operating System:

NOEL F. MCGINN

The Bureaucratic Organization of the French National System of State Education

This chapter focuses on one technology for the operation of national state education systems—the bureaucracy. The particular historical example chosen—the French National System of state education created formally by Napoleon I—has at least two merits. First, most public educational systems, particularly in the developing countries of the world, use today an organizational technology remarkably like that which appeared in France 150 years ago. The French example can be used to understand the education operating systems of other countries.

Second, although there is relatively little research on bureaucracy in education (Anderson, 1968, and Katz, 1971, are exceptions), it has been well studied in other kinds of organizations, and we have a good understanding of its characteristics, benefits, and drawbacks. Even though little research has been done on the transfer of this organizational technology from the education systems of central countries to those of peripheral countries, there is a conceptual model that permits useful inferences. Chapter 9 is a test of that assumption.

Two major features define a state educational system as *national.* First, it is universal, that is, found in all parts of the nation. Second, it is uniform in its organization across constituent elements of the nation. Several countries of the world have private national systems of education, e.g., the schools run by the Catholic Church. And a handful have state educational systems controlled at the provincial or local levels.

The major distinctions between state and private education systems are that (1) the former are owned and operated in the name of all the people and groups in society, and not by and for particular individuals, groups or corporations, and (2) state systems are designed to incorporate all persons, at least at the initial or entry levels. As we shall see, this latter feature is directly related with the technology that the French state developed to manage its educational system.

The earliest modern state system of education may have been that of Prussia. Other countries had public schools, and some had national systems of privately-owned schools, but the Prussians, under Frederick II, appear to have been the first to create a public system that in principle was to enroll all children. On the other hand, Prussia was not a nation-state; the French system that emerged under Napoleon therefore is recognized as the first national state system of education. Today most countries have national state systems of education, with remarkable similarities in their content and organization, attributed to the influence of a world system dominated by the early-industrialized countries (Meyer and Hannan, 1979).

The purpose of this chapter is to provide a basis for analyzing the transfer of the bureaucratic technology of organization in education from France (and other early-industrialized countries) to the developing world. The chapter has four major parts. First, the chapter contrasts bureaucracy with other technologies for the operation and management of the state and its organizations. Second, it reviews possible explanations for the emergence of organizational technologies in education. In a third section, these hypotheses are tested through a review of the history of the development of bureaucracy as the dominant technology in France in the early nineteenth century. Finally, the chapter suggests some reasons why bureaucracy continues to be the dominant technology of educational management.

Technologies for the Management and Control of State Organizations

Therborn has identified four major technologies of state organization: seigneurial or aristocratic; bureaucratic; technocratic; and cadre. Their differences can be summarized as a function of three variables: the basis of loyalty to the ruling person or group; the basis for distinguishing between levels of authority within the organization; and the means by which leadership is actually exercised (Therborn, 1978). The categorical scheme is useful to highlight the major features of the bureaucratic technology of organization.

The feudal state was held together on the basis of hierarchical relationships of personal loyalty, justified through a code of honor that specified ideals for which persons were to strive. Law was based on custom, and no special training was needed to manage the affairs of state. The efficacy and efficiency of this technology of social organization is testified by the pockets of feudal organizations still found today. Much of the elements of the "prismatic society" claimed by Riggs to be the dominant form of state organization in developing countries are consistent with the feudal technology of management (Riggs, 1964). The charismatic leader continues to be a force in modern society as well, despite the general dominance of the bureaucratic technology. For example, the failure of planning is generally ascribed to the presence of personal relationships or "irrational" politics based on personal or group loyalties rather than on allegiance to more abstract rules (Caiden & Wildavsky, 1974).

The term bureaucracy is used in several ways in social science (Crozier, 1964): as a pejorative to describe the frustrations experienced by clients of large organizations; to refer to government by offices or "bureaus"; and in the sense originally intended by Max Weber, as a form of organization that stresses specialized knowledge as the major basis for identifying the hierarchy of authority in an organization, as well as the basis for legitimizing that rule (Weber, 1962). It is this third definition that is followed in this chapter.

The effectiveness and efficiency of the bureaucratic technology of management and control depends on the imposition of "calculable rules" and a system of formal rationality that applies equally to all the members, including the rulers. Laws are based on reason and experience; special training is necessary both to learn the laws, and to learn how to apply them (e.g., to work through inconsistencies). The utilization of rules makes personnel management "impersonal" and regards workers who perform the same tasks within the organization as interchangeable. As the organization grows in size, it grows in complexity. The efficiency achieved through division of labor is enhanced by creating even more specialized roles. Because fewer persons are capable of carrying out these tasks, the bureau establishes a hierarchical system of controls and rewards that channels "talented" persons into the most specialized positions.

Weber understood the bureaucracy to be a system of exploitation, in which through emphasis of obedience to rational and public rules, the masters of the organization were able to hide from public scrutiny their actual goals for the organization. He referred to the bureaucratic social structure as a "crypto-plutocratic distribution of power" (Weber, 1968: 989) within society. Administrative secrecy about the actual performance of the bureau (as opposed to the rules that govern the conduct of its members) was seen by Weber as a fundamental and essential part of the efficacy of this technology as a means of extracting and accumulating resources (Antonio, 1979). In bureaucracy, centralization of decision-making is justified in terms of formal rationality, but also contributes to the maintenance of secrecy over the actual operations of the bureau.

A third kind of technology for organizational management has emerged in the nineteenth century, and in the past several decades has become dominant in most large organizations, including government.

Therborn calls this technocracy, to denote that the basis for authority is now technical skill and technical knowledge, rather than membership in a rules-governed office or bureau. Like bureaucracy, technocracy:

> is characterized by specialization, impersonality and stratified monopolization of intellectual knowledge by professionals. But it does not rely to the same degree on calculable rules and fixed hierarchies . . . Its rationality is substantive rather than formal; and, instead of juridical knowledge, it promotes technical and scientific expertise applied with discretion and consideration of actual effects, rather than with calculable legal precision. The stable hierarchy is broken up by ad hoc committees, working parties, and special enquiries (Therborn, 1978: 54).

Management by objectives, contingency planning, situational planning, the task force, are characteristic of the technocratic approach to management. Planning in bureaucracies specifies the sequence of actions to reach long-term goals; technocratic planning relies more on a situational approach in which plans are revised frequently in response to information about the organization's performance. Staff officers in bureaucratic organizations are chosen for their training in and knowledge of organizational procedures and rules; staff officers in technocracies are generally specialists in a discipline with no particular knowledge of or training in management per se.

The emergence of technocratic forms of organization has generally been conflictual: technocratic management is proposed by groups not currently in power seeking to displace groups whose power is in part based on the structures and process of bureaucratic management. The groups espousing the two technologies often differ in class origin, political ideology, and levels and kind of education. Examples of the struggle for dominance within ministries of education of "technocratic" versus "bureaucratic" groups are Benoit (1974, 1975) and McGinn and Street (1982).

The fourth form of organizational technology has not yet appeared in any of the world's education systems, and therefore is described only briefly here. Therborn argues that the collective mass organization employs a distinctive managerial technology in which

> The central figure is not the priest shepherding his flock towards salvation, nor the feudal seigneur, capitalist manager-technocrat or rule-applying bureaucrat, but the organizer. His principal ability is that of ideological and practical mobilization for common goals. He also has a special kind of knowledge which has as its objective class organization and class struggle; or, to put it more generally, social

organization and the social struggle of which he is himself part (Therborn, 1978: 57).

This technology of social organization may have been dominant in China during the Cultural Revolution (1966-1976) or in the long struggle that led up to the establishment of the People's Republic. It also characterizes some political organizations in Socialist countries, as well as mass organizations in pre-revolutionary societies.

The neat distinctions made by Therborn blur in reality for at least two reasons. First, two or more technologies may be employed within a single organization. Even as the French state adopted bureaucracy as the official technology of management in the early 1800s, some institutions persisted with a charismatic, personalistic technology of management.

Second, the practice of individual technologies of management does not always adhere to every detail to the "ideal type" description of that technology: bureaucrats do not always behave as they preach. (Or, in other words, persons in organizations may use more than one technology according to the problems the organization faces. This is the finding of Peterson (1984) who looked at the methods used by managers in elementary school districts of varying sizes in the United States. In general, there is heavy reliance by superintendents on bureaucratic methods—such as direct supervision and central control over curriculum—but higher status and larger districts are more likely to also rely on more technocratic methods—such as asking principals to set and meet performance objectives.) Despite the ambiguities of the concept, it is however possible and useful to define the essential features of bureaucracy as an operating system.

Explanations of the Emergence of Bureaucracy

What are the causes of the transition from the relative dominance of one technology of management to another? Specifically, why did bureaucracy emerge as the dominant technology of educational organization (replacing personalism) in France at the beginning of the nineteenth century? There are at least 4 possible explanations.

1. Bureaucracy was chosen as a technology of management to match the specific tasks of educational institutions.
2. Bureaucracy was chosen because of a general belief that it is the most appropriate technology for all organizations.
3. Bureaucracy emerged as dominant through an evolutionary process in which "natural selection" substituted bureaucracy for the more traditional technology of organization.

4. Bureaucracy was constructed as the outcome of a conflictual process in which bureaucratic practices enabled one group to achieve dominance over others.

These explanations are not mutually exclusive, but they do point to different kinds of social processes.

1. The first explanation requires an assumption that those who designed the operating system of education had a clear conception of the special tasks of education. Concepts such as education for the New Society, the "making of Frenchmen," (Baker & Harrigan, 1980), "the well-educated gentleman," and the use of examinations to certify that a person is "educated," all indicate a belief in the ability to specify what knowledge, skills, and attitudes a student should learn through education. This belief makes the major task of education the transmission of a given curriculum or content, a specification in advance of what is to be learned. If, in addition, it is assumed that all students *can* learn what is presented to them if certain methods are followed by teachers, and that it is possible to identify and train persons who will impart the curriculum as pre-defined, then bureaucracy, as a technology of organization emphasizing calculable rules, makes eminently good sense. If those responsible for the organization of the French national education system had a clear conception of the implications of their theory of education, and consciousness of the special merits of bureaucracy as a technology of organization appropriate to the special tasks of education, then the first explanation would be correct.

2. The second explanation will be considered validated if we can show that bureaucracy was seen as superior to other technologies of organization for all institutions. The following evidence is pertinent. The rationalism of the definition of educational technology provided in Chapter 1 was also the dominant mode of thought in France in the late eighteenth and early nineteenth centuries. People *knew* that their world was an orderly system governed by innate laws that could be detected by observation of the regularities of the system. *Science* was understood as a process of discovery of knowledge, through the use of the senses, and the organization of that knowledge into *theories* understood not as speculations about reality, but descriptions of the laws governing that reality. In such a world, it made sense to have goals and objectives— and not just dreams or ideals—and to plan one's advance toward them. For the French who had just overthrown the Ancien Regime, it made sense to formulate a Constitution that specified the rules to be followed in order to produce a society characterized by liberty, fraternity, and equality. Many believed that bureaucracy would increase equity through the regulation of recruitment, examinations, and promotion of State personnel (Markoff, 1975).

While the first and second explanations are reasonable, they leave unexplained how it was that people came to believe that the world is orderly, and that they knew enough in order to impose in advance the rules that if followed would result in increased efficiency and equity. The third and fourth explanations respond to these questions. Both argue for a process of gradual development of bureaucracy as a dominant technology, a process in which changes in social behavior and social structures produced by multiple causes led to the design of a new form of social organization. These explanations assert that the dynamic of human history involves praxis, or reflection on action; that human history is not a history of ideas but of actions that generate ideas. Bureaucracy was a discovery, but not an invention of Weber. For example, the Roman government at the time of the Empire was bureaucratic in form (Antonio, 1979); Jacoby describes the emergence of bureaucracy under Frederick William I (1688-1740) of Prussia (Jacoby, 1973). There were strong elements of bureaucracy in the regime of Louis XVI prior to the Revolution.

3. The third explanation argues that bureaucracy emerged as the dominant technology of organization (first in the Church, then in industry) because organizations with a bureaucratic operating system were more successful in the struggle for existence than were organizations structured according to a different technology.

The "ecological theory of bureaucracy" posits that either an organization adapts to changes in its environment or "dies." Langton (1984) analyzes the development of the British pottery industry in the late eighteenth century (1760-90), with particular attention to the emergence of the Wedgwood firm as the leader in the industry. Langton argues that it was the principles of Darwinian evolution, rather than foresight on the part of Josiah Wedgwood, that led to the domination (for a short period of time) of the pottery industry by the Wedgwood firm. These principles are variation, or innovation; heredity, or organizational continuity; and natural selection, or differential reproduction. Wedgwood did not know, when he began to experiment with new forms of organization for production, that they would be more effective and efficient than others. But the introduction of variation into what had been a uniform process of pottery production led to differential rewards by the environment (market) to some forms as compared to others.

Wedgwood's major innovation was, following analysis of the methods of production of the best workers, to detail in writing the specific actions all workers should take in the production process. This included specification of the hours of arrival and departure from the factory, the time to be taken for rest periods, the sequence of steps to be used in preparing the clay, the glaze, etc. These specifications were in the form of rules to which each candidate for employment had to agree. Deviations from the rules were punished with pre-determined sanctions, without regard to the person involved.

The imposition of owner-specified work rules, instead of reliance on the traditional personalist, or artesanal approach to production in which each worker determined his/her own pace, product, etc., permitted Wedgwood to standardize the quality of the product of his workers and over time to improve the general level of quality. Conflict with workers was reduced, as the Firm justified its actions by reference to a set of impersonal rules to which all employees agreed at time of contract. With experience, rules that did not contribute to improved efficiency were replaced, just as were inefficient workers. The Wedgwood firm not only became a symbol of high quality in pottery, but also generated larger profit margins than did other, non-bureaucratized firms. Those less efficient firms failed and were eliminated, i.e., they were not able to reproduce themselves.

> Wedgwood . . . found bureaucracy to be very rewarding because it allowed him to get, in many senses of the word, much more out of his workers and consequently out of the environment than traditional modes of organization (Langton, 1984: 349).

Over time, Wedgwood lost its position of advantage, however, as other firms, through modelling (or rational imitation) and vicarious reinforcement adopted the same bureaucratic technology. By the beginning of the nineteenth century almost all pottery production in England was through relatively large, centrally-managed firms that employed workers as units of production controlled by work rules.

This same process occurred in other industries, and in France and the rest of Europe as well. Over time, as successful capitalists and their intellectuals had an opportunity to reflect on the process, a theory of bureaucracy was developed to explain the success of capitalist firms over more traditional forms of ownership and production. The next generation of capitalists then adopted that theory as the basis for the organization of their own productive processes. What in the twentieth century was called "scientific management" (Braverman, 1974) had its roots in the bureaucratization of industry in the late eighteenth. (For a critique of the ecological theory of bureaucracy see Perrow, 1985.)

4. The fourth explanation of the emergence of bureaucracy as the dominant technology in the education system of France addresses the question: Why was the French operating system for education at that time so much more bureaucratic than others, e.g., the English system? This hypothesis explains the differential rather than universal appearance of the bureaucratic technology.

In general, two major forms of educational organization developed in Europe, as a function of the relative power of the Church and the State with respect to other groups (Archer, 1979). In countries like England

and Denmark, new groups in society controlled enough resources that they could replace the schools controlled by the Church with their own. These groups in general did not control the State, and the State's role was as a mediator between the Church and the new social groups. Over time (about the end of the nineteenth century in England) the social cost of competing education systems became such that the groups involved asked the State to act as a mediator, and to create a decentralized system of public education.

In France and Russia, on the other hand, the new groups that acted through or took control of the State did not have enough resources to create an education system parallel to that of the Church. They could not replace Church schools with their own, but they were able to substitute State control for Church control of education. The emergence of a national public system of education with a bureaucratic form of control was the means by which this was accomplished.

Three major factors were at work. First, when the State was forced to assume control of a system that it had not itself created (and which in fact it could not operate solely with its own personnel and its own financial resources), it became necessary to substitute "entrepreneurial" with "managerial" management systems (Archer, 1979: 150). This led to an attempt to unify (or centralize direction of) the system in order to maximize control.

Second, as the State grew in size it relied more on the education system in order to produce the human resources it needed to reproduce itself and its ability to control society. Education was re-designed to prepare the elites and specialized functionaries who would carry out tasks according to the dictates of the State. Training and certification were the major methods used to insure that the State would acquire the human resources it needed.

Third, because the State did not have sufficient resources of its own to provide education demanded by groups outside the State, it chose to permit management of some parts of the system by other groups, under supervision. At the same time, demands for education by many sectors was met by differentiation of the system (e.g., tracks in the secondary level), which increased managerial difficulties. To maintain control, the State attempted to regulate the inputs into the system (e.g., teacher certification) while at the same time imposing uniform standard for outputs (e.g., national examinations). This imposition of controls through regulations had the effect of increasing the autonomy of the organization itself. Organizations emerged as populated with "bureaucrats," with functionaries seeking to perpetuate the organization whose rules, originally designed to insure that the State's wishes would be fulfilled, now served in some measure to protect the interests of the functionaries.

These four perspectives have different implications with respect to the kinds of problems that will be faced, and generated, by the use of the bureaucratic technology. I will return to them at the end of the chapter when we discuss the kinds of problems faced by the system in France.

The Bureaucratization of Education in France

We are accustomed to speaking of "bureaucracy" in terms of governmental inefficiency in the handling of routine matters (Crozier, 1964). But the term introduced by Weber refers to a technology of organization that dramatically increased the efficiency of the French State with respect to control of education in the eighteenth and nineteenth centuries. Bureaucratic organization enabled first the King, and then the Emperor, and later the government of the Republic, to increase their control over all educational activities, to capture and mobilize more resources, and to use those resources more efficiently for objectives set by the State. It may be that citizens found the growing set of rules and procedures troublesome and time-consuming, but the State found them essential. This section describes the process by which bureaucracy emerged as the dominant technology in education.

It is important to keep in mind that bureaucracy was not the only technology that could have developed, or have been developed. Katz (1981) describes how ruling groups in the United States in the second half of the nineteenth century chose bureaucracy over three alternative forms of education: paternalistic voluntarism, democratic localism, and corporate voluntarism. With proper allowances for differences in time and place, these three alternative forms also existed in France prior to the nineteenth century (and, as discussed in Chapter 9, were tried in various French colonies). Bureaucracy at first substituted for and later suppressed these other ways of organizing education.

The starting point is hard to fix. I have already noted that bureaucracy as a technology of organization was only named by Weber; the Romans and perhaps the Egyptians before them had organized their states along bureaucratic lines. As early as 1600 Henry IV was specifying detailed rules for the organization and management of the University of Paris, indicating books (but not textbooks) to be read; requirements to be a professor; the uniform to be worn while teaching; the principle of graded instruction ranging from the youngest to the oldest; selection of students by examination and religion; rules for student behavior; methods of finance; and the responsibilities of the rector and the deans. But the Crown, or State, so far had little control over educational activities in elementary schools and colleges, the greatest part of education in France.

The major source of concern to the Crown (as to ruling groups later in the United States) was democratic localism, in the form of the lay, public "colleges" for boys and young men operated in all the cities of France as early as 1600. These colleges provided what today would be called a "liberal" education, rather than specific training for an occupation. The French universities, on the other hand, organized by the Church in a form of corporate voluntarism, were professional schools more closely akin to American graduate schools. The colleges were thriving institutions, even though they had few bureaucratic elements, and did not constitute an education system. In each municipality they were supported by the local bourgeoisie, charged no tuition, and were taught by well-educated men who made up their own curriculum, largely based on teaching of Greek and the study of the Classics. The growth of democratic localism, particularly in regions of France known for Protestant and secessionist tendencies, alarmed both the Church hierarchy and the Crown. Municipally-controlled schools were flooding France with educated persons with democratic, free-thinking ideas. In the mid-1500s the Church hierarchy had tried to stem this tide by pressuring the burghers to let the Jesuits run the colleges. The offer was tempting, as many of the municipalities were strapped for funds, but most burghers were resistant to the threat of domination by Jesuits from Spain and Italy.

Henry IV's advisor, Richelieu, recommended that the teachers in colleges be made employees of the State, which would permit controls over their behavior. He, and other members of the Church hierarchy, believed there were too many colleges

> even in the smallest towns of the Kingdom, to the great detriment of the State . ... it is the ease of access to this bewildering number of colleges that has enabled the meanest artisans to send their children to these schools, where they are taught free of charge— and that is what has ruined everything (quoted in Huppert, 1984: xii).

Elementary schools—which provided basic literacy and numeracy to children of peasants and artisans in a form of paternalistic voluntarism— were of little concern, given that their "graduates" seldom assumed positions of importance in society. The Crown could not afford to assume control of municipal colleges through subsidization, however, and instead encouraged religious orders (at first the Jesuits, later Oratorians and members of the Christian Doctrine community, called "Doctrinaires") to negotiate with the cities for the management of their colleges, with the stipulation that the religious functionaries be French citizens. Given a shrinking economy, severe problems of internal college discipline generated by a change in public morality and respect for authority, and pressure from the Crown, some of the cities yielded. In fact, some of them were already experiencing declining enrollments. Over the next century, most of the secular municipal colleges disappeared; those that remained declined in quality until they resembled elementary schools rather than colleges (Huppert, 1984).

The Crown's alliance with the Church had other consequences for education. Early in the eighteenth century, when the Pope sought to suppress the Jansenists (who questioned the nature of the divinity of Jesus, but who also were developing as a political force that questioned Royal authority), Louis XIV sided with Rome. To reduce the Jansenists' use of schools to prepare future leaders, Louis in 1719 sought to eliminate locally-financed colleges by guaranteeing a subsidy from the State. At the same time, professors in these colleges would become employees of the State, responsible to the Crown.

Within the next 30 years the number of colleges run by municipalities and non-Church groups dwindled even further. In many cases, management of the colleges passed to the Jesuits, Oratorians, and Doctrinaires. Their colleges were "public" in the sense that they were supported with public funds, but in fact they were confessional, and had replaced the public schools run by local governments. Many of them charged fees but provided scholarships for those unable to pay.

Under the religious communities, colleges began to acquire a recognizable form of organization. The religious communities rewrote the content of programs so that there was uniformity across the schools under their control. Some of the communities certified the ability of teachers by granting of a license. Seminaries began to offer special courses to their students as preparation for teaching in the community's colleges. Some of the religious communities began to experiment, grouping children by age, anticipating the system of grades used today. Examinations were made uniform across colleges within each community, permitting comparison and competition across schools for prizes awarded by the King. Regulations for students were made uniform, as were sanctions for failure to comply. Each community developed its own system of financial accounting, as well as titles to distinguish the various ranks of teachers and administrators in the colleges (Palmer, 1985).

As a consequence of political circumstances that went far beyond the boundaries of France (and to the delight of the Jansenists), the King in 1764 was obliged to expel all Jesuits, who returned to Rome from around the world. The impact on education was dramatic. Overnight the State found itself the manager of 105 colleges, requiring more than 1,250 new teachers. The response was a bundle of proposals to fill the vacuum that had been created. These included a national, uniform system of education; the preparation of textbooks under government supervision; and the establishment of teacher training institutions. There was strong support for State involvement in the management and improvement of existing colleges, but not for their expansion, nor for State involvement in elementary education. Some in the Royal government thought there were already too many educated. The compromise was a program that provided 60 scholarships per year awarded through a national examination, for admission to a State college to train teachers.

A diagnosis of education in France, presented to the Parliament of Paris in 1768 (and published in 1785), provided a series of recommendations for the improvement of education. These included standardization of the size of the colleges; creation of educational districts; creation of secondary schools that would feed into the colleges; supervision of secondary schools by the colleges, and the colleges by the university; and establishment of teacher training institutions in each district. A proposal by the Catholic bishops called for a national standard for mealtimes and class hours; dates of vacations; books for each grade; specification of duties of principals; and specification of ventilation of dormitory quarters in boarding schools. Another group proposed a council of public instruction that would have authority over the university, colleges, and lesser schools. In 1784 the government specified the maximum age for enrollment in the levels of colleges (Palmer, 1985).

Immediately prior to the Revolution, interest in education was high, and every group had proposals for its reform. Some felt that the diversity present in the existing, unregulated elementary schools and colleges was good, not only from the point of view of providing a choice for parents among different contents and styles of education, but also in terms of encouraging innovation and creativity in the improvement of education. But the majority of sentiment was in favor of increased uniformization of education, across a wide spectrum of political beliefs. Some Catholic theologians criticized the proliferation of questionable schools that might be "open doors to the spirit of novelty and error" (Palmer, 1985: 72). The bishops had no objection to a national system of education; their assumption was that if created it would be dominated by the Church. The Crown believed that a well-managed education would contribute to curtailing the forces of dissent that were growing in the country. Even among those soon to be revolutionaries, education was seen as a vital force for the modernization of France. Standardization was believed to be essential to that process.

Representative of this latter group was Destutt de Tracy, who proposed a theory he called *ideology* which held that empirical knowledge was sufficient to understand all the major problems facing humanity, and that schools could be effective devices for teaching that set of facts that all persons should know in order to live harmonious and productive lives. The laws of science and the economy (he was an admirer of Adam Smith) could be embodied in rules that would lead to healthy societies.

> Law-makers and government are the true preceptors for the mass of the human race, and the only ones whose lessons are effective (quoted in Palmer, 1985: 4).

Education, especially with the priests removed, was the ideal mechanism for transmitting the facts that would produce the desired social order.

The power of these ideas persisted despite the violence, turmoil, and chaos generated by the Revolution. The Revolution's Declaration of the Rights of Man and the Citizen stated, "There shall be created and organized a system of Public Instruction, common for all citizens, and free for those subjects of knowledge that are indispensable for all men" (quoted in Palmer, 1985: 81). Talleyrand wrote in his Report of 1791, "Society is a vast workshop. It is not enough that all should work in it; each must be in his place." (Palmer, 1985: 95).

The Revolutionary government created a Committee on Public Instruction, with the mandate to replace the corrupt system of the monarchy with one in keeping with the new France. All institutions would have to be reformed at once, it was felt, with a single grand plan, a general law of education that covers all facets. The Council proposed that all existing educational institutions, from universities to the lowest primary schools, be suppressed, and new institutions created in their place.

The major target was the Church. Properties taken from the Church were either sold, or turned into endowments to support the new schools. The Revolutionary government organized a National Church among those priests and few bishops who supported the Revolution. Priests became employees of the State and received a salary. When the hierarchy opposed this move, the Revolutionary government required a loyalty oath of all clergy, including teachers.

The Revolutionary government had two major concerns in education; equality and the mobilization of the French people to resist the growing threats to the Revolution from outside. Elementary schools were therefore of more concern than colleges, and the task was to build a national system of uniform primary education that would produce a nation of Frenchmen willing to defend the Republic against its enemies. A major obstacle was language; French was not spoken in all parts of France. Legislation dictated that French would be the language of instruction in all schools. New textbooks were drafted, with careful attention to inclusion of Revolutionary and patriotic themes. Thousands of young men were mobilized for work as teachers in the provinces. A crash program taught them the essentials of teaching. A 1792 plan proposed a uniform primary school for children 6-11 (but not yet divided into grades); one secondary school per district (approximately 31,000); institutes that would replace the colleges, with a four-year course, for youths 15-18; the lycée, that would replace the university, and a National Society of Arts and Sciences, divided into four major specializations or disciplines, that would supervise the content of the teaching institutions and appoint professors for the lycées. The lycées in turn would supervise the institutes. Teachers for primary schools were to be trained in normal schools, borrowing a term introduced only a few years earlier in Austria (Palmer, 1985). The normal school was designed to give these neophyte teachers a uniform set of skills and knowledge, to normalize instruction.

The Revolutionary government also proposed the use of entrance examinations that would replace degrees, which were seen as "titles" that might not reflect a person's true ability. These examinations were intended to measure ability, rather than achievement, in acknowledgement of the poor state of instruction.

Like many of the proposals of the Revolutionary government, few of the democratic reforms of education were actually implemented. Many schools that had closed in reaction against the excesses of the Bourbons were never reopened; those that did provided an education not only lacking in technical quality, but often reproducing many of the earlier ills.

The bourgeoisie among the revolutionaries called for a strong hand on the tiller of state. That hand was Napoleon's. Dominant among his advisors were Enlightenment rationalists, many of whom had advised the Crown. They were strongly nationalistic and supported a common language of instruction and a common curriculum as devices for nation-building. They were anti-clerical, but not anti-religion. They criticized the Church hierarchy when it supported external enemies, but saw in the Catholic religion a common source of values that favored order and obedience. Education was critical for the formation of loyal citizens who would build the nation-state by their productive work.

In order to take control of education, Napoleon's advisors decided they needed:

1. top down control
2. to eliminate competition from private (i.e., Church) sources of education
3. compliance of teachers
4. content that engendered submission to the State by those who completed primary school, but training in leadership for those studying in colleges and lycées

5. recruitment of the most highly qualified persons as both students and as teachers
6. alliance with a powerful group outside the State (Vaughn and Archer, 1971).

Top down control was effected by the creation of the Imperial University in 1806. The University was not so much a teaching institution as a ministry (or bureau) of education in charge of the national system. The University was directed by a Grand Master, assisted by a council representing various sectors in French society (including the Church and private enterprise), all appointed by the Emperor. The University was responsible for the regulation and supervision of all teaching establishments in France, including those in private hands. The University also was given an exclusive right to grant degrees (in effect, preventing the establishment of rival "universities"). In 1808 educational regions, called "academies," were created through which branches of the central University exercised regional control.

Religious communities continued to operate primary schools, but now under the explicit and active supervision of the State, and as public institutions open to all children. An Imperial Catechism was written to reinforce national values through association with religion. Church involvement in secondary schools and lycées, however, was forbidden. State financial support of primary education was sharply limited, so that Church participation could be seen as a requirement in order to increase enrollments.

Legislation specified the content of curriculum for all institutions. The curricula were written by the directors-general of the University, specialists in each of the major subject areas (eight in the secondary schools and lycées, four in primary schools). The secondary schools and lycées were seen as institutions that would prepare students for specified occupations in the State; no effort was made to expand enrollments.

Teachers in public schools were regarded as State employees, which meant requirements of loyalty to the State, training by the State, and supervision in their performance. A national teachers' college, the Ecole Normale, served both to train teachers and to monitor all other teacher training institutions. Certification no longer was based on personal references or examination, but on completion of academic programs specified and controlled by the State. For example, teachers of students in the first three years or forms of secondary had to be graduates of a baccalaureate program (complete secondary). Teachers for the next two years of secondary had to have a license, equivalent to a university degree. Students studying for the baccalaureate were to be taught by professors with a doctorate. The Ecole Normale focused not just on content, but also on the development of an esprit de corps based on shared values.

Selection of students for scholarships to the Ecole was by national examination.

Supervision of teachers and schools was carried out by inspectors-general from the University, one for each major subject area. These were assisted by staff appointed at the departmental and district level, so that it was possible to keep track of activities in each school in France.

A major concern for supervision was to insure a correspondence between the various levels of institutions beginning with secondary schools. Students were to be selected into these institutions by examinations, and promoted on the basis of merit. Regulations specified ages of entrance for each kind of institution.

The State assumed responsibility for the organization but not the provision of educational finance. Most central State funds were spent on secondary schools and lycées. Funding came from bonds, fees for examinations, 5 percent of all fees paid by students at secondary or higher institutions, the sale of properties of nationalized private or Church schools, and a compulsory municipal contribution. Municipalities were held responsible for the maintenance of secondary schools, lycées, and university buildings in their region. State regulations controlled the amount of revenues that private schools could generate, and were from time to time manipulated to reduce the number of these institutions. In fact, the central government spent little of its own money on education, but exercised control over the financing of the entire system.

Further Bureaucratization after Napoleon

Despite radical differences in political ideology, and the shift from Empire to Monarchy to Republic and back to Empire, the education system of France continued to employ the bureaucratic technology of management. There are at least two explanations for this persistence. The first argues that many of the social groups that had favored the introduction of bureaucracy in the government of Napoleon I continued in power despite the Emperor's overthrow and the restoration of the Bourbon kings. Bureaucracy had been shown to be effective as a means of control, both in the Napoleonic government and in the industries and commercial establishments of the bourgeoisie; its maintenance would favor their interests under a new ruler. In effect, this argument says that once bureaucracy had emerged as an effective technology of management, belief in its effectiveness by powerful groups external to the government became the major cause of its persistence.

A second argument maintains that the major reason why bureaucracy persisted despite changes in governments and political ideologies was the presence of a large group of persons within the state apparatus with a

vested interest in its persistence. Bureaucracy meant not only the creation of a specialized group of managers of the educational system, but
also the professionalization of teachers. Both groups benefitted from the
formalization of an ideology in which education becomes essential for
the progress of individuals and society, and in which only specialists
from within the system are capable of evaluating its effectiveness.

Once again, these arguments are not necessarily contradictory. They
can be combined into a single thesis that bureaucracy persisted (and in
fact expanded in French education) because it was seen as favorable to
their own interests by groups which in combination were dominant in
French society. These alliances are unstable, however, and from time to
time previous supporters of bureacracy move to weaken its control in
order to enhance their own positions. The persistence of bureaucracy
until recent years is a reflection of the strength of the coalition of social
forces that benefitted from it.

The monarchy that replaced Napoleon had no illusions that all
Frenchmen welcomed them. Education was seen as one means of changing attitudes to favor the new order. There was initial criticism of the
centralization that Napoleon had imposed, but the new government
quickly saw that its objectives too could be achieved more effectively by
tight central control over schools and teachers. The Crown did not share
the Revolution's commitment to universal education, and enrollments
declined; but it did share a belief that any investments in education
should benefit the State. Although the content of education was to be
changed, it would be changed by the State. The basis of education, it
was decreed, was religion, the State, law, and the constitution (Ponteil,
1966: 160). In 1816 the new government decreed that all teachers would
require certification by the State. Briefly closed, the Imperial University
was re-opened with essentially the same structure, but many of its
professors were replaced by men loyal to the Crown and the Church. In
1824 a ministry of public instruction was created that assumed many of
the coordinating tasks of the University.

The Revolution of 1830 restored the bourgeoisie to power, with a
consequent restatement of the importance of education as a means to
train future workers and citizens. The Guizot law of 1833 required every
commune to organize a primary school, but attendance was neither
compulsory nor free (Anderson, 1975). More importantly, the State
created a corps of inspectors to insure that the communes complied with
this decree. Every department in France was ordered to build a normal
school that would follow the national curriculum. Although training for
teachers still focused on subject knowledge and rudimentary skills, the
result was creation of a sense of profession and common identity among
teachers who looked to the central government for protection against
local pressures for moral and ideological conformity.

Many of those teachers joined the ranks and leadership of the 1848 Revolution, a fact not lost on the conservative government of Louis Napoleon that followed shortly. The teachers were branded "communists" and agitators. The education law of 1851 increased the regulations with respect to training and selection of teachers, and gave control over teachers to local civil authorities and priests. Many teachers were purged at the same time that salaries were raised. The long-term effects were increased professionalism of teachers. The law increased the participation of the Church hierarchy in management of education and relaxed restrictions on creation of private schools, but at the same time increased the bureaucratization of education by extending the range of educational activities specifically regulated. The 20 rectors of the regional academies (local representatives of the Imperial University) were replaced with 87 departmental rectors. The rectors' advisory councils were instructed to inform on the condition of schools, necessary reforms, discipline, administration, budgets and accounts (of lycées, colleges, normal schools, and primary schools), school fees, and sanctions to be applied for infractions of the regulations. Although the content of the law has been characterized by some (e.g., Ponteil, 1966) as a triumph for the reactionaries, bureaucracy remained and even prospered as the dominant technology of management.

As knowledge about the differential efficiency of educational practices became more widely known, and the "science" of pedagogy became established, regulation of the process of teaching and learning increased. For example, prior to the 1830s the dominant method of teaching in primary schools was the Lancasterian, or "mutual" method developed to allow teachers to handle very large classes by assigning older or brighter students to work as "monitors" with those less well-prepared. Under this arrangement teachers taught all levels of students in a single room, moving from group to group; students were not separated by levels of knowledge or skills. The Christian Brothers, on the other hand, had developed a system of "grading" students by the level of achievement or knowledge, which then permitted a single teacher to instruct an entire class simultaneously and permitted the use of graded textbooks written for children with specified levels of knowledge and reading ability. By the 1860s research had shown the graded (or "simultaneous") method of instruction to be superior; the ministry of public instruction organized primary schools into elementary, middle, and higher divisions, with subdivision into separate classes where appropriate. Class sizes were specified, and children could enrol or be promoted only at the beginning of the year. Wedgwood's techniques for pottery could now be applied to children.

With the overthrow of the Second Empire and founding of the Third Republic in 1870, education received a further boost as anticlerical

Noel F. McGinn

positivists used the technology of bureaucracy to reduce the influence on education of the Catholic Church, and in general to reduce inequalities in access to education. Once again, the content of education changed less than did its structures; regulations increased, sometimes as a result of increased technical knowledge about education, often in response to political pressures. The net effect of each change in government was an expansion of bureaucracy, even when governments shifted from Left to Right and back. With each elaboration of regulations, the rationale for existing rules was more deeply embedded in the ideology of the system, obscuring both the original technical or substantive reason for those rules, as well as their contribution to control by the State over workers and students in the system. Reformers in France, as elsewhere today, defined educational quality in terms of inputs to the system, but were blocked by their own myths and bureaucratic controls from an evaluation of the effectiveness of their programs. In France, as later in the colonies (see Chapter 9), politicians struggled and generally lost in their efforts to reassert control over an increasingly autonomous state bureaucracy. (The collusion between educational managers and teachers in the avoidance of evaluation of the efficiency and effectiveness of educational institutions in the United States is described in Meyer and Rowan, 1978.) Curricula, perhaps appropriate in one era, persisted into the next, despite increasing complaints that graduates knew little of what was important for productive work or democratic practice. By the end of the nineteenth century French education, for all its rigor and discipline, lagged far behind Germany, particularly in science.

The Future of Bureaucracy in Education

By the end of the nineteenth century the national state education system was common in the world, and bureaucracy was well established as the dominant technology of management. At this point in the twentieth century, this kind of education operating system is clearly predominant. Only a few countries in the world do not have a national ministry of education that specifies:

1. the content of education
2. methods to be used in teaching
3. procedures and criteria for the selection, training and supervision of teachers
4. criteria and procedures for the selection, supervision and certification of those who are taught
5. methods and sources of finance
6. methods for system management

Most of the few exceptions are large countries whose states or provinces have ministries of education that centralize authority for their region. In only a handful of countries are issues of content, methods, teachers, students, finance, etc., not regulated directly by a central government—the United States and Australia come to mind—although even in those instances a higher government agency specifies many of the conditions of operation of the local system. And independent of the degree of centralization, bureaucracy is accepted as the most appropriate technology of management, even if it is not always applied faithfully.

The review of the history of French education in the nineteenth century supports the following explanation of the emergence of bureaucracy as the dominant technology of management. Bureaucracy was imposed on French education by groups that sought control over all aspects of the system in order to carry out larger political and economic objectives. These groups were disposed to favor bureaucracy as a managerial technology for education because their general world view and ideology favored central control, because they assigned to education a reproductive rather than creative or innovative task, and because the very imposition of bureaucratic regulations enabled them to wrest power away from competing groups. At least one of the competitors—the Church—also favored bureaucratic management, but found it used against itself. Other groups, favoring personalism, democratic localism, and other managerial forms, could not mobilize sufficient resources to win out over those groups favoring bureaucracy. Belief in the efficacy of bureaucracy grew over time as groups controlling the State learned how to use it to enhance their interests. Bureaucracy did not win out because it was a better technology of management, but because the social groups that took power believed (and learned) that it was an effective means to maintain that power.

Bureaucracy, and the operating systems of national public education systems are, however, under increasing criticism today. The principal group of critics propose technocracy, in the sense of the term as used by Therborn, as an alternative technology of management. Although the rationale for change is technical, the net effect of a shift to technocratic management would be a shift of the locus of control of organizations, from those who work within (e.g., educators, teachers) to groups external to the organization.

In most countries, the dominant group espousing technocracy as a technology of management of education holds a world view and social science perspective similar to that of the positivists and Ideologues of the nineteenth century. This group begins with a theory of how society should operate, and then looks for ways to manage social organizations consistent with the theory's specifications. The dominant perspective emphasizes the choice of consumers in a market setting as a method to insure overall system efficiency. The rationale is that consumer demand will force suppliers of education to produce that kind of education which "society" finds most useful. Educational managers are encouraged to respond to market demands with respect to the outputs of education, and to use whatever means is effective to produce a saleable education. The effect of the implementation of these proposals would be to shift control of education away from educators and teachers to those groups in society with control over economic resources. Some of the proponents of the technocratic approach are explicit about their ambition to replace those groups that maintain control of education through bureaucratic processes and structure.

No countries as yet have adopted technocracy as the technology of management of their public education system. There have been some reforms in aspects of North American education which are technocratic—e.g., performance pay for teachers, educational vouchers for parents—but as of yet there are no local school districts which have permitted teachers to use whatever methods they wish so long as their students achieve certain learning objectives. Some international assistance agencies have been insistent in their recommendations that poor nations increase diversity through increased support for private education, but no country with a well-established bureaucracy has moved away from strong central control although some have enhanced central control through de-concentration of their administrative apparatus (see McGinn and Street, 1986). Only for a few brief historical movements have some countries abandoned bureaucracy as a technology of educational management—the Cultural Revolution in China was one short-lived experiment.

There are at least two reasons for this. First, bureaucracy has a large constituency. It is defended by those who see in its rules and regulations protecting the weak and defenseless the history of a century of struggles to extend social justice. It is also defended by those with less sense of history who understand clearly that their current benefits depend on maintenance of the *status quo*. That group includes not just barely-paid-enough teachers with no employment options, but also politicians and their backers who gain from distribution of the spoils of employment and contracts. It is defended by parents who have swallowed whole a particular myth of education—one that says that to be educated a child must learn these things and not those, using these methods and not those, earning these titles and not those—and who have no opportunities (given the focus of functionalist research) to question the validity of the myth. Second, in most developing countries there is little information available to demonstrate the inadequacies of bureaucratic management in technocratic terms. Few national ministries provide information about the performance of the education system in terms of national goals; children may fail but the system is unquestioned.

Bureaucracy continues, therefore, not because in fact it has been shown to be an effective way of producing a high quality education, but because it is believed to be an effective means of social control. The chapter that follows describes the persistence of French colonial governments in the bureaucratic organization of their education system in Vietnam, despite resistance from both French and national teachers, and despite evidence that alternative approaches to education would be more effective for the achievement of educational objectives.

References

Anderson, James G. (1968) *Bureaucracy in Education*. Baltimore: Johns Hopkins Press.

Anderson, R. D. (1975) *Education in France, 1848-1870*. Oxford: Clarendon Press.

Antonio, Robert J. (1979) The contribution of organizational efficiency to the decline of the Roman Empire, *American Sociological Review*, **44** (6), pp. 895-912.

Archer, Margaret Scotford (1979) *Social Origins of Educational Systems*. Beverly Hills, CA: Sage Publications.

Baker, Donald N. & Harrigan, Patrick J... (1980) *The Making of Frenchmen: Current Directions in the History of Education in France, 1679-1979*. Waterloo, Ontario: Historical Reflections Press, University of Waterloo.

Benoit, Andrew (1974) *Changing the Educational System: A Colombian Case Study*. Munich: Weltforum Verlag, Arnold Bergstrasser Institut.

Braverman, Harry (1974) *Labor and Monopoly Capital*. New York: Monthly Review Press.

Caiden, Naomi & Wildavsky, Aaron (1974) *Planning and Budgeting in Poor Countries*. New York: Wiley.

Crozier, Michel (1964) *The Bureaucratic Phenomenon*. Chicago: University of Chicago Press.

Huppert, George (1984) *Public Schools in Renaissance France*. Urbana, Illinois: University of Illinois Press.

Jacoby, Henry (1973) *The Bureaucratization of the World*. Berkeley, CA.: University of California Press.

Katz, Michael B. (1971) *Class, Bureaucracy, and Schools: The Illusion of Educational Change in America*. New York: Praeger Publishers.

Langton, John (1984) The ecological theory of bureaucracy: The case of Josiah Wedgwood and the British Pottery Industry, *Administrative Science Quarterly*, **29**, pp. 330-354.

Markoff, J. (1975) Governmental bureaucracy: general processes and an anomalous case, *Comparative Studies in Society and History*, **17**, pp. 479-509.

McGinn, Noel & Street, Susan (1982) The political rationality of resource allocation in Mexican public education, *Comparative Education Review*, **26** (2), pp. 178-198.

McGinn, Noel & Street, Susan (1986) Educational decentralization: weak state or strong state? *Comparative Education Review*, **30** (4), pp. 471-490.

Meyer, John W. & Hannan, Michael T. (1979) *National Development and the World System: Educational, Economic, and Political Change, 1950-1970*. Chicago: University of Chicago Press.

Meyer, John W. & Rowan, Brian (1978) The Structure of Educational Organizations in Marshall W. Meyer & Associates, *Environments and Organizations*. San Francisco: Jossey-Bass. 78-109.

Palmer, R. R. (1985) *The Improvement of Humanity: Education and the French Revolution*. Princeton, NJ: Princeton University Press.

Perrow, Charles (1985) Comments on Langton's "ecological theory of bureaucracy," *Administrative Science Quarterly*, **30**, pp. 278-283.

Peterson, Kent D. (1984) Mechanisms of administrative control over managers in educational organizations, *Administrative Science Quarterly,* **29**, pp. 573-597.

Ponteil, Felix (1966) *Histoire de l'Enseignement en France; les Grandes Etapes, 1789-1964.* Paris: Sirey.

Riggs, Fred Warren (1964) *Administration in Developing Countries: The Theory of Prismatic Society.* Boston: Houghton Mifflin.

Therborn, Goran (1978) *What Does the Ruling Class Do When It Rules? State Apparatuses and State Power under Feudalism, Capitalism, and Socialism.* London: NLB.

Vaughn, Michalina & Archer, Margaret Scotford (1971) *Social Conflict and Educational Change in England and France, 1789-1848.* Cambridge: Cambridge University Press.

Weber, Max (1962) *Basic Concepts in Sociology.* New York: Philosophical Library.

Weber, Max (1968) *Economy and Society.* New York: Bedminster Press.

CHAPTER 9

The Transfer of an Education Operating System: French Educational Management Organization in the Colonies

GAIL P. KELLY

In 1917-18 France developed a school system in Vietnam adapted from the French model. The French called these schools "Franco-Annamite" or "Franco-native." They taught a curriculum that emphasized French versions of Vietnamese culture and society and Western-style subjects such as mathematics, hygiene and general science.[1]* The transfer of the schools was accompanied by the implantation of a French-style educational bureaucracy modeled after the metropolitan ministry of education. The educational bureaucracy was called the Office of Public Instruction. I will show in the pages that follow that the decision to build a French-style educational bureaucracy in Vietnam was politically rather than technically motivated. A centralized Office of Public Instruction was called for because of irreconcilable political conflicts over schooling within Vietnam that threatened the government's stability. This case study of the Office of Public Instruction emphasizes the political nature of educational transfers. It also deals with the political struggles for control over educational transfers like the Office of Public Instruction once implanted and with the use of such an educational transfer as a bureaucracy to reduce political issues to technical issues, thereby defusing conflict in the broader society.

While this is a case study of bureaucratic transfer from France to one of her colonies in the first decades of the twentieth century, the case study has relevance today for the way we think about the transfer of educational technologies. Transfers occur within the context of unequal power relations, both among nations and within them. The choice of what technologies to transfer and what technologies not to transfer cannot be separated from the social contexts in which those technologies are put.

The paper begins with a discussion of the importation of French

*Superscript numbers refer to Notes at end of chapter.

bureaucratic technologies to colonial Vietnam and the reasons for developing a French-style ministry of education situated in Hanoi. It will then turn to the struggles to control the Office of Public Instruction and will end with a discussion of the ways in which the Office was used to render political issues technical issues in an attempt to minimize social conflict. The discussion is based on archival sources, government documents, school inspection reports, and annual reports of the Office of Public Instruction.

The Vietnamese Context and the Imposition of Bureaucracy

In 1858 the French embarked on the conquest of Vietnam, a long-standing independent nation-state. After protracted armed resistance, the French took control of the southern part of the country which is called the colony of Cochinchina. In subsequent years of battle, French armies subdued the North, which was renamed Tonkin, and in the 1880s French hegemony was assured as the Vietnamese monarchy accepted French "protectorate" status over Annam, the central part of the once independent country.

Vietnam, upon conquest, had its own system of education. Rudimentary education was widespread, taught in village schools, staffed by Vietnamese who aspired to become civil servants in their nation's bureaucracy.[2] A national academy, situated in Hué, trained those who had passed the provincial examinations. The Vietnamese monarchy had traditionally controlled education through a Ministry of Education and Rites which administered examinations and ran the National Academy.

In the years of protracted warfare Vietnamese village schools were abandoned in Cochinchina.[3] The village teachers had organized their students and other villagers to fight for the monarchy against French incursions. When the Vietnamese monarchy ceded Cochinchina, the scholars retreated north to carry on the struggle. No indigenous schools remained as the French consolidated their hold on Cochinchina and the French built their own schools at the village level to substitute for the abandoned ones. In Tonkin and Annam, however, when the French gained control, indigenous schools stayed intact. Until 1919 the Vietnamese monarchy continued to administer the examinations to recruit civil servants.

The motive of the French was to maintain control over the colony so that the colonial government could pursue its political and economic purposes peacefully and efficiently. They had no clear-cut educational policy until 1917. In that year Albert Sarraut, the governor-general of French Indochina (an amalgamation of Cambodia, Laos, Annam, Tonkin, and Cochinchina) promulgated a set of decrees that brought into being a comprehensive educational system that would serve the youth of the three Vietnamese states of Annam, Cochinchina, and Tonkin.[4] The school system consisted of five years of primary education, five years of higher primary and three years of secondary education. A university was established in Hanoi that housed faculties of Indochinese Studies, Medicine, Pedagogy, Public Works, Veterinary Sciences, Post and Telegraphs and Pharmacy. There is little doubt that the system was modeled on metropolitan France's and not on Vietnam's long-standing indigenous system of village schools and national academies. The new school system was to teach in French. The focus was on moral education and vocational training. The schools were to be staffed by trained teachers who were well acquainted with the new pedagogy, and quality control was to be sustained through a newly established series of competitive degree examinations.

Contending groups within the colonial society—each for its own reasons—resisted the introduction of the innovation. As a result, the new school system was heralded in amongst heated controversy about what kind of education Vietnamese should have. The French resident community (*colons*) expressed hostility towards the very idea of providing Vietnamese with anything more than the most rudimentary education.[5] They demanded that Vietnamese be prevented from obtaining French education, which supposedly turned them into *deracinees* and malcontents. The *colons* disliked the new schools because they taught in French and because the 1917-18 Code provided for post-primary education. Particularly odious to them was the university, which, as far as they understood, was destined to train an elite.

While the *colons* were unhappy with the 1917-18 Code, the new Vietnamese elites—large landowners, civil servants and entrepreneurs— of Cochinchina greeted the new schools with skepticism.[6] Their own children attended French schools that had been formed to serve the French community. They believed the new schools were inferior to metropolitan schools and resisted any attempts to make them the sole educational route for Vietnamese. They argued that these schools were fine for the masses, but elite education was still French education and that Vietnamese should have freedom of choice in matters concerning their children's education.[7]

Vietnam's traditional elite were even more disdainful of the new code of public instruction. The new schools threatened to undermine indigenous education which for the Monarchy was national education. The Monarchy, despite French pressure, had maintained the traditional system of village schools in Annam. Through the first decades of the twentieth century the French government sought to reform the village level schools of Annam, and also of Tonkin. Its approach initially was one of friendly persuasion. Workshops were held to instruct village teachers in a new curriculum which was supposed to be "modern," consisting of Vietnamese written in the Roman script, mathematics, hygiene, and French. Retraining was hardly successful. Henri Russier, a school inspector on a tour of Annam in 1915, reported to the Governor-General in Hanoi that the schools were dismal. "Their teachers . . . (are) neglectful and lazy . . .".[8] He found as well that most ignored the new curriculum and lapsed into their old ways. Russier argued that the schools would remain in the hands of the "nasty" traditional teachers as long as no mechanism was in place to control what and how they taught. Some "means of control other than encouragement" was needed, he wrote in his report to the Governor-General.[9]

The Vietnamese Monarchy, for its part, resisted any attempts to legislate change in the schools, and this resistance began well over ten years before Sarraut issued the Code of Public Instruction. In 1907, a Committee for the Improvement of Native Education was organized by the French Resident in Annam. The Committee was composed of three Vietnamese ministers, several French administrators of the civil services, French teachers, several Vietnamese teachers and one missionary. The French proposed reforms in the linguistic medium of the school; the Vietnamese representatives hotly opposed them. When the director of the French civil service in Annam suggested that science and agriculture be added to the curriculum of the village schools, the Court's ministers and Vietnamese representatives refused to consider such proposals.[10] Whenever the Vietnamese Court had a chance to comment on proposed reforms, it opposed them. This opposition occurred in Tonkin as well, where Vietnamese mandarins who collaborated with the French argued that traditional education ought to be left intact. Nguyen-Huu-Thu, who commented on proposed educational reforms at the request of the French Resident at Nam Dinh, politely pointed out that the reforms the French proposed would provide a superficial education devoid of proper moral basis and recommended that good enough be left alone.[11]

The resistance of Vietnamese traditional elite to French reforms surfaced openly in 1917 and 1918 when the Vietnamese Monarchy was asked to promulgate the Code of Public Instruction in Annam. The Court's Council of Ministers stone-walled the proposal, refusing in session after session to consider the decree. By 1919 the Court still refused to act on the decree. At this point, the Governor-General interceded and told the Resident that he would promulgate the decree with or without the Court's consent. The Governor threatened to abolish the Court's ministry of education—which he did at a later date—and put educational matters in the hands of individuals technically capable and willing to see that school reform would indeed occur. The Court reluctantly promulgated the new decrees, and power over education was taken out of its hands.[12]

The French authorities, in effect, substituted force for friendly persuasion to ensure that the innovation was adopted.

The Vietnamese context, in short, was one in which educational policy was contested from all sides—by French *colons*, Vietnamese elites, and villagers. The new school system also was being imposed on a society which already had its own schools, ones which the new system of education was designed to replace. In Annam, a ministry of education was attached to the Vietnamese Court. The Court and its bureaucracy claimed that it was the sole legitimate power in directing the course of educational development. Further, Vietnamese expected schools to provide them with access to power; such expectations had been historically attached to education and the new system was contrary to such notions, being developed as Governor Albert Sarraut put it, to provide "a simple education, reduced to essentials, permitting the child to learn all that will be useful for him to know in his humble career of farmer or artisan to ameliorate the natural and social conditions of his existence."[13]

Given the disputes over the Code of Public Instruction, it is little wonder that when, in 1919, the ministry of education and the Minister of the Colonies in Paris demanded that all French colonies develop a means for managing the schools, the Government of Indochina adopted the ministry concept.[14] Not all of France's colonies chose to transfer the metropolitan technology for school administration, for there were options other than the ministry available for superintending.

Alternative Forms

Other administrative forms were available, but local conditions rendered them unacceptable to people in the colonial society who wielded significant political power. That is, a centralized bureaucracy was not the only possible form French policymakers had for administering education. In fact, there were two other options which were extant in other French colonies and which also had been tried, in varying degrees, in French Indochina. The first option was to have no bureaucracy at all and to rely on trained teachers or Frenchmen loyal to the State's educational policy. In Cochinchina this had been the mode of administration up to 1914. While the local government provided funding for teachers' salaries, for the most part the day-to-day business of education was in teachers' hands. The teachers up to World War I were predominantly French. Some were trained teachers on loan from the metropole, others were wives of French businessmen and civil servants, and still others were French demobilized army officers. Vietnamese teachers brought into service were supervised by French nationals. This system of educational administration was also in vogue in French West Africa where Frenchmen, many of whom were actually trained as teachers, until the 1920s were in the majority, assisted by a handful of African graduates of the Ecole William Ponty, the major teacher-training institution in West Africa.

This mode of administration, with some modification, remained throughout the interwar years in West Africa; in Indochina it was discarded for several reasons. First, a lack of clearcut administrative control over education meant that Vietnamese were free to open schools on their own. In Cochinchina, several Vietnamese had opened prestigious French-private schools like the *Ecole des Jeunes Filles Indigènes*.[15] It also meant that Vietnamese were free to purchase French education, which many did by either obtaining entry to the schools designated for French nationals or by going to France to study.[16] The lack of control over what kind of education Vietnamese might receive became a political problem, because French-educated Vietnamese tended to demand the same rights as Frenchmen and access to positions in the colonial civil service that Frenchmen held. Another reason for the abandonment of informal modes of educational control had to do with Vietnamese demand for the expansion of education and the lack of French manpower to staff the schools. The crisis of personnel was exacerbated by World War I, when many French returned home to fight in Europe. Increasingly Vietnamese were recruited into teaching and remained unsupervised by any French nationals. Given Vietnamese traditions of teacher autonomy at the local level, the government feared that the school system might go out of control.

A second alternative for educational administration was to place education firmly in the hands of the state without the intervention of an educational bureaucracy. This was tried in Vietnam before 1919 in Tonkin and led to all sorts of problems. The control of education in the hands of the political authorities—governors, mayors, residents and the like—had made education even more of a political issue than it might otherwise have been and often heightened conflict between the French and Vietnamese as well as between the colonial government and French nationals residing in Indochina. A mode of educational administration such as this was viable only where conflict over education was minimal, as in West Africa. In West Africa, where such a system had been tried, the local French administration refused to build schools since they put greater priority on road construction and on the police. Despite the fact that African demands for education remained quite low until the 1930s, the central government in Dakar insisted that schools be built so that local elites could learn to speak French. The Governor-General had to prod administrators to open schools.[17] Political administration could effectively control schooling in West Africa because the colonial state's right to control education was not questioned. Such a system was doomed to failure in Vietnam where most Vietnamese questioned the colonial government's right to meddle in their nation's education. Furthermore, in Vietnam, political administrators had viewed education as a political good which they could use to win over reluctant Vietnamese elites or reward Vietnamese who had served the administration well. In Tonkin this had meant that the French administrators had often insisted that the French *lycée* in Hanoi make room for the sons of Vietnamese collaborators, regardless of whether these children spoke French or had passed the entry examination.[18] Such practices provoked the *colon* community which insisted that their schools were overcrowded by Vietnamese and that educational quality had declined.[19] The *colon* community insisted that the government adopt an educational policy that would keep Vietnamese out of their schools.

The other problem with placing schools under the control of French political administrators without the intervention of an educational bureaucracy was that Vietnamese perceived educational questions to be political questions. The Court of Annam, for example, saw issues like language choice, teacher education, curriculum emphases as political issues and argued that the French administration was seeking to undermine its authority by intruding in these matters.[20] Additionally, Vietnamese elites became disaffected from schooling because they saw it as part of colonial politics, of domination, designed to keep them in servitude.[21] The school system, in short, lacked legitimacy in Vietnamese eyes as long as it was attached to political administration. Albert Sarraut, as Governor-General, understood that Vietnamese acceptance of the new schools would not be possible without distancing schools of political administration.[22] It was Sarraut who, in response to Paris's call for a plan to administer colonial educational system, brought into being the centralized educational bureaucracy, modeled on the metropole's.

The Office of Public Instruction and the Struggle for Control Over School Management

In 1920 the Office of Public Instruction for Indochina was established in Hanoi. Initially its powers were less than well-defined vis-a-vis political authorities. The Office had the power to oversee secondary, higher and vocational education and control the content and personnel of primary education.[23] However, as we shall see, the Office of Education periodically adopted additional characteristics of the French Ministry of Education whenever local conditions called for increased central control over educational practice.

The Office of Public Instruction was headed by a Director, who was appointed by the Minister of the Colonies and the Governor-General, and three inspectors. The Inspectors in Arts and Sciences were appointed by the Governor-General while the third inspector, the inspector at large, was appointed by the Director of Public Instruction.

The Office had three bureaus—secretariat, personnel, and budget—
which were staffed by tenured civil servants. The Secretariat initially was
responsible for school publications and texts, curriculum development,
school records and higher education. The Personnel Bureau focused on
teacher qualifications, salaries, degree granting and testing as well as
teacher promotions. The Budget Office confined itself to drawing up
budgets, equipment purchases and facilities development. By 1926 the
Secretariat began to maintain teachers' records and set examinations. In
1939 the Personnel Bureau assumed private school inspection and the
Budget Bureau took to surveilling students attending school in France as
well as general political surveillance of students in Indochina.

It did not take long for a struggle to emerge over who was to control
the newly established educational bureaucracy—the political administration or professional educators. This struggle was one over who should
control the technology of administration and how legitimacy of the new
school system could best be established. It emerged over the selection of
Directors of Public Instruction and in the division of labor between the
Office and the political administration in setting educational policy and
practice.

The Struggle over the Director

The Director of Public Instruction was by law appointed by the Minister
of Colonies in France in conjunction with the Governor General of
Indochina. And as the years passed it became clear that the particular
personalities of the men who assumed that position influenced the form
and functions of the educational bureaucracy.

The first Director was Coqnacq, a medical doctor from the French
colonies in the West Indies. Coqnacq emerged as Governor of Cochinchina and doubled as Governor of Cochinchina and Director of Public
Instruction until 1923. Coqnacq may have had the confidence of the
Governor General and the French nationals residing in Indochina—he
was infamous among Vietnamese elites in Cochinchina for his remarks
to the effect that the country needed no intellectuals. Coqnacq resigned
from his post amidst controversy about his role in land swindles in the
Mekong Delta as well as Vietnamese protests about his good faith in
providing quality education for their children.[24] His successor was
Joubin[25] who, as a Rector of the Academy and inspector of schools in
metropolitan France, was selected precisely because the whole school
system lacked legitimacy in the eyes of the Vietnamese elite. Albert
Sarraut, who nominated Joubin, wrote in October 1922, that the Vietnamese were suspicious about the school system created by the 1917
Code of Public Instruction. He argued that a French metropolitan in-

spector of education or a French professor *agrégé* who had no colonial ties and no prior involvement in Indochinese politics might be able to placate the Vientamese community as well as French residents.[26]

Joubin's career in Indochina was short-lived. In 1924 he was replaced by Blanchard de la Brosse. De la Brosse, like Coqnacq before him, had served as Governor of Cochinchina. De la Brosse, however, did have a background in education. He did his utmost to "decentralize" primary education and put power in educational matters back into the hands of colonial politicians. The schools abandoned the French medium in the first three years of education, much to the glee of the French community in Hanoi and Saigon.

In 1926 de la Brosse was replaced by Thalamas, a Professor at the Academy of Paris, who like Joubin lacked colonial experience. His appointment, however, roused the ire of the Catholic Church in Hanoi because of his belief in secularism and his faith in bureaucracy.[27] Particularly irksome to the Church was his tract on Jeanne d'Arc which attacked the Catholic Church for its role in her martyrdom. The choice of Thalamas was a well-considered one. By 1924 the political authorities in Indochina intended to bring in a Director of Public Instruction who would not only be acceptable to Vietnamese, but who would control the Catholic Church which had come into conflict with the government's attempts to spread secular Franco-Vietnamese schools.[28] Thalamas remained at his post until 1929.

Between 1929 and 1932 the Office was headed by colonial politicians, among them was Tholance who had served as mayor of Hanoi. Tholance represented the *colon* community, and he completed the task of structurally differentiating education for Vietnamese from that of Frenchmen. Under his leadership Vietnamese were banned from French *lycées* in Indochina. The years 1932 to 1939 marked the ascendency of the career pedagogue from outside the colony in the directorship. In 1932 J. J. A. Bertrand, an inspector of schools from metropolitan France, assumed the post of Director of Public Instruction.

The struggle over the leadership of the educational bureaucracy occurred because the colonial state was ambivalent about the technology of educational management it had imported. While the political context had led to the development of an educational bureaucracy to control a school system which was highly contested, the state feared that it might not be able to control the bureaucracy it had created. The choice of Director of Public Instruction was an assertion of the state's right to control pedagogues who had little experience with the political missions of the schools in a colonial society. This same struggle for control of the bureaucracy the government had transferred from metropolitan France to the colony extended to conflicts over the division of labor between political bureaucracy and educational bureaucracy which were acted out in the 1920s.

The Division of Labor Between Political and Educational Bureaucracies

The 1920 legislation that gave rise to the Office of Public Instruction gave that office the sole authority over education at all levels. This was in the tradition of the metropolitan ministry. However, by 1921, a decree from the Governor-General attempted to curtail the Office's power. The 1921 decree made the Governor-General, the *Résidents* and their cabinets responsible for the financing, opening, and administration of schools. The Office's duties were to be confined to pedagogical control.[29] The Office was to set standards for teacher hiring and promotion (the political authorities, however, selected the teachers). The Office was to develop curricula and texts; the political administration, however, had power to ban books from school. The Office supervised school inspection as well and after 1924 took responsibility for monitoring private schools in conjunction with the political authorities. While the Residents and Governors could make policy decisions affecting the Office, the Office did not have to follow such decisions if they could be defined as existing within the "pedagogical and technical" domains. The Director of Public Instruction was given the power to approve as well as dissent from legislation and policy set by political authorities.[30]

The division of labor between the educational bureaucracy and the political authorities that was set in 1921 was continually renegotiated. That renegotiation took several forms. First, political authorities sought to wrest control over education from the Office of Public Instruction, arguing that the Office's meddling in personnel and curricula matters had caused major political problems, especially in elementary and primary education. At issue was the Office's attempt to set standards for the teaching profession. At the time of the 1917-18 educational reform, there was a severe shortage of normal school graduates, as well as Vietnamese who had completed primary school and had some teacher education. The bulk of the teaching profession in Annam and Tonkin consisted of the *thây do* and *giao sú*—individuals who had traditional education, but had no Western-style education credentials. In 1917, 1,320 of these teachers were in service.[31] The Office of Public Instruction insisted that these teachers be phased out and replaced by well-trained normal school and primary school graduates. In order for this to occur, the political authorities were charged with funding a massive expansion of education, especially at the post-primary level. Needless to say, the *Résidents* were not enthusiastic about coming up with such funds. In addition, the Office had set the salaries of certified teachers relatively high and through the institution of teacher career ladders meant to control teacher behavior by promising good teachers advancement and substantial raises. The insistence of the Office that qualified teachers be put into service and paid a reasonable wage threatened to saddle political administrators with on-going fiscal crisis.

The matter of qualified teachers created serious political problems as well as fiscal ones since the traditional teachers, whom the office was attempting to undermine, had a great deal of power at the village level. The Residents in Annam and Tonkin complained loudly about the displacement of the traditional teacher and the potential political disaffection of the mass of rural villagers because of this.[32] Pasquier, the Resident of Annam in 1922, insisted that Annam was an independent country and had the right to hire whomever it wanted as teachers.[33]

Curriculum matters were also a sticky point. The Office of Public Instruction, charged as it was with such "technical" matters as the curriculum, tried to see to it that a "Franco-Vietnamese" curriculum, like the one foreseen in the 1917 Code, was taught. Pressure from the Office to do so evoked an angry response from the Vietnamese monarchy in Hué, which argued that the new curriculum was irrelevant to Annam. The monarchy apparently convinced the French Resident, Pasquier, that this was the case. Pasquier then petitioned the Governor-General in Hanoi to repeal the Code of Public Instruction.[34] He argued that Annam was an independent country with its own customs and mores: "Every one requests that their children be raised to respect the traditions of the past, in adoration for their king and in observance of rites and customs." Pasquier also believed the Office of Public Instruction had ignored the political nature of educational decision-making. "This is above all a political question. If we don't watch out, we will soon see our schools deserted and clandestine schools opening their doors. The people will go where the mandarins tell them to go, or otherwise, confusedly, they will believe themselves to be responding to a secret desire of a spirit and go elsewhere."[35]

In 1924, a massive educational reform occurred, indicating the victory of the politicians over the educational bureaucracy, no doubt brought about with the connivance of the Director of Public Instruction, himself a former governor. The 1924 reforms took control over elementary and primary education out of the hands of the Office of Public Instruction and placed it in the hands of a newly organized Education Services.[36] The Education Services were each headed by a chief who was appointed by the *Résident* (in the case of Cochinchina, the Governor) of each of the states in the federation. The chiefs reported directly to the political authorities; the Office of Public Instruction had no control over them. The Office's powers were then restricted to post-primary education. The newly created chiefs in Annam and Tonkin proceeded to create elementary schools that used traditionally trained teachers and taught a curriculum that had little to do with that foreseen by the 1917 Code. These schools and the salaries of their teachers were paid for by villages and not by the state governments.[37]

While the decentralization of 1924 represented the attempt of the political bureaucracy to dominate educational policy, the Office of Public Instruction regained considerable power over primary education as the political bureaucracy began to understand it needed a bureaucracy of educational experts to meet political goals. The Office, as will be shown later, had shown itself capable of defusing political conflict over educational issues such as linguistic medium, which an educational policy emanating directly from political authorities never could. In the period after 1924 the Office of Public Instruction reasserted its control over primary education. It did this initally through its power over post-primary education. The Office controlled access to primary superior, secondary and higher education. It insisted that no one be admitted to primary superior school without a primary certificate and it devised and administered the primary certificate examinations. The Office also began to monitor individual students in the primary schools run by local education services. In order to sit for the primary school certificate examination (as well as the primary-superior examination, the baccalaureate, the teacher certification examinations), students were required to produce a *certificate de scolairité*. Students were not allowed to sit for examinations unless their school certificate indicated that they had gone to a school that followed the guidelines set forth in the 1917 Code of Public Instruction.[38] In 1924 the certificate was replaced by a *livret scolaire* maintained by the Office.[39]

Another way that the Office of Public Instruction in cooperation with the Governor-General regained control over education was through curricular development activities. Its testing program was one means of control—others were through the production of pedagogical journals and textbooks. Its *Bulletin of Public Instruction*, issued monthly during the school year, contained detailed lesson plans which covered all years but the first three of education. The journal also contained extensive articles on teaching methods and educational theory. The Office had a virtual monopoly over textbook production. In 1924 it established a textbook commission that contracted for new school texts, charts, and maps. By 1926 the Office's commission gained full power over selecting texts for public school use and it could also ban texts from use in Indochina.[40]

The textbook commission contracted for a number of works that, unlike metropolitan texts, would convey a Franco-Vietnamese curriculum. Its major emphasis was on commissioning texts in Vietnamese written in Roman characters for the first three years of education, which was in theory out of its control. Before 1924, the Office of Public Instruction issued but one text for the first three years of education. In 1925 and 1926, after the first five years of schooling were brought under the aegis of the local education services, the Office issued 11 new texts, some in editions close to 200,000.[41] By 1930 the Office of Public Instruction had published 4,884,000 copies of texts; in 1930 alone 755,000 were issued for Vietnamese language instruction, mathematics and rudimentary hygiene and moral education.[42] The Office's domination over textbook publishing and curriculum at the primary level was maintained throughout the interwar years. By 1938 the Office had published and created an additional 3,000,000 or so primary texts.[43]

In short, over time the political administration came to see that the Office of Public Instruction was the most effective and efficient means for mediating the conflicts over the schools that characterized the interwar years. The Office of Public Instruction in the long run could assert its authority over the schools because it alone could claim to possess technical expertise in matters such as matriculation, certification and curriculum development. The political administration found, after 1924, when it had forced decentralization of education and asserted its own hegemony over primary education, that it could not put into practice the educational policies it chose to pursue. The political bureaucracy depended on professional educators to figure out how a new curriculum that distinguished education for Vietnamese from that of French could be constructed and how teachers could be trained to transmit that curriculum.[44] Pedagogues like Thalamas, Bertrand and the many inspectors of public instruction which staffed the Office of Public Instruction possessed such expertise. In addition, political authorities came to rely on the Office and its "experts," who were removed from the realm of colonial politics, to defuse diverse political demands on education. The Office of Public Instruction played such a role by making political issues technical ones which could be solved by experts in the educational bureaucracy and not by parents, French *colons* or Vietnamese elites.

The Office of Education's Role in Converting Political Issues into Technical Issues

As was pointed out earlier, the schools brought into being by the 1917/18 Code of Public Instruction were deeply contested by a wide spectrum of colonial society. Pressures to rescind the Code were quite strong. The Office of Public Instruction over time served to quell much of the controversy surrounding the Code by insisting that some of the more politically irksome features of educational policy were in fact technical matters and were grounded in pedagogy rather than in politics. The way the Office served this function is illustrated by looking at the role of the Office in taking the language medium of instruction out of the political arena.

The 1917 Code of Public Instruction specified that education, wherever possible, should be given in the French language. This decision initially was a political one, for in the Councils for the Improvement of Native Education that met in the first decades of the twentieth century the issue of language came up repeatedly.[45] Indigenous schools had taught in Vietnamese written in Chinese characters, and there was much support in rural areas as well as in the Court of Annam for continuing instruction in this mode. However, French administrators believed that such a course was politically dangerous, since literacy in Chinese characters might open Vietnamese to seditious writings coming from China.[46] The alternative was to teach in Vietnamese written in Roman script which had been developed by missionaries. This course was favored by the *colon* community, but was contested by both newly emergent Vietnamese elites and by the Vietnamese monarchy. The newly emergent elites argued that there was no literature in the new script and that instruction in the Vietnamese language cut Vietnamese youth off from science and technology. They argued that only French language education was capable of bringing Vietnam out of the dark ages and into the modern world.[47] The Court of Annam was less than enthusiastic about instruction in the new script since it held to the position that traditional Vietnamese values could only be taught through the Chinese characters.[48] Substitution of the new script for Chinese characters was seen as undermining the political authority of the Court.

A third alternative, which was adopted initially in the Code of Public Instruction, was French medium education. This choice was made to calm Vietnamese urban elites and landowners who feared the new school system was destined for their children who currently were enrolled in French schools. While the choice of French medium instruction was an attempt to soothe this elite, it raised the ire of the *colon* community, which saw the linguistic medium as opening French metropolitan education to Vietnamese.[49] The Vietnamese Court also objected to French medium education since it saw French even more of a threat to its power than Vietnamese written in Roman script.[50] The debate over language heated up after the Code of Public Instruction was promulgated.

The Office of Public Instruction, however, after its institution in 1920 began to pose the language question not as a political issue, but as a technical one that was best left to experts in pedagogy. In 1921 school inspectors issued reports that the standards in the new schools were abysmal due in large part to the adoption of French as the language of instruction. The reports pointed out that most Vietnamese teachers, while they could barely speak French, were teaching in French. Schooling, they argued was a farce and would remain so as long as French language medium instruction was maintained.[51] Even in schools where the teachers could speak French reasonably well, instruction amounted to nothing more than vocabulary drills, and the children reportedly learned nothing. Inspectors like Lafferanderie argued for mother-tongue education on pedagogical grounds which were hard to refute. He wrote:

> Taking into account realities in which nine times out of ten the native child of modest means lives and the fact that he has but a short time to acquire the knowledge indispensable to him . . . the teaching of this knowledge (must) be given in the only language in which he can rapidly acquire it, the mother tongue.[52]

Language choice was effectively transformed into an issue of educational efficiency, not one of who would hold power in society.

The inspectors attached to the Office of Public Instruction further charged that those who wanted to maintain French medium education in Franco-Vietnamese elementary schools were those who had little interest in children's education. They were "profiteers" who wanted to squeeze money out of the government for textbooks they had written to teach Vietnamese French and French teachers who feared for their jobs in schools based on a language they could not speak.[53] In 1924 the language of instruction in the first three years of education was changed to Vietnamese written in Roman script. There was little controversy after the change was made, simply because the pedagogues had reduced the issue of language to a technical question, best resolved by professional educators who had the true interests of the children at heart.

The reduction of political issues to technical issues was not confined to the linguistic medium of instruction. The Office effectively limited educational expansion, which was demanded by Vietnamese and opposed by French *colons*, and managed to minimize conflict over the extension of schooling. The Office did this by changing the discourse about the quantity of education to the quality of education. The Office supported the idea of mass education but it imposed a series of degree examinations in the name of standards which limited Vietnamese access to primary, primary superior and secondary education.[54] The Office also undermined the mass extension of elementary education by insisting in the name of quality that certified teachers be hired. However, the Office fixed teachers' salaries so high that villages after 1926 confronted with the finance of elementary education, found themselves unable to support new schools.

The implantation of an educational bureaucracy, despite the many conflicts over who would control it, in the end served to defuse political demands made on the schools from all quarters of colonial society. The bureaucracy presented itself as comprised of impartial experts who were removed, like many Directors of Public Instruction, from colonial politics and who made decisions on scientific pedagogical grounds, rather than on political grounds.

The Transfer of Bureaucracy in Perspective

This case study of the transfer of school management practices is a study of technological transfer. Bureaucracy, after all, is a technology for managing institutions and the transfer of a centralized bureaucracy from France to Vietnam represents a transfer of an educational technology. In the case study explored here, we have shown that policymakers in colonial Vietnam had a range of technologies for school management to draw from. They chose to import a Ministry, but they could have chosen, as did policymakers in West Africa in the same time period, to manage the schools differently. The decision to transfer a centralized educational bureaucracy was not a technical one that was necessitated by a growing school system. Rather, it was a political decision, designed to legitimate power relations in a divided society and defuse political conflict. The use of technology, in short, was political as was the choice of what technology to transfer. While the government of colonial Indochina opted to transfer a technology, once that technology was transferred, a series of struggles ensured over who was to control the technology; ultimately these struggles were resolved, given the use to which bureaucracy was to be put. In Vietnam, the bureaucracy was necessary to legitimate a contested educational system and to mute the debate about education by rendering political matters technical ones.

The study of the transfer of school management practices from France to her colonies does have relevance for our understandings of technological transfers today from industrialized nations of North America and Western Europe to the Third World despite the fact that Third World nations are not ruled directly by foreign powers today as was Vietnam in the period considered here. Technological transfers do occur in political contexts. Decisions to seek new technologies and the choice of which technology to transfer are not necessarily technical issues. Rather these decisions are related to power relations both within and between nations. The choice of technology to transfer may well be related to the political uses of that technology and technological transfers may themselves set off political disputes over who will control the technology for what end. Technology may change its forms as a result of the political conflicts surrounding its transfer from one political context to another. The Office of Public Instruction in Indochina did not end up the same as the French ministry of education on which it was modeled and it played a somewhat different social and political role than its metropolitan counterpart. How transferred technology is transformed by the political struggles that surround their implantation is certainly a question future research might investigate.

Notes

The following abbreviations have been used in the notes:
SOM—Archives Nationales de France, Section d'Outre Mer
JOIF—*Journal officiel de l'Indochine française*
BGIP—*Bulletin général de l'instruction publique* (Indochine)

1. For a more detailed description of the schools, see Gail P. Kelly "Colonial Schools in Vietnam: Policy and Practice," in P. G. Altbach and G. P. Kelly, *Education and Colonialism* (New York: Longmans, 1978) pp. 96-121.
2. This discussion of Vietnam's pre-colonial schools is based on Tran-Van-Trai, *L'Enseignement traditionnel en An-Nam* (Paris: P. Lapagesse, 1942); Buu Bong, "The Confucian Tradition in the History of Vietnamese Education," Unpublished Ph.D. dissertation, Harvard University, 1958; Nguyen-Khac-Vien, "Marxism and Confucianism in Vietnam," in Nguyen-Khac-Vien, *Tradition and Revolution in Vietnam* (Berkeley: Indochina Resource Center 1974), pp. 15-75.
3. See Milton Osborne, *The French Presence in Cochinchina and Cambodia: Rule and Response, 1858-1903* (Ithaca: Cornell University Press, 1969).
4. Gouvernement général de l'Indochine, française, *Code de l'instruction publique, 21 Décembre 1917 et 1921.* Hanoi: Imprimerie d'Extreme-Orient, 1921.
5. For *colon* reactions, see Gail P. Kelly, "Educational Reform and Re-Reform: Politics and the State in Colonial Vietnam," in Colin Brock and Witold Tulasiewicz, *Cultural Identity and Educational Policy* (New York: St. Martin's Press, 1985) pp. 11-40.
6. *Ibid.*
7. See, for example, "Hier et Aujourd'hui-coup d'oeil sur le niveau intellectuel et la vie materielle du peuple annamite avant et après de la conquête française," *La Cloche fêlée*, 2è Année (24 Décembre 1925) p. 1; Nguyen-Phan-Long, "Ayons une veritable élite," *L'Echo Annamite*, 5è Année (Nouvelle série) No. 53 (13 Juin 1924) p. 1.
8. Henri Russier (L'Inspecteur de l'Enseignement en Indochine), Rapport à M. le Gouverneur général de l'Indochine, Saigon, 13 Juillet 1915 au sujet d'une inspection des écoles de l'Annam, No. T 21. SOM, Fonds du Gouvernement général, 51.079.
9. *Ibid.*
10. Comité de perfectionnement de l'enseignement en Annam, Compte rendu, Séance du 25 Mai 1907, SOM, Fonds du Gouvernement général, 48.091.
11. Nam Dinh, 1 Octobre 1915, Quelques aperçus sur l'enseignement indigène, Nguyen-Huu-Thu, SOM, Fonds du Gouvernement général, 48.043.
12. See No. 1222 Hanoi, le 30 Juin 1919, Le Gouverneur général de l'Indochine p.i. à M. le Resident Supérieur en Annam a.s. projet d'ordannace royale à l'enseignement primaire en Annam. SOM, Fonds du Gouvernrment général, 51.080.
13. Sarraut is quoted in "La ville-ouverture de la 4è Session du Conseil de perfectionnement de l'enseignement indigène," *L'Avenir du Tonkin*, 30è Année, No 5466 (9 Avril 1931) pp. 2-3.
14. See Projet de loi fixant l'organisation de l'instruction publique aux colonies, 28 Octobre 1919 and Projet sommaire de l'organisation de l'administration de l'instruction publique aux colonies, Juillet 1919, SOM, Nouveau Fonds 259-2223 (1).
15. The history of this school was spelled out in a series of articles in *L'Echo Annamite*, a Cochinchinese newspaper run by Vietnamese members of the Constitutionalist Party. The school was the scene of a number of student strikes. See, "Au collège des jeunes filles indigènes," *L'Echo Annamite*, 4è Année, No. 427 (11 Janvier 1923) p. 1; "La verité sur la grève au college des jeunes filles indigènes de Saigon," *L'Echo Annamite*, 7è Année (Nouvelle série) No. 550 (10 Avril 1925) p. 1.
16. See, for example, 9 Septembre 1914, Van Vollenhoven le Gouverneur General à M.

le Resident Supérieur au Tonkin, No. 1719 a.s. de l'admission des élèves annamites dans les écoles françaises, SOM, Fonds du Gouvernement général 51.221; Rapport à M. le Gouverneur général de l'Indochine, No. 1.397G (Inspection conseil de l'enseignement), 24 Octobre 1924. SOM, Fonds du Gouvernement général 51.221: Rapport sur l'enseignement à distribuer au lycée de Hanoi, SOM, Fonds du Resident supérieur du Tonkin R24, No. 36.311.

17. See especially A. Mairot, "Inspection de l'enseignement, mission d'inspection dans le Gouvernement de la Guinée française," *Journal officiel de l'Afrique occidentale française*, 1re Année, No. 31 (5 Août 1905) pp. 396-99: "Inspection de l'enseignement— Rapport sur une mission d'inspection dans le Gouvernement du Haut-Sénégal et Niger," *Journal officiel de l'Afrique occidentale française, Partie non-officiel*, 1re Année, No. 30 (29 Juillet 1905) pp. 384-87.

18. See, 9 Septembre 1914, Van Vollenhoven, le Gouverneur général, à M. le Resident supérieur au Tonkin, No. 1719 a.s. de l'admission des élèves annamites dans les écoles françaises, SOM, Fonds du Gouvernement général 51.221.

19. Rapport a M. le Gouverneur général de l'Indochine, No. 1.397G (Inspection conseil de l'enseignement), 24 Octobre 1924, SOM, Fonds du Gouvernement général, 51.221.

20. Co Mat Vien, Kinh thu Tru Kinh Kham-su-dai than Tissot dai tien thanh giam, Hue, 14 Juillet 1919, SOM, Fonds du Gouvernement général, 51.080; No. 113 Resident supérieur en Annam, Hué, 14 Février 1914, SOM, Fonds du Gouvernement général, 51.080.

21. See, for example, Bui-Quang-Chieu, *France d'Asie—L'Indochine moderne—ou ne pas être vers-la Domination* (Toulouse: Imprimerie du Sud-Ouest, 1925); Bui-Quang-Chieu, "Pour la domination indochinoise," *Viêt-Nam Hon*, 1re Année, No. 1 (Janvier 1926) p. 4; Van-The-Hoi, "Il y a élite et élite," *L'Echo annamite*, 1re Année, No. 106 (7 Octobre 1920) p. 1.

22. See, for example, Décret Nominant le Recteur le l'academie de Lyon Directeur de l'instruction publique en Indochine, 28 Octobre 1922, *BGIP, partie officielle*, 2è Année, No. 6 (Février 1923) p. 97.

23. "La Direction de l'instruction publique en Indochine," *L'Echo Annamite*, 1re Année No. 70, (6 Juillet 1920) p. 2. This is a reprint of the Arrêté of 20 May 1920 establishing the Office of Public Instruction in Indochina. The *arrêté*, interestingly enough, was published in the *Journal officiel de France* and not the *Journal officiel de l'Indochine française*.

24. For Coqnacq's corruption, see Walter Langlais, *Andre Malraux and the Indochine Adventure* (New York: Praeger, 1966). Coqnacq's statement "This country needs no intellectuals" was widely reported in the Vietnamese press. See Nguyen-Phan-Long, "L'Instruction de la jeunesse annamite," *L'Echo annamite*, 3è Année, No. 362 (1 Août 1922) p. 1.

25. See Decret nominant le Recteur de l'academic de Lyon Director de l'instruction publique en Indochine, 28 Octobre, 1922, *BGIP, Partie Officielle*, 2è Année, No. 6 (Février 1923) p. 97.

26. *Ibid.*

27. See, for example, M. Dandolo, "A propos de M. Thalamas," *L'Avenir du Tonkin*, 42è Année, No. 8772 (27 Juin 1925) p. 1.

28. On Catholic Church–state conflict, see Protestations des Êveques du Tonkin et du Nord Annam Contre le Reglement général de l'instruction publique, 10 Mars 1919 et 20 Février 1919, SOM, Fonds du Gouvernement général 51.222; Phat-Diem, le 8 Decembre 1923, Marcou Vicariat apostolique du Tonkin maritime à M. le Resident supérieur, SOM, Fonds du Gouvernement général 51.566; Minute No. 1712 sa, Hanoi, le 4 Novembre 1924, Le Gouverneur général de l'Indochine à M. le Ministre des colonies, Objet: Missions catholique du Tonkin, SOM, Fonds du Gouvernement général, 51.566.

29. "La Direction de l'instruction publique en Indochine," *L'Echo Annamite*, 1re Année, No. 70 (6 Juillet 1920) p. 2. This is a reprint of the Arrêté of 20 May 1920 establishing the Office of Public Instruction in Indochina which appeared in the *Journal Officiel de France*.

30. 20 Juin 1921, Rapport au Gouverneur général suivi d'arrêtés: (1) Portant modification

du Reglement général de l'Instruction publique," *JOIF*, 33è Année, No 52 (29 Juin 1921) pp. 1257–1271, see especially article 4.

31. Gouvernement général de l'Indochine, *Rapports au Conseil du gouvernement, session ordinaire. Deuxième partie: Fonctionnement des divers services indochinois* (Hanoi: IDEO, 1924).

32. See, for example, Circulaire No. 1085–C, Le Chef du Service de l'Enseignement p.i. au Tonkin aux mesdames les institutrices et messieurs les instituteurs indigènes, Hanoi, 19 Avril 1927 (signé Berit-Debat), *Hoc Báo, Cong Van Sô*. 35 (2 Mai 1927) pp. 417-18.

33. No. 2A, Hué, 2 Janvier 1922, Le Resident supérieur en Annam à M. Le Gouverneur général de Indochine, SOM, Fonds du Gouvernement général, 51.080.

34. *Ibid.*

35. *Ibid.*

36. 15 Avril 1924, Arrêté portant création dans chaque pays de l'Union d'un poste de Chef local du service de l'enseignement, *BGIP, Partie officielle*, 3è Année, No. 10 (Juin-Août 1924) pp. 170-71.

37. See Circulaire—Le Resident superieur au Tonkin à MM les administrateurs, maires, residents, chefs de province et commandants des territoires militaires, 2 Décembre 1926 (Signé Robin) a.s. création et organization des écoles communales du Tonkin, *Hoc Báo, Cong Van, Sô* 19 (10 Janvier 1927) pp. 225-28: Arrêté No. 4146 autorisant les communes du Tonkin ne disposant d'aucune école officielle à ouvrir des écoles élémentaires publiques confiées à des maîtres n'appartenant pas aux cadres reguliers de l'enseignement, *Bulletin de l'amicale du personnel indigène de l'enseignement au Tonkin*, Vol. 17, No. 14 (Juillet 1926-Juin 1927) pp. 217-18; Annam, 16 Septembre 1927, Circulaire relative aux écoles élémentaires communales. *BGIP, Partie officielle*, 7è Année, No. 6 (Février 1928) p. 124–25.

38. 21 Mars 1924. Circulaire au sujet de la production d'un certificate de scolairite et de conduite a exiger des eleves changeant d'establissements Scolaires, *BGIP, Partie officielle*, 3e Annee, No. 10 (Juin-Aout 1924) p. 173. The certificate, which reextended the Office's power over the primary school, was brought into being as a response to the student strikes of the 1920s. Students who were expelled from schools in Cochinchina or Annam often tried to gain entry to another school under an assumed name in Tonkin. The certificate kept by the Office as the centralized bureaucracy in education was seen as a way to prevent student strikers from re-entering the school system. The re-establishment of Office of Public Instruction control over primary education was an unintended result of the need to control student activism.

39. Gouvernement général de l'Indochine, Direction de l'instruction publique. *Arrêtés 1. fixant les nouveau horaires des programmes de l'enseignement primaire supérieur franco-indigène; 2—fixant les nouveaux horaires et programmes de l'enseignement secondaire franco-indigènes, 3—instituant un livret scolaire pour l'enseignement secondaire français ou franco-indigène* (26 Décembre 1924). Hanoi: IDEO, 1924, especially pp. 84-91.

40. See 14 Octobre 1924, Arrêté portant création à le Direction de l'instruction publique d'une commission de reception de manuels scolaires et de tableaux muraux destinés à l'enseignement primaire élémentaire indigène, *JOIF*, 36è Année, No. 8 (18 Octobre 1924) p. 1999; 17 Novembre 1928, Arrêté modifiant l'article 21 de l'arrêté du 27 Janvier 1925 et l'Article 269 du Reglement général de l'instruction publique en Indochine, *JOIF*, 40è Année, No. 93 (21 Novembre 1928) p. 3443; 10 Mai 1925, Arrêté rélatif à l'elaboration de manuels scolaires et de tableaux muraux destinés aux élèves des divers cours de l'enseignement primaire franco-indigène, *JOIF*, 38è Année, No 39 (15 Mai 1926) p. 1302.

41. See manuels scolaires de la Direction de l'instruction publique, *BGIP, Partie générale*, 10è Année, No. 9 (Mai 1931) pp. 144-48.

42. Indochine française, Direction générale de l'instruction publique *Les manuels scolaires et les publications pédagogiques de la Direction générale de l'instruction publique* (Hanoi: IDEO, 1931) ff. p. 22 (Tableau).

43. Gouvernement général de l'Indochine française, *Rapports au conseil du gouvernement.*

Session ordinaire, Deuxième partie: Fonctionnement des divers services indochinois (Hanoi: IDEO, 1938) p. 142.

44. A similar point was made by Guy Benveniste, *The Politics of Expertise* (Berkeley; Glendessary Press, 1972).

45. See Gail P. Kelly, "Colonial Schools in Vietnam. . ." *op. cit.*

46. See "La session du conseil de perfectionnement de l'enseignement indigène en Indochine," *L'Asie française*, 10è Année, No. 116 (Novembre 1910) pp. 464-68; G. Prêtre, "L'Enseignement indigène en Indochine," *L'Asie française*, 12è Année, No. 137 (Auguste 1912) p. 311.

47. See, for example Bui-Quang-Chieu, *France d'Asie* . . . *op. cit.*

48. No. 1222, Hanoi, le 30 Juin 1919, Le Gouverneur général de l'Indochine p.i. à M. le Resident supérieur en Annam a.s. d'un projet d'ordonnance royale à l'enseignement primaire an Annam, SOM, Fonds du Gouvernement général 51.080. See also "La session du conseil de perfectionnement de l'enseignement indigène en Indochine," *Bulletin du Comité de l'Asie française*, 10è Année, No. 116 (Novembre 1910) pp. 464-68.

49. *Ibid*. See also "La ville—ouverture de la 4è session du Conseil de perfectionnement de l'enseignement indigène," *L'Avenir du Tonkin*, 30è Année, No. 5466 (9 Avril 1913) p. 3. Mat Gioi, "Lettre de Mat Gioi," *L'Avenir du Tonkin*, 30è Année, No. 5438 (6 Mars 1913) p. 1 (Mat Gioi is the pen name for Crayssac, a colonial poet and fiction writer who worked for the French colonial service.)

50. See Unsigned memo to the Governor Général, 1931, SOM, Fonds du Gouvernement général 51.174.

51. See Brachet, Inspecteur de l'instruction publique de l'Indochine (Ordre des Sciences) a M. le Recteur d'academie, Directeur général de l'instruction publique en Indochine. Rapport sur certaines questions concernant l'enseignement primaire en Cochinchine. SOM, Fonds du Gouvernement général 51.208; Blanchard de la Brosse, *Une année des réformes dans l'enseignement public en Indochine (1924-25)* (Hanoi: Imprimerie d'Extrême Orient, 1925). Hanoi, 13 25 Novembre 1921. Rapport sur l'Instruction publique en Indochine, execution des prescriptions de la circulaire ministerielle du 10 Octobre 1920, SOM, Fonds du Gouvernement Général 2721; Nguyen-Van-Ngoc, Su Phat o Hoc Duong, *Hoc Báo, Luang Thuyet*, Sô 26 (27 Février 1922).

52. No. 691-C. Le Chef du service de l'enseignement au Tonkin à MM. les directeurs et mesdames les directrices des écoles du Tonkin. Objet, L'instruction élémentaire et l'enseignement du Français, 31 Mars 1925. SOM, Fonds de la Residence supérieure du Tonkin R1 36.313.

53. See Blanchard de la Brosse, *Une année de reformes dans l'enseignement public en Indochine (1924-25)* (Hanoi: Imprimerie d'Extrême Orient, 1925); Rapport sur l'instruction publiques en Indochine, execution des prescriptions de la circulaire ministerielle du 10 Octobre 1920, SOM Fonds du Gouvernement général, 2721: Le Gouverneur général de l'Indochine à M. le Ministre des colonies, Mars 1926, No. 442-IP a.s. de l'arrêté du 18 Septembre 1924 reglementant l'usage de la langue indigène dans les trois premiers cours de l'enseignement primaire et consacrant dans tous les cours de cet enseignement les modalités de l'enseignement du Français et de l'enseignement en Français (signé Marlin), SOM, Fonds du Gouvernement général, 51.174.

54. For a fuller discussion of the Office's role, see Gail P. Kelly, "Franco-Vietnamese Schools, 1918 to 1938," Unpublished Ph.D. Dissertation, University of Wisconsin, 1974.

CHAPTER 10

The Meaning of Educational Technology in the Modern World

VICTOR N. KOBAYASHI

In this concluding chapter we provide some perspectives on educational technology, its creation, development, and cross-cultural transfer, other than those raised previously, while also summarizing some of the ideas that have been presented. In addition, we raise questions about the meaning of this technology in present-day education.

Operating Systems as Educational Technology

We have used the term *educational technology* in this book to include *operating systems* as well as what the term conventionally evokes in one's mind: objects, thingish tools, such as textbooks, film projectors, computers, television sets, and the like. The major type of operating system that we have investigated is the educational bureaucracy, a technology that has spread throughout the world as part of what we mean by a modern mass national system of education. Although there may be ideological differences between nations, such as Marxism or liberalism, all modern nations organize their schools on the bureaucratic pattern.

Bureaucracy and Education

Educational bureaucracies have certain patterns in common, while also having features that are unique to specific cultures. Furthermore, persons directly involved in the various versions of bureaucratic systems, especially in the higher positions, for better or for worse greatly influence the direction and shape of educational development in the twentieth century throughout most of the world. As both Noel McGinn and Gail Kelly have pointed out in their essays, the development of bureaucracy, at least in the nations they studied, France and Vietnam, respectively, was closely related to political and economic interests having large-scale control over a nation.

Despite the pervasiveness and seeming indispensability of educational bureaucracies, however, we must keep in mind that there has been a minority tradition of criticism of bureaucratic approaches to the organization and management of education. The gist of the criticism is that bureaucracies, by their very nature, operate in and create climates unsuitable for the highest and noblest aim of education, that of liberating the human mind. Our purpose here is not to elaborate on what is meant by this idea of "liberating the human mind," but to assume that philosophical ideals such as "truth," "freedom," and "humanity" are strongly linked to conceptions of "education," although it is not the aim here to discuss these ideals in detail, despite their fundamental importance.

Noel McGinn has mentioned the case of the Cultural Revolution in China, where the bureaucracy was attacked for retarding the progress of communist reforms. We also need to be reminded that in the West in the sixties, there was a revival of interest in the reconstruction of education so that it would be freer, less nationalistic, less bureaucratic in control. The movement was different from, but reminiscent of, the worldwide "New Education Movement" (or Progressive Education movement, as it was called in the United States) of the twenties and early thirties. In some parts of the industrialized world, there was a reaction to bureaucratic approaches to education, and a call for greater decentralization of authority and greater freedom for teachers and pupils from the constraints of the official school system.

Summerhill school in England was in many ways the most radical protest against the bureaucratic approach to education, in its attempt to return to reduce formal education to direct face-to-face encounters between teachers and pupils in a small, self-regulated community (that was nevertheless embedded in a society composed of large bureaucratic organizations, including those that governed the mainstream school systems). Founded in 1924 in England, it became a model for the 1960s free-school reformers in Canada and the United States who attempted to establish "Summerhill" type alternative operating systems. The reformers, however, found it difficult to maintain such schools over a long period of time; such schools seemed to depend upon the leadership of unique charismatic personalities like Summerhill founder A. S. Neill and his wife.

Bureaucracies have the built-in strength of assuring their survival over a long period of time, despite the individual characteristics of the personalities who may lead them. They are designed so that positions can be held by interchangeable, replaceable persons. The capacity of educational bureaucracies to endure is an asset as well as a liability: bureaucracies stand for conservatism, regularity, routine, and stability, while at the same time, because of these very qualities, they become easily moribund and a major obstacle to revitalization efforts in education.

Other critics of the influence of bureaucracy on education during the 1960s included persons such as Paul Goodman, who drew on ideas from John Dewey and the Russian anarchist Peter Kropotkin, or Ivan Illich with his ideas of "Deschooling Society." Critics such as these argued that bureaucratic systems of mass education were not only an unwieldly means for providing "education" which in its basic form is something that takes place between students and teachers; bureaucratic systems also themselves conveyed a teaching message, that of making the systems' participants accept a submissive posture towards official agencies, and of making learners become dependent on external authorities for what was to be learned and how. The critics were not arguing (using the language adopted in this book) about the efficiency and effectiveness of one educational operation system over another in producing desired effects upon its students; they were arguing that the operating systems were not merely technology, that is instruments that were mere means to accomplish certain educational ends, but themselves had certain educative (or mis-educative) effects, and had to be critically appraised in terms of what effects they fostered as technology, regardless of the content they were intended to convey to, or to promote in, learners. One version of the criticism was that of Paulo Freire (1970), who called for an education that empowered the oppressed, particularly those in the Third World.

This argument, of the incompatibility of bureaucracy and education, of course, was the basis of Dewey's plea that it was not enough for schools to teach the scientific method and to teach about democratic values; the schools had to operate and be managed scientifically, that is, be more experimental themselves, and they had to be organized democratically, in order for genuine scientific and democratic values to be learned by children. The school had to strive to become a workable democratic community itself and free itself from the dominant authoritarian model, while also conducting its affairs in an experimental, scientific manner. At the same time, however, Dewey's pragmatism and emphasis on deliberate planning and control through rational processes were congenial with the rationale for bureaucracies, and may have helped, perhaps unwittingly, lay the groundwork for the idea of the technocracy, mentioned in Noel McGinn's chapter.

A different argument is found in Jacques Ellul's *The Technological Society* (1967), where he argues that there is an illusion that technique (including technology) serves human ends, when, in fact, it creates instead an artificial and self-serving environment that meets only its own needs, while diminishing our humanity. Ellul was critical even of some of the progressive education movements, with their *techniques de l'école nouvelle*. He criticized both liberal and traditional educators, including Montessori, because (1) they emphasized psychopedagogic techniques that had to be exercised over all children in order for society to be

democratically reformed, (2) they, in the end, supported social co
formity to a technical society by emphasizing psychological happine
through adaptation to society, and (3) they made usefulness in a techni
al society the predominant end of instruction (Ellul, 1967: 344-349
Similar criticisms were voiced by Lewis Mumford (1970).

Educational Technology and Twentieth-Century Dehumanization

Finally, another criticism of educational bureaucracies, closely related to
the protests discussed above, lies in the fact that they are viewed as
technologies, as tools to accomplish some other end outside of themselves. Because bureaucracies are not things, and are made up of human
beings who perform certain specified functions, there is a tendency to
view those in a bureaucracy also as means, as things that are used to
accomplish certain objectives, rather than as persons. This aspect of
bureaucracies is the one aspect causing them to be viewed as "dehuma-
nizing." Of course, luckily, real persons who work in bureaucracies in
reality don't operate completely as objects, as means, and don't completely treat each other without regard to individual personalities. Also,
one is reminded of Lewis Carroll's *Alice in Wonderland*, where in
playing the game of croquet, flamingoes were used as the mallets, while
hedgehogs were used as the balls; thus, when the flamingoes were
swung to hit the hedgehogs, the flamingoes avoided hitting the hedgehogs while the hedgehogs dodged the mallet-flamingoes. The animals
refused to become objects, become mere means to some other person's
purposes. Of course, from another point of view, bureaucracies become
self-serving, and thus become inefficient in accomplishing the goals that
they were created to serve.

The Persistence of Traditional Operating Systems

Another point that must be made is that alternatives to the dominant
operating system of educational bureaucracy continue to exist today,
partly as a result of the persistence of traditional forms of educational
organizations from the past into the present, despite the growth of huge
educational bureaucracies. With the tremendous changes brought about
by industrialization and high technology, many peoples are concerned
about the preservation of traditions, such as those in the area of crafts,
dance, folk arts. Bureaucratic systems do not seem to serve education in
these areas very well, and the conventional school system does not
provide an appropriate environment for the preservation of them,
although many attempts have been made and continue to be made.
There is the strong possibility that conventional school environments,
complete with their bureaucratic features, are not conducive to the

maintenance of certain traditional arts. Although the formal schools may include some aspects of the traditional arts in their curriculum, the primary vehicles have been through non-formal educational institutions. Thus, older systems that helped perpetuate traditional arts may still have a place in the contemporary world.

In Japan, the *iemoto* system, based on the leadership of a grand master, with disciples ranked in order of seniority and sometimes ability, related to each other in a fictive kinship system, survives, and even thrives in the teaching of certain arts, such as the tea ceremony, flower arrangement (*ikebana*), and traditional performing arts. Their operations are routinized and punctuated through regular rituals and ceremonies that bond the practitioners together and affirm the aesthetic and spiritual principles of the *iemoto* traditions. Some of the *iemoto*, such as the *Urasenke* school of the tea ceremony and the Sogetsu school of flower arrangement, are extremely prosperous today and co-exist side-by-side with the conventional schools in the official system. More people have practiced the tea ceremony in the present age than in previous periods of Japan's history. Not only has *Urasenke* flourished in Japan, but it has gone international, with branches formed overseas. There are also signs that some of the arts introduced into Japan from the West, and practiced with intense appreciation, are being taught in schools organized in *iemoto*-like patterns. One example is the teaching of jazz singing, where the leading senior disciple is given the name of the founder in a special ceremony.

For the last few decades, Hawaii has been undergoing a revival of interest in its Polynesian heritage, with growth in the popularity of *halau*, a kind of academy, headed by a *kumu* and organized somewhat like the Japanese *iemoto*. Thus, many of the different traditional Hawaiian dances (hula) and chants are being nurtured through more traditional-based educational operating systems, outside of the conventional formal school system. There also has been an effort to incorporate some of the carriers of traditional Hawaiian arts, the *kupuna* (elders), into the classrooms of the state schools.

In the Islamic world, too, that extends from Morocco to Indonesia, traditional Quoranic schools continue to persist and are fiercely supported, despite the secularizing and modernizing pressures that call for schools that teach practical subjects required for industrialization and scientific and technological development (Ashraf, 1985). Hindu ashrams also continue to be supported in India.

Another traditional type of educational operating system that has declined, but continues to persist, is apprenticeship. In parts of the United States, Canada, and Europe, the apprenticeship system continues to survive and is advocated by craftspersons as a way of promoting craftsmanship in such arts as pottery, woodwork, and glass blowing.

An encyclopedic book on the place of apprenticeship in contemporary society has been supported by the National Endowment for the Arts, and the US Office of Education (Williams, 1981). Similar movements of alternative but more traditional and indigenous systems of education that coexist with the mainstream modernized school system may also be found in other countries that have a strong interest in preserving some aspect of their cultural heritage, or in reviving traditional arts and crafts, without being hard-core Luddite in their resistance to contemporary industrialization and technologization. The basis for these types of educational systems seems to be a concern for something deeply spiritual—in the case of Japan, a spirit that is closely related to the sacredness of the moment that is celebrated by Zen Buddhism, or in the case of the crafts apprenticeship movement, a sense of sacredness of doing something skillfully, with great care and respect for the material as well as for the human body in the crafting of objects. The secularized and impersonalized bureaucratic system seems unsuited for such educational endeavors. Then, too, some of the traditional forms have also taken on some of the characteristics of bureaucratic operating systems, and thus may in the near future become increasingly secularized and lose their spiritual or religious qualities. Mass tourism also has been a mixed blessing, aiding the economy, sometimes encouraging the arts, while also having the potential of endangering craftsmanship.

The New Media as Educational Technology

Besides calling attention to alternative operating systems in contemporary education, our discussion of educational bureaucracies as creating a particular kind of educational climate, regardless of the school curricula fostered by them, suggests another important point. Throughout this book, we have discussed various technologies, including bureaucracies, as means to accomplish something deemed educational, without considering what exactly is meant by "educational." Thus, we could consider an "advanced" technology as one that accomplished its educational objectives in a more efficient and effective manner, compared to something less "advanced"; we also assumed that technology contributed to some sort of movement to a more "developed state" of education, and therefore of the society also, regardless of whether the society was communist, capitalist, agrarian, etc.

In this way, educational technologies that enabled a large mass of the target population to learn certain specified skills, behaviors, values, and knowledge, in the fastest, and in the most cost-effective way, would be considered more advanced than one considered less advanced. From this point of view, television and radio and print have been hailed as major tools for mass education, as well as for mass communication in general.

The messages these media carried could be educative or miseducative, but these were not within our major concern, because we were only interested in the means that were most potent and widespread, regardless of the ends for which the technologies were put to use. It was not necessary to specify the skills, values, dispositions, to be fostered by education, because we were only looking at the major tools, the means, used to accomplish whatever educational effects were considered desirable. It also seemed convenient to leave ends out of our discussion, because they would open a Pandora's Box of arguments about what specific educational values were desirable and feasible to promote.

In this concluding chapter, however, we are now forced to pursue a slight opening of the Box, because we must now consider the possibility that technologies are not ideologically or philosophically neutral. The domain of this book is thus widened to include something more complex than what we originally set out to explore: the shifting context of technology. We do this being fully aware that a slight opening of Pandora's Box may be the same as a full opening: its entire content gets released in either case.

The Shifting Contexts of Technology

We have seen earlier, as in the chapters on educational print materials, that publishing has been undergoing rapid change, as electronic computers and laser technology have been applied to publishing. Our exploration of educational technology requires us also to shift the context of how we perceive educational technology, in order to add to a fuller, rounded out view of educational technology. Thus, in this concluding chapter, we explore other perspectives that can be taken to understand educational technology. To accomplish this task, we will consider educational technology in terms of the following theses, some of which have been already hinted at by this and earlier chapters:

1. Educational technology itself carries certain educational values that vary with the specific technology used.
2. The technology itself, as it becomes predominant, changes the consciousness of the society, and is morphogenetic, that is to say, helps to shape the form of the culture of which it is a part.
3. Any aspect of the environment, both natural and cultural, including any technology itself, has the potential of being studied as "educational technology."

1. Educational technology itself carries certain educational values that vary with the specific technology used. Our discussion in this chapter on bureaucracies is one illustration of this point. Another example does not

deal with educational technology, but with weaponry. However, it is also a dramatic example of transfer of technology, and how a culture might consider a foreign, but more effective technology, but nevertheless reject it because it would be considered less effective as a technology *in other domains* of human concern in which it may also be considered a technology. In feudal Japan, the major weapon technology for the military were swords, spears, bow and arrows, and the like. The gun was first introduced in 1543, when Portuguese firearms were purchased by a feudal lord. Within ten years, the Japanese were producing large amounts of their own guns, and by 1560, they were in wide use in major battles. However, despite the proliferation, by 1637, the Japanese had stopped using guns, a situation that lasted over 200 years, until after the forced opening of Japan to the West by Commodore Perry in 1853. Among the reasons Japan turned away from the gun were the symbolic value of the traditional sword for the samurai class and the aesthetic relationship between swords to the human body, as opposed to that between the gun and the body. Considerations other than the effectiveness of the gun as a weapon then were at play in the case of Japan's long history of "giving up the gun" (Perrin, 1980). This example also provides evidence of exceptions to the often suggested "law," that, as Jacques Ellul has stated it, "In a given civilization, technical progress is irreversible" (Ellul, 1967: 89). The evidence is welcomed, because it offers some hope to those who fear the proliferation of nuclear weaponry throughout the world.

Another example, also from Japan, but occurring in very recent times, that illustrates the carrying of certain values in a technology, is the use of the abacus. With the advent of inexpensive hand-held electronic calculators, Japanese educators were fearful that these products would replace the abacus used by children learning how to add, multiply, subtract, and divide. However, what occurred in Japanese schools was for the abacus to continue to be used, because of its educational value in learning analogic relationships between the moving of beads of the abacus and arithmetic manipulation of numbers. Electronic calculators, of course, are widely used in Japan, but coexist with the abacus. Studies indicate, too, that experts of the abacus interiorize the manipulation of the abacus such that they can mentally perform calculations using large numbers faster than they can on the actual abacus (Hatano and Inagaki, 1986). An electronic calculator's operations, because they are neither visual nor tactile would be impossible to interiorize.

The most striking example of a technology that carries values of the most profound sort is that of writing and print. We are only recently beginning to fully appreciate the ramifications of the development of writing, and the invention of the printing press, although as Eric Havelock (1963) has pointed out, Plato, in his criticism of the poets and their ways of thought, had seemed to be aware of the significance of writing, at a crucial moment in the history of Western thought, when there was an awareness of the transition from orality to literacy in Western culture. Writing made possible the development of critical reflection, for when it was possible to put language into written form, one could pause, reread, think, and consider what has appeared several sentences previously, and ponder the relationship to material appearing later in the text. As Walter Ong has said in his study of how literacy affected human consciousness, "Writing . . . was and is the most momentous of all human inventions. It is not a mere appendage to speech. Because it moves speech from the oral-aural to a new sensory world, that of vision, it transforms speech and thought as well" (Ong, 1982). Plato, at the same time was also critical of writing, which was thing-like rather than mind-like. He also argued (through Socrates in his dialogues) that writing destroys memory, and prevents the interactive dialogue between persons that speech provides. But as Walter Ong (1982: 80) points out:

> One weakness in Plato's position was that to make his objections effective, he put them into writing, just as one weakness in anti-print positions is that their proponents, to make their objections more effective, put the objections into print. The same weakness in anti-computer positions is that, to make them effective, their proponents articulate them in articles or books printed from tapes composed on computer terminals. Writing and print and the computer are all ways of technologizing the word. Once the word is technologized, there is no effective way to criticize what technology has done with it without the aid of the highest technology available. Moreover, the new technology is not merely used to convey the critique: in fact, it brought the critique into existence. Plato's philosophically analytic thought . . ., including his critique of writing, was possible only because of the effects that writing was beginning to have on mental processes.

Literacy made possible new constructions such as the novel and the essay. It made it possible for us to "refer back" to something, to have history in the sense of a record based on written documents as evidence, rather than on individual memory and the transmission of important past events through such devices as Homeric ballads or Polynesian genealogical chants. It made possible lists and also scripts, and by extension, formal logic, recipes, encyclopedias, libraries and archives, schools, textbooks, newspapers, memos, policy statements, constitutions, and educational and other bureaucracies. As literacy became interiorized, our thought processes changed. Literacy, combined with mass printing, transformed human consciousness and changed the form of culture and the direction in which culture developed (Ong, 1982).

Dennis Harper in Chapter 2 has pointed out the proliferation of research on computer education in the advanced industrialized nations in the last five years, and has pointed out the optimistic as well as the pessimistic views of the effects of computers on society in the future. But another type of question might be raised: Are there any values that a computer-dominated life favors? Philosopher Philip J. Bossert, who grew up with computers (his father worked with the early computers) and who continues to work with computers in philosophy, argues that the high speed of massive data processing is a mixed blessing, for it may result in a breed of human beings who are less patient with the normal human pace of life:

> The durations which we come to consider as normal after working with high-speed computers on a regular basis are for the most part much shorter durations than those within which human beings are accustomed to responding. The speeding up of our environments with nanosecond and picosecond processors saves us time but it can also result in a loss of patience with those around us who continue to think and act in human time (Bossert, in Kobayashi, 1987: 14).

Bossert also points out the "overcommunicated, information-overloaded, overly complexified and over-stimulated environments" created by high-speed computers that have access to telecommunications systems, and the excitement and stimulation that these environments offer; although he is basically optimistic about the potential of computers, he worries that the new environments created by the new electronic technologies also have the possibility of inducing nervous exhaustion and alienation:

> With so much information transmitted to us through the various media, many of us react with an indifference to most types of information and, in some cases, suffer a debilitating numbness in the face of important decisions. With so much information available to each of us, there begin to emerge very specialized and limited "colonies of consciousness," within which we feel comfortable communicating, but between which communication—from parent to child, spouse to spouse, neighbor to neighbor, employee to employee—is increasingly difficult if not impossible. Those who attempt to accommodate and process the overload of information in a timely fashion often suffer what is called "burnout." The regular "living presence" via electronic media of world events in our living rooms and offices can threaten us with feelings of insignificance, while the increased complexity of these option-rich in-

formation environments causes many to withdraw to the simplistic, to seek easy answers, and to embrace the security of cure-all systems which have a solution to everything. And, at the extreme, we see an increase in personal aberrations such as drug and alcohol abuse, spouse and child abuse, as well as at the collective level, an increase in terrorism of all sorts as people collapse under the pressure of such environments and lash out to destroy that which threatens them (Bossert, in Kobayashi, 1987: 14-15).

As the chapters on television and computers in this book indicate, electronic technology is rapidly being adopted into the schools and colleges of many nations. Since the invention of photography, thousands of visual images are now accessible to us, and in fact are difficult to avoid, as they flicker on the TV screens as we switch channels, or as we are blitzed with photographs of various sorts in newspapers, magazines, and posters displayed in public places. If writing changed our consciousness, what does this massive infiltration of photographic and electronic imagery into our minds mean? Philosopher Frank Tillman argues that our conceptual world is being dominated by these mediated images, with a decline in meaning based on direct eyewitness experiences (Tillman, 1987). The world of our associations has widened exponentially, as we see the earth from a satellite, see violence in the streets of a faraway city, or see a volcano erupt on an island we have never visited. These images, by their very number and their variety are changing the substance, the conceptions, and abstractions involved in our thought.

Then there are those who see a decline in our ability to reflect and think about the complex issues of our time as a result of too much television in our lives. In 1982, the National Institute of Mental Health found that high school seniors spent more time watching television than being in their classrooms. The effects of so much television in our lives are not clear. But many may agree with Neil Postman in his argument that Americans are "Amusing Ourselves to Death," as the medium of television conditions people to new expectation patterns, and replaces the valuable skills that deep literacy involves. TV must continually hold our attention, so that we do not turn off the set or our minds, or switch to another channel. Postman sees television as changing American society, as what is visually entertaining sets the standards of discourse for politics, government, education, and even religion. Government by public relations has become commonplace, and clever one-liner made-for-TV quips that catch audience attention become regarded as political commentary, replacing the deep probing of issues that once were the standard of political discussion. Educational programs take on the techniques used in TV commercials to attract and keep the attention of children.

For Postman, complex social and political issues that need to be given serious consideration by an informed electorate are trivialized by the show-business demands of new generations brought up on commercial television, rather than on the intellectual demands that literacy makes on people. Postman recalls the days of the Lincoln-Douglas debates, which he calls "The Age of Exposition," when the standards of public discourse over serious issues emanated from the examples set by serious writing. Such a period is rapidly passing away, replaced by a TV mentality, with fast editing, expensive special effects that even modify live footage through computerized manipulation of the videotape track, and so meets the audience demands for novelty and instant gratification. Democratic institutions are endangered by these unhealthy trends, as we proceed not into Orwell's *1984* (which has already passed) but into Aldous Huxley's *Brave New World* (Postman, 1986).

These considerations also highlight our first thesis (that educational technology itself carries certain educational values that vary with the specific technology used) as well as our second one, that is: A particular technology, as it becomes predominant, changes the consciousness of the society, and is morphogenetic, that is to say, helps to shape the form of the culture of which it is a part.

Discarded Technology, Discarded Values

Again, but in a different context, we must make the point that when new technology improves in one major respect over another technology, the older technology may still be of profound value in other respects, and therefore ought not to be automatically discarded. Conventional thinking sometimes argues that when a new technology is introduced, it replaces the older one. But this is not necessarily the case. New technology may displace the older, but the old may continue to survive, finding another ecological niche in the evolving culture. Domesticated horses still have a place in our culture, despite being replaced by automobiles as a major means of transportation; and then too, old models of cars still have a place as treasured antique "classics" and are valued along with the latest high-tech models. Radio was not replaced by TV, but coexists with it. Film coexists with TV, while at the same time the two technologies are merging, with high-resolution, high-definition video with magnified screen projections that mimic cinema. Films are made to be later shown on TV, and marketed also in videotape and laserdisc form. Already, high resolution video can be transformed into high quality film.

Another example is that of poetry. The unfortunate suggestion is sometimes made that poetry was more important in preliterate times, in exclusively oral cultures, because it provided mnemonic devices to help human memory transmit valuable information into the present. Poetry, from this point of view, is prose put into a form that could be more readily remembered in a culture that has no writing to preserve the word. But poetry has continued to flourish centuries beyond the invention of writing and the printing press, which made knowledge more "permanent" and less vulnerable to the weakness of human memory. Poetry continues to be valuable to the survival of a healthy culture, even if its role as a mnemonic aid in the transmission of past information is no longer important. One could even say that the invention of writing liberated poetry. For one thing, poetry no longer required rhyme and other formulaic devices, straight-jackets that were dictated by the needs of an oral culture dependent on mnemonic aids.

A similar case may be made for orality. Literacy doesn't need to replace completely the consciousness of an oral culture. A literate culture has many advantages over one that is primarily oral, but the kind of consciousness nurtured by preliterate orality still has an important place in the contemporary world. Indeed, Martin Buber's evocation of the I-Thou relationship is in many ways a reminder for us to return to the spiritual sense of an oral culture, where presence, immediacy of the moment, listening, the voice, and being in touch with the living person was sensed fully and savoured. For, as Walter Ong has written, speech is sound, and "Sound exists only when it is going out of existence" (Ong, 1982: 32). We are also reminded by Zen that we need to regain, to renew, from time to time the aesthetic sense of life and the sense of relationship we had to the universe as prelinguistic beings. In our ardor to convert children into literate beings, we must at the same time attempt to preserve those aspects of their pristine preliteracy that are so important to our mental and spiritual health.

Loosening the Boundaries of "Educational Technology"

The third hypothesis, that any aspect of the environment, both natural and cultural, including any technology itself, has the potential of being studied as "educational technology," is one that was suggested by Rousseau when he called for education based on experience and the senses, rather than based on textbooks and academic imparting of knowledge. Some of Rousseau's ideas in the *Emile* (1762) were elaborated upon and applied by Pestalozzi in his work as a teacher, where learning through the senses was emphasized so that any object, anything in the environment, had the potential for being educational, for being the starting point in an encounter with learning through experiential elaboration.

This point often seems obvious to us today, but historically, schooling often became so preoccupied with the academic, with textbooks and set curricula, that teachers had to be reminded of this perspective. Thus,

English teachers are urged to use trade books such as novels and plays, rather than rely exclusively on textbooks, in class. Even today there are workshops for teachers on using the newspaper as a teaching tool for social studies. Magazines, comic books, as well as textbooks can be used as material to be analyzed, for learning about contemporary values; or, if a textbook is 100 years old, from another era, it can be used as a source for learning about values and attitudes that were held in that era. Documentary and feature films as well as "educational films" also fall in the category of educational technology: they can be used as actual products that express a culture, rather than as a means to learn something outside of themselves. Thus, a miseducative television commercial might become material for a class interested in analyzing how commercials manipulate their audiences; or a film produced in Nazi Germany might be used to study propaganda films as well as the metaphors utilized by the Nazi regime in affirming certain thought patterns.

Our third hypothesis also suggests that even educational technology itself is something that can be the object of study, exploration, and experimentation. Many innovative artists have used material designed for a particular use and converted it to their own use. Thus, the Korean-born Nam June Paik has played with television sets, rehooking their electronic connections, using multiple sets simultaneously, and has become one of the leading innovators in the new electronic arts. In the 1960s overhead projectors were used to produce "light shows" by putting transparent trays filled with liquid over the projector beam, and then dripping various dyes to create a "psychedelic" effect. Today's playful equivalents experiment with laser beams in musical performances. Norman McLaren took old film stock which he scratched and projected to produce an artistic movie. The underlying statement of these artists was to loosen the boundaries of what technology was for. From this perspective, therefore, educational technology loses its distinctive boundaries as a category and opens up into something threateningly creative, but wonderfully playful and liberating. The Pandora's Box has been opened.

Transfer of Technology

Our final set of comments are reflections on the transfer of educational technology across cultures. A first point is that it is possible for a new technology developed in modern Western nations to be quickly picked up by "underdeveloped" cultures that then excel in the use of the new technology. A good example is the case of cinema. The Edison Kinetoscope opened in New York in 1894, but was imported only two years later into a Japan that had only just begun its modernization efforts. The Kinetoscope was quickly followed by the French Cinematographe Lumiere and then other new cinematic technology, and all of these quickly became popular in Japan (Anderson and Richie, 1982). Japan quickly began to produce its own films, first by imitating Hollywood, but soon by creating films that had distinctive Japanese characteristics. By the 1920s and 1930s some of the films reached world-class aesthetic standards. At the end of 1936, there were 1,627 cinema theatres (84 percent with "talkie" equipment) and an attendance rate of 226,060,000 for the year, three times the total population. As for educational films, the ministry of education began producing films for classroom use in 1923 (Yamakawa, 1938). But it was not until the 1950s with Kurosawa's *Rashomon* that Western audiences recognized the high aesthetic standards of some of the Japanese film makers.

India today produces the largest number of titles of films and perhaps has the largest audiences in the world. Films are produced nationally as well as regionally, in different languages; and although most of the films, as in any other country, are not of much artistic merit, India has produced outstanding internationally recognized film makers, such as Satyajit Ray and Mrinal Sen, who bring a distinctive Indian sensibility to their films. China, Hong Kong, and also Taiwan have significant film industries today, and have produced some outstanding films of both artistic and social significance, as well as films of high production quality.

Another new technology developed in the West, but quickly adopted by an Asian nation, was radio. Japan did not adopt radio broadcasting for school and home use until the 1930s. But radio spread so quickly that in two years, 40 percent of all the primary schools in Japan were using radio. Educators visiting Japan were often shown the accomplishments of the Japanese in the area of broadcast—and were most impressed. The Japanese also conducted scientific research to determine the effectiveness of the educational programs and what seemed to work; for example, the effectiveness of the rate of speech in communication over radio was determined for children of different ages (Aoki, 1938: 76-78). Programs for various subjects, including music, science, morals, history, and geography were designed. With just one receiver, speakers could be connected and placed in each classroom. The Broadcasting Corporation of Japan (the predecessor of today's major national educational network NHK) produced not only programs for children in school and for adults, but also teaching materials that accompanied the radio programs. "Teacher's Hours" were also broadcast to help prepare teachers for the next day's broadcast lessons for the students. Well-known Japanese leaders spoke over the radio to schoolchildren on the mornings of the first and third Mondays of each month, and they frequently exhorted them to study hard, work patiently, and support the national cause.

One of the most effective and successful uses of radio was for morning exercises along with lectures on moral and nationalistic education. They began in 1931, first in the Tokyo area, but then spread nationwide to include both children and adults; a mass national physical culture movement developed, with a hundred million participants, including factory and office workers, teachers, children, mothers—practically everyone—exercising in unison during the summer for outdoor exercises (Shimizu, 1938: 78-100). With all of Japan being in the same time zone, the centrally controlled government-operated broadcast system was used for mass propaganda purposes to mobilize national effort and create a sense of nationalism, which also was utilized to support Japan's military expansionism.

The order in which technologies grow and develop in another culture need not follow the historical sequence taken in the culture in which the technology was developed. Although television proliferated in American homes after the development of the telephone, in Japan when television was introduced, TV sets were acquired by most households before a telephone was installed. Then, too, there may be advantages in being "behind" in the race to have the latest educational technology; nations—or school systems—that did not utilize computers on a wide scale ten years ago, can now purchase the latest, more sophisticated generation of computers, often at less cost.

Finally, a word must be said about new metaphors of how the human mind works, and how humans learn, emerge as technology changes. The metaphor of the mechanical machine might underlie the way we have developed bureaucracies and ideas of how the human mind calculates and works; but today, the computer and electronic processing are becoming the guiding metaphors for our concepts about new social structures as well as about how the human mind thinks and learns: the entire domain of "artificial intelligence" feeds on this new metaphor.

Clearly, people make technology, and technology makes people. As we approach the age of high technology and information overload, basic human problems nevertheless remain the same. There is no progress when it comes to how each of us deals with the responsibility of existence; as Bossert puts it:

> The problems will be essentially the same as those which have confronted the realm of information and knowledge throughout history: Who is in charge? How do you verify the truth or validity of knowledge and information? How is access distributed—according to who can pay or according to who needs it (or who wants it)? Who is allowed to input data and information to the network? etc. But the possibilities for greater understanding, greater creativity, better communication and greater realization of human potential are also there. As always, the technologies can only support us; they cannot relieve us of our ultimate responsibility as

human beings to make the final choices (Bossert, in Kobayashi 1987: 17).

References

Aoki, Seishiro (1938) Psychological studies in school broadcasting, *Proceedings of the Seventh Biennial Conference of the World Federation of Education Associations*, Vol. IV. Tokyo: World Conference of the Japanese Education Association.

Ashraf, S. A. (1985) *New Horizons in Muslim Education.* Cambridge: Hodder & Stoughton.

Barrett, William (1979) *The Illusion of Technique: A Search for Meaning in a Technological Civilization.* Garden City, New York: Anchor Books.

Ellul, Jacques (1967) *The Technological Society.* New York: Vintage Books.

Freire, Paulo (1970) *Pedagogy of the Oppressed.* Translated by Myra Berman Ramos. New York: Herder & Herder.

Goody, Jack (1977) *The Domestication of the Savage Mind.* New York: Cambridge University Press.

Goody, Jack and Ian Watt (1968) The consequences of literacy, in J. Goody, ed., *Literacy in Traditional Societies* (2nd ed.). Cambridge: Cambridge University Press.

Hatano, Giyoo and Kayoko Inagaki (1986) Two courses of expertise, in *Child Development and Education in Japan,* edited by Harold Stevenson, Hiroshi Azuma, and Kenji Hakuta. New York: W. H. Freeman and Co., pp. 262-272.

Havelock, Eric (1978) *The Greek Concept of Justice: From Its Shadow in Homer to Its Substance in Plato.* Cambridge, Mass.: Harvard University Press.

Havelock, Eric (1963) *Preface to Plato.* Cambridge: Mass.: Harvard University Press.

Illich, Ivan (1970) *Deschooling Society.* New York, Evanston, San Francisco, and London: Harper and Row.

Kobayashi, Victor (ed.) (1987) *Literacy and Orality: The Transformation of Thought.* Honolulu: University of Hawaii Foundation and the Third International Conference on Thinking.

McLuhan, Marshall (1962) *The Gutenberg Galaxy: The Making of Typographic Man.* Toronto: University of Toronto Press.

Mumford, Lewis (1970) *The Myth of the Machine: The Pentagon of Power.* New York: Harcourt Brace Jovanovich, Inc.

Nakayama, Riuji (1938) Position of educational broadcasting in Japan's radio program, *Proceedings of the Seventh Biennial Conference of the World Federation of Education Associations,* Vol. IV. Tokyo, Japan: The World Conference Committee of the Japanese Education Association, pp. 71-76.

Nishimoto, Mitoji (1938) "Special features of school broadcasting in Japan", *Proceedings of the Seventh Biennial Conference of the World Federation of Education Associations,* Vol. IV. Tokyo, Japan: The World Conference Committee of the Japanese Education Association, pp. 59-69.

Obi, Hanji (1938) Position of educational broadcasting in modern education in Japan, *Proceedings of the Seventh Biennial Conference of the World Federation of Education Associations,* Vol. IV. Tokyo, Japan: The World Conference Committee of the Japanese Education Association, pp. 52-59.

Olson, David R. (1986) The cognitive consequences of literacy, *Canadian Psychology,* 27:2, pp. 109-121.

Ong, Walter J. (1982) *Orality and Literacy: The Technologizing of the Word.* New York: Methuen.

Perrin, Noel (1980) *Giving Up the Gun: Japan's Reversion to the Sword, 1543-1879.* Boulder, Colorado: Shambhala.

Postman, Neil (1986) *Amusing Ourselves to Death: Public Discourse in the Age of Show Business.* New York: Viking Penguin.

Tillman, Frank (1987) Photographic/videographic imagery and conceptual thought, paper for the Third International Conference on Thinking, Honolulu, Hawaii. (To be published in forthcoming *Proceedings of the Conference*, edited by Donald Topping, Victor Kobayashi and Doris Crowell, Hillsdale, New Jersey: Lawrence Erlbaum Associates.)

Williams, Gerry (ed.) (1981) *Apprenticeship in Craft*. Goffstown, New Hampshire: Daniel Clark Books.

Yamakawa, Takeru (1938) Film education in Japan, *Proceedings of the Seventh Annual Conference of the World Federation of Education Associations*, Vol. IV. Tokyo: World Conference Committee of the Japanese Education Association.

Index

274

Index

Photoelectric cell 95
Photographic slides 16, 20-21
Photographs 1
Political conditions 12-13, 44-45, 69-72,
  108-113, 132-135, 163-164, 170, 184-
  185, 206-207, 233-252
Political science 206-207
Portugal 121, 260
Print materials 1-4, 6-9, 14-15, 18, 37, 39-
  40, 143-195, 259
Print media *see* Print materials
Print technology 147-157, 167, 174, 178-179
Problem solving 36
Professional organizations 113-114
Programmed instruction 19, 21
Progressive education 254
Publishing technology 147-157, 166-168

Radio 1-2, 4, 6-7, 12, 14-16, 18, 21, 91-142,
  267-268
Radio Sutatenza 129
Random-access memory (RAM) 32
Raster image processing 152-153, 156
Readability 193
Reading instruction 5, 13, 72-88, 127
Read-only memory (ROM) 32
Record keeping 20
Regionalism 134-135
Religious influences 16-17, 209, 219-225,
  227-229
Remedial teaching 5
Research and development 19, 21-22, 37-
  43, 69, 115
Research-literature search 69-72
Robotics 29
Romans 218

Satellites 57-58, 159
Saudi Arabia 14, 97, 106
Science education 5, 41, 122, 136, 190
Self-instructional media 3, 20
Sesame Street 110
Singapore 4, 14, 157, 182-183, 185, 187,
  189
Social studies 5, 41, 122, 190, 194
Socratic method 1, 204
Soviet Union 27, 95, 97-98, 106, 186, 217,
  255
Spain 106
Special education 41
Speech instruction 122
Speech processor 57
Sri Lanka 187, 189
Sudan 97-98, 189
Summerhill 254
Supervision of education 225

Swaziland 106
Sweden 14, 100-101, 106
Switzerland 106

Taiwan 81
Tanzania 106
Tape recording 1, 7, 17
Teacher education 136-137, 190, 224, 237
Teacher placement 70-72
Teacher resistance to innovation 116-118
Technical conditions 77-88, 107, 185-186,
  243-248
Technocracy 210-213, 230
Telescola 121
Television 1-4, 6-8, 12, 16, 18-19, 21, 39-
  40, 43-44, 52, 91-142, 156, 161, 253,
  263-264, 268
Test-item bank 199-200
Text materials 2-3
Text technology 191-194
Textbooks 2-3, 6, 12, 19-20, 46, 116, 144-
  146, 151, 154, 159-175, 179-195, 203-
  204, 244-245, 253, 266
Thai language 83
Thailand 127, 184, 189
Third World 159-195
Tonkin 234, 243
Transistor 27
Translations 28, 86-87
Tunisia 188-189
Typewriter 149-151

Underdeveloped societies *see* Developing
  societies
Unesco 130-131, 190
Unicef 130
United Kingdom *see* Great Britain
United States Agency for International
  Development (US-AID) 130, 138
United States of America 4, 14, 27, 35-36,
  49, 52, 94-96, 106, 110-113, 120, 130,
  138, 155, 157, 160, 177-178, 186, 191,
  218-219, 229, 254, 257-258
University of Mid-America 120-121
Uruguay 189

Vacuum tube 27, 95
Values and technology 264-265
Venezuela 189
Videocassette recorder (VCR) 97
Videodiscs 96, 123, 156
Video-recording 96-97, 102
Videotapes 20, 96-97, 129
Vietnam 189, 231, 233-253
Vocational education 116, 199